FINAL CUT PRO 5
EDITING ESSENTIALS

Tom Wolsky

CMP**Books**

San Francisco, CA

VISUAL & PERFORMING ARTS

Published by CMP Books
an imprint of CMP Media LLC
600 Harrison Street, San Francisco, CA 94107 USA
Tel: 415-947-6615; Fax: 415-947-6015
www.cmpbooks.com   email: books@cmp.com

Managing editor: Gail Saari
Layout design: Madeleine Reardon Dimond
Cover design: David Hamamoto

Distributed to the book trade in the U.S. by:
Publishers Group West
1700 Fourth Street
Berkeley, CA 94710
1-800-788-3123

Distributed in Canada by:
Jaguar Book Group
100 Armstrong Avenue
Georgetown, Ontario M6K 3E7 Canada
905-877-4483

For individual orders and for information on special discounts for quantity orders, please contact:
CMP Books Distribution Center, 6600 Silacci Way, Gilroy, CA 95020
Tel: 1-800-500-6875 or 408-848-3854; fax: 408-848-5784
Email: cmp@rushorder.com; Web: www.cmpbooks.com

Library of Congress Cataloging-in-Publication Data

Wolsky, Tom.
   Final Cut Pro 5 editing essentials / Tom Wolsky.
      p. cm.
   Includes index.
   ISBN-13: 978-1-57820-286-7 (alk. paper)
   ISBN-10: 1-57820-286-8 (alk. paper)
   1. Video tapes--Editing--Data processing. 2. Digital video--Editing
--Data processing. 3. Final cut (Electronic resource)   I. Title.
   TR899.W69 2005
   778.59'30285536--dc22
                                       2005027312
Printed in the United States of America
05 06 07 08 09   5 4 3 2 1

CMPBooks

Reviewers' comments about the author's previous books

"It takes a pro to teach Final Cut Pro, and Tom Wolsky delivers. His years of TV and film experience make him uniquely qualified to demystify Final Cut Pro and teach good editing techniques. Every editor needs this book."

 — Jim Heid, Avondale Media

"If you want to learn editing with Final Cut Pro, look no further. Tom Wolsky brings a depth of experience to digital editing that few others share. He has proven himself an excellent teacher at Stanford University's Academy for New Media, and I will encourage, if not require, future students of the Academy to read this book."

 — Phil Gibson, president, Digital Media Academy

"Tom Wolsky's longtime professional career with ABC News in London — and his later teaching position and full-time studio work in California — takes this work far beyond the simple "how to" books that address Final Cut. In Tom's hands, the subject becomes a look into the process of professional editing and project management as well. Because of this, we believe that he knows Final Cut in many ways better than the people that write the program."

 — Ron and Kathlyn Lindeboom, founders, creativecow.net

"*Final Cut Pro 3 Editing Workshop* shows off both Tom's complete expertise with FCP and his skill as a writer. He has always written in a clean, understandable manner with the ability to demystify his subject matter."

 — Ken Stone, www.kenstone.net

For B.T. Corwin
With Love and Gratitude

Table of Contents

Introduction

Thanks to modern technology, anybody with even a modest budget can acquire the means of production to make movies. Affordable camera, lighting, editing, and other equipment of professional quality can produce images better than seen on most home television sets, and these are now available to anyone on a modest budget. Simply possessing these professional level tools is not enough, of course. Even I can buy a tool belt with a hammer and a wide range of the power tools, but I would still not be a carpenter, let alone an artist in wood. The same is true of video production. Acquiring and learning how to use the tools is only part of the process. You have to also learn the craft.

This book, I would like to think, is one of the steps in the process. Another might be a course of study, such as a film school program or the traditional method of apprenticeship, learning from a master. I have been fortunate enough to learn from both, first at the London School of Film Technique (now the London International Film School) and later with master editors. Starting in Stan Hawks' and Arthur Solomon's cutting rooms, I worked with many talented BBC directors and with a many great camerapeople and editors in England on independent productions and at ABC News in London and New York.

Though this book is about editing with Final Cut Pro 5, the essentials of editing don't change when you use different applications. All that changes is how you use the tools to create the effect that you want. This book is intended to cover the editing aspects of working with this powerful application. The animation features, special effects, and other additional applications that are now included with Final Cut are subjects for another book. This book is very much derived from my earlier books, but has been updated to include the newly available features and techniques, particularly the introduction of FCP's powerful multicam editing functions.

This is a book about editing and is not intended to be a manual, or to supersede or replace the FCP manual. If you want to know how every control, slider, and button in FCP functions, a voluminous manual is supplied with the application.

This book is organized as a series of tutorials and lessons. I hope I have written them in a logical order to lead you from one topic to a more advanced topic. The nature of your work with Final Cut Pro, however, may require the information in Lesson 5, for example, right away. You can read that lesson by itself and make that scroll you need right now. There may, however, be elements in Lesson 5 that presuppose that you know something about using the **Viewer** in conjunction with the **Canvas**.

The book can also be read in the more traditional manner, from start to finish as you absorb the material, without doing the lessons. It doesn't need to be read in linear fashion beginning with this page, though for a new user to Final Cut Pro, it might be better if you did.

In this book I offer a good many opinions on how I like to produce, even how I think scripts should be written, scenes shot and finally edited. I want to emphasize that these are only a single individual's views and are not necessarily the best way to work or the best way for you to work. Everybody has different experiences, both in the field and in the cutting room. How you work depends on many factors, not least of which is your experience and the types of projects you're working on. These latter often dictate your workflow. I'm only offering suggestions for a variety of work scenarios. I hope you find one that's beneficial for you.

Who Is This Book For?

This *Editing Essentials* is intended for all FCP users, but primarily those new to the application and who want to learn how to edit with it. Because FCP has expanded into a Hydra of different applications, each complex in its own right, a single book that covered all these subjects would be monstrously large as well as expensive. This volume covers the editing portions: capturing your material, organizing, editing, adding transitions, basic titling and sound techniques, and outputting from the application.

What's on the DVD?

The DVD contains some of the lessons, projects, and clips used in the book. Not all of the lessons require materials from the DVD. For some, such as Lesson 1, you don't need any at all. For others you may want to substitute your own material, clips you want to work with or are more familiar with. I hope you find this book useful, informative, and fun. I think it's a good way to learn this kind of application.

The also contains to other folders called *Transitions* and *Extras*. *Transitions* contains small QuickTime preview movies of FCP's standard transitions. *Extras* has:

- Avid keyboard shortcut layout to customize your keyboard to the Avid model

- FCP Rescue 5 for trashing your preferences (see page 6 in the first lesson)

- A folder of standard Photoshop frame sizes to use as templates

- A Timecode Calculator to take the headache out of calculating drop frame and other timecode durations.

Acknowledgements

First as always my gratitude to all the people at CMP Books who make this book writing process relatively painless: Paul Temme, associate publisher; Dorothy Cox, senior editor; and Gail Saari for their guidance and help. Many thanks and gratitude to Madeleine Reardon Dimond for coming back to work through the copy editing and layout. My thanks to David Hamamoto for his wonderful work on the covers.

Special thanks to Lanny Cotler for again allowing me to use a portion of *Heartwood*, an independent production directed by Lanny Cotler and Cotler, produced by Steve Cotler and Cotler Brothers Productions, and starring two-time Academy Award winner Hilary Swank, Eddie Mills, and the late Jason Robards.

My grateful thanks to the musicians and organizers of the Stanford Summer Jazz Workshop for allowing us to tape their performance at the Coffee House, especially Ambrose Akinmusire, trumpet; Patrick Wolff, tenor sax; Ryan Snow, trombone; Sam Grobe-Heinte, piano; Josh Thurston-Milgrom, bass; and Adam Coopersmith, drums. For their hard work in shooting this material, my thanks to B.T. Corwin, Sjon Ueckert, and Ross Hardy.

So many helped in making this book possible: Sidney Kramer, for his expert advice; Anders Holck Petersen for allowing me to include FCP Rescue 5; Eric Fry, for his Timecode Calculator, and many others who don't even know it, all those wonderful people in the FCP forums such as 2-pop, the Apple Discussion forums, the Creative Cow forums, Michael Horton's LAFCPUG (Los Angeles Final Cut Pro User Group) forum, Ken Stone, and others. The list of names of contributors of ideas and discussions would be endless, but a representative few to single out would have to include Jerry Hofmann, Philip Hodgetts, Dan Brockett, Charles (Chawla) Roberts, David Bogie, Bret Williams, Walter Biscardi, Marco Solorio, Nick Meyers, and many, many more.

The most important thanks are due to my partner B. T. Corwin for camera work and perseverance in arranging the multicamera material. As always, her insights, her endless encouragement, her engineering technical support, and her patience with me made this book possible. Without her, none of this would have been possible. Finally, again my thanks to the wonderful people of Damine, Japan, who welcomed us into their homes and whose lives provided the source material for these lessons.

Lesson 1

Capturing Your Material

Firing Up the Application

Launching a new application for the first time is always an adventure, especially one as complex as Final Cut Pro 5. To start up the application either double-click on the icon in the *Applications* folder (Figure 1.1), or better yet, make an alias in the **Dock** and just click once on that. After a new installation or after you have trashed your *Final Cut Preferences* file, you will first be greeted with the preferences screen in Figure 1.2, which now includes many more presets.

The default setting is **DV-NTSC** with audio at 48kHz. You have a **DV-PAL** option as well as the two **OfflineRT** options, which are used to capture material at low resolution to conserve drive space, as well as HDV and Panasonic HD presets. Besides those in the default popup, even more choices are available. If you click on the little **Show All** checkbox in the upper right of the window, you will see a much longer list of options (Figure 1.3).

The second popup makes you choose a scratch disk (Figure 1.4). The popup defaults to your system partition and offers you the choice of any hard drives on your system. Notice the new function that allows you to not only set an available hard drive or partition, but now actually allows you to specify a folder for your

1.1   Application Icon

1

1.2 Start-up Dialog

```
Cinema Tools - 23.98fps from DV NTSC
Cinema Tools - 23.98fps from DV PAL
Cinema Tools - 24fps from DV NTSC
Cinema Tools - 24fps from DV PAL
Cinema Tools - DV NTSC NDF
DV PAL 24 @ 25
DV-NTSC
DV-NTSC 24p (23.98)
DV-NTSC 24p (23.98) Advanced Pulldown Removal
DV-NTSC Anamorphic
DV-NTSC FireWire Basic
DV-PAL
DV-PAL Anamorphic
DV-PAL FireWire Basic
DV50 - NTSC
DV50 - PAL
DV50 NTSC 24p (23.98)
DV50 NTSC Anamorphic
DV50 PAL Anamorphic
DVCPRO - PAL
DVCPRO - PAL (No Device)
DVCPRO - PAL 48 kHz Anamorphic
DVCPRO HD - 1080i50
DVCPRO HD - 1080i60
DVCPRO HD - 720p24
DVCPRO HD - 720p30
DVCPRO HD - 720p60
HDV - 1080i50
HDV - 1080i60
HDV - 720p30
HDV-Apple Intermediate Codec 1080i50
HDV-Apple Intermediate Codec 1080i60
HDV-Apple Intermediate Codec 720p30
MPEG IMX 8-Bit NTSC - 50 Mb/s - 48 kHz
MPEG IMX 8-bit PAL - 50 Mb/s - 48kHz
OfflineRT - DVCPRO - PAL
OfflineRT HD - 23.98
OfflineRT HD - 24
OfflineRT HD - 25
OfflineRT HD - 29.97
OfflineRT HD - 30
OfflineRT NTSC
OfflineRT NTSC 24fps
OfflineRT NTSC 24p (23.98)
OfflineRT NTSC Anamorphic
OfflineRT PAL
OfflineRT PAL Anamorphic
Uncompressed 10-bit NTSC 48 kHz
Uncompressed 10-bit PAL 48 kHz
Uncompressed 8-bit NTSC 48 kHz
Uncompressed 8-bit PAL 48 kHz
```

1.3 Available Presets

1.4 Scratch Disks

scratch disk if you wish. You should choose your separate, dedicated media hard drive, not the system drive that holds your operating system and your applications. The system drive is where you save your documents and your project files, but your media should go on a separate large, fast hard drive.

Understanding the Interface

When the application is fully launched, it opens to fill your screen as in Figure 1.5.

The Primary Windows

The screen is divided into four primary windows, with two large empty screens as your principal monitors:

- The **Viewer,** the empty black window in the middle of the screen, allows you to look at individual video clips.

- The **Canvas,** the empty monitor on the right, is the output of your material as you edit it. The **Canvas** is linked directly to the **Timeline.**

- The **Timeline** for your video is the window with the horizontal tracks that stretch across the bottom of the screen. This is where you lay out your video and audio material in the order you want it. A **Timeline** sequence can be any duration up to 12 hours.

- The **Browser** is the fourth window at the top left.

Think of the **Browser** as a giant folder. This is where your project materials are listed and organized. You can create folders called

1.5   The Final Cut Pro Interface

bins, and you can nest folders within folders, just like you can on a Mac desktop. This is not where your clips are stored; it is only a list. The data that makes up your clips is stored on your media hard drives. In the **Browser** you can have a variety of different types of files, obviously video files, but also audio files and graphics or still images. You'll also notice in the interface the vertical bars that contain the **Tools** and **Audio Meters**.

Figure 1.5 shows the default configuration, called **Standard**. You can choose a number of preset window arrangements from the **Windows** menu by selecting **Arrange**. You can recall the **Standard** arrangement at any time with the keyboard shortcut **Control-U**.

Windows can be resized by grabbing the edges where the cursor changes to a **Resizing Tool** (Figure 1.6). When you pull with the **Resizing Tool**, the windows will move proportionately, expanding and contracting as needed to fill the available space. You can arrange the windows to your specific needs. You can save these arrangements and call them from the menu (Figure 1.7). Notice that any saved arrangements appear at the bottom of the list with keyboard shortcuts for really fast access.

1.6   Window Resizing Tool (above)

1.7   Windows > Arrange (right)

Window Help	
Minimize	⌘M
Send Behind	
Arrange	▶
✓ Tool Palette	
✓ Viewer	⌘1
✓ Canvas	⌘2
Tool Bench	⌥5
✓ Timeline	⌘3
✓ Audio Meters	⌥4
✓ Browser	⌘4
Effects	⌘5
Favorites	⌘6
Export Queue	
Timeline: Sequence 1 in Untitled Project 1	
Browser	
Canvas: Sequence 1 in Untitled Project 1	
Viewer: Slug	

Arrange	
Custom Layout 1	⇧U
Custom Layout 2	⌥U
Audio Mixing	
Color Correction	
Multiple Edits	
Standard	^U
Two Up	
Save Window Layout...	
Load Window Layout...	⌥⇧U
BT's_Spread_Browser	^⇧6
QuickView_Viewer_Canvas	^⇧7
Tom's_Audio	^⇧8
Tom's_Compositing	^⇧9
Tom's_Long_Browser	^⇧0

We will look at these windows in detail in the next lesson, but first we need to get some material captured and into your project. Before we begin that process, we should save our project. This is important because FCP will use the project name to create a folder inside the *Capture Scratch* folder. *Capture Scratch* is where your media will be stored. The application creates it inside the designated scratch disk, which we set up when the application was first launched.

To save the project, go to the **File** menu and select **Save Project As**. Give the project file a name and save it on your system hard drive. It defaults to going into your home *Documents* folder. This isn't a bad place for it. If other users need access, the project file will have to be in the *Shared* folder or in some other location.

Setting up the Application

Digital video editing is divided into three phases:

- Getting your material into the computer
- Editing it, which is the fun part
- Getting it back out of your computer

This lesson is about the first part, getting your material into your computer. First you have to set up your application correctly. In Final Cut Pro, as in most video editing programs, that means setting up your preferences. These fundamentals are absolutely necessary for Final Cut Pro to function properly. Set it up right, get your material into your project properly, and you're halfway home. You cannot overestimate how important this is.

To set up your preferences correctly, you need to understand something about the workflow of video editing and to make some decisions about how you want to work. You have to make a fundamental choice before you start: do you want to work online or offline?

At its simplest level, offline is working with a copy of your material that is never intended to be seen by anyone other than the editor, producer, director, and those working on the project. It's the equivalent of a work print in film cutting, which used be to mostly in black and white, full of china graph marks, dust, scratches, and tape joins. In video it's usually a low-quality, low-resolution copy of your material. The online version is what is intended to be seen by your audience.

In computer-based editing, *offline* has come to mean the process of digitizing your video material at low resolution, thereby conserving drive space, while allowing the editor access to a huge

➤ *Note*

Offline Confusion: Confusion about the term offline has been compounded because FCP often uses the word to mean a clip that's in your **Browser** or **Timeline**, but whose source file is missing or deleted from your hard drive. When I speak of offline and of OfflineRT (real time), I mean the workflow and not the missing media.

What is Timecode?

Timecode is a series of numbers that are written on your videotape whenever you make a DV recording or record on a professional device. The numbers represent time and on most consumer cameras begin at 00:00:00:00, zero hours, zero minutes, zero seconds, and zero frames. On professional cameras the start number can be set to anything time you like. A timecode number is assigned to every frames of video—25 frames per second in the European PAL system, 30 frames per second in the North American and Japanese NTSC system.

For NTSC this is a problem, because the true frame rate of all NSTC video isn't 30fps but 29.97fps. Because of this, NTSC has created two ways of counting timecode called Drop Frame and Non-Drop Frame.

Non-Drop Frame displays the numbers based on a simple 30fps frame rate. The problem with this is that when your timecode gets to the one-hour mark, one hour of real world time hasn't passed yet. It's still almost four seconds from completing the hour.

Drop Frame uses a complex method of counting that compensates for the difference between 29.97fps and 30fps. No actually frames of video are dropped. DF drops two frames a minute in its count, except every 10th minute. This means that at the one-minute mark, your DF video will go from 59;29 to 1:00;02. There is no 1:00;00 or 1:00;01. Notice the semicolons. The convention is to write DF timecode with semicolons, or at least one semicolon, while NDF is written only with colons.

The DV standard uses Drop Frame timecode as its counting method, though some prosumer and all professional cameras can be switched between the two.

amount of material. After editing the offline material, an edit decision list (EDL) is produced. The EDL is used to redigitize the material in an edit suite capable of finished resolution quality. In Final Cut Pro, the process remains within one edit suite. FCP is both the offline and the online suite. This simplifies the process and allows greater capabilities because you have the full resources of the application available to you, which you don't when exporting to an EDL. After the material has been redigitized at its high, final resolution, the finish work is done, tweaking the color and effects so that every shot is as perfect as can be.

So this is the decision you have to make when you first set up your preferences: will you start by working in offline, capturing your material at low resolution first and then recapturing at high resolution, or will you capture at your final resolution from the beginning?

System Settings

Before we can bring material into the computer, we should set up our system controls. There are now three separate sets of preferences. There are the **User Preferences**, which let you set up your computer to your taste, and there are the **System Settings** and the **Audio/Video Settings**. Let's start by looking at the **System Settings** panel, which opens first to the **Scratch Disks** panel.

Preferences Folder:

Once you've worked with your system a little bit and decided you really like **the preferences you've cre-ated, it is** a good idea to save them. This **will** also **save** any Favorites you **created.** So after you've made a few transitions or effects **favorites** that you like, **you may want to** back up your prefs again.

If you have any problems with FCP, one of the first remedies anyone will suggest will be to trash your *Preferences* files. If there's a problem, these often get corrupted. If you need to trash your preferences, you have four files to throw away. The first is inside the *~/Library/Preferences* folder (in UNIX, ~ stands for Home) and is called *com.FinalCutPro.plist.* The other three are inside *~/Library/Preferences/Final Cut Pro User Data.* You need to discard the *Final Cut Pro 5.0 Prefs, Final Cut Pro Obj Cache,* and *Final Cut Pro Prof Cache.* These should be moved to the **Trash (Command-Delete)** and the **Trash** emptied (**Command-Shift-Delete**).

The best way to trash your preferences and to back up a clean current version of your preferences is to use Anders Holck Petersen's FCP Rescue 5. You can find a copy of this freeware in the *Extras* folder of the DVD that came with this book.

1.8   System Settings

Open **System Settings** from the **Final Cut Pro** menu, or use the keyboard shortcut **Shift-Q**. This brings up a window with six tabs (Figure 1.8).

Scratch Disks

Let's look at the lower portion of the window before we tackle setting the disks. Except for some specialist systems, make sure that the **Capture Audio and Video to Separate Files** box is left unchecked. This box is primarily a legacy of older systems that worked better with separate files on separate drives. If yours is one of the few capture cards that prefers this option, check this box. In all other cases, particularly for DV, leave it unchecked. For DV material the same drive should always be used for both video and audio. For high-resolution work at high data rates, setting audio to a different disk drive helps achieve better performance because the heads need to serve only video or audio, not both. With multiple tracks of audio in a sequence, the drive-handling audio has a great deal of work to do. Having a separate drive deal solely with the high data rate video portion of the signal makes it easier on the system to achieve playback without dropping frames.

The *Waveform Cache* and the *Thumbnail Cache* default to the drive that you set when you first launched the application. This would be the drive or folder you set for your media drive when you first launched the application. These and the *Autosave Vault* probably should remain on your dedicated media drive. The reason many recommend this procedure is that if your internal system drive fails, your backups will still be preserved. Similarly if your media drive fails, your main project file, being on a separate drive, will still be available to you.

Minimum Allowable Free Space On Scratch Disks defaults to proportion of your drive, usually quite a small one. Arguably this low setting will cause the hard drive to become heavily fragmented and slow down. Some go so far as to say that you should leave 25% of your drive free. For large drives, this seems a bit excessive. If you have a large single partition above 50GB, perhaps you could set this number to 1G.

Unless you have a particular reason, you should leave **Limit capture/export segment size to** unchecked. This feature limits the size of segments FCP can capture or export. If your drives have been initialized as HFS+, this should not be a problem. FCP should capture large clips without segmentation.

The **Limit Capture Now To** box is a legacy of older versions of the software. Unless you have a specific reason to set a value there is no longer a need to use it as FCP no longer checks for available hard drive space before beginning capture.

Note
Naming Drives and Partitions: It's not a good idea to use a numbering scheme like 1, 2, and 3 for drives or partitions. Nor is it a good idea to name drives or partitions Blue, Blue 1, Blue 2, etc. Some FCP users seem to have trouble with drives that use a name that is included in part of another name. The application seems to be much happier with unique drive names such as Larry, Mo, and Curly.

Let's get back to the main body of the **Scratch Disks** window. Here you assign scratch disks for your captured material and for your render files. Normally you set your project's video, audio, and render files in the same location. Set each drive you want to capture to, and the application will fill that drive and then move on to the next. You can set up to 12 separate drives or partitions.

By default, FCP assigns separate render folders for audio and video. When you click the **Set** button, a navigation window allows you to select the location for these files. Usually I pick the drive I want to use for a project. I used to create separate folders for different projects, but FCP does this internally with the *Capture Scratch* and *Render* folders. Apparently this structure will never change, so I gave up trying to tame it and yielded to its work flow.

When you set the drive, FCP creates these folders: the *Capture Scratch* folder, the *Render Files* folder, and the *Audio Render Files* folder. *Render Files* contains the video renders; *Audio*, the audio renders. As you capture or digitize material, it is stored in *Capture Scratch*. Within each of these folders will be separate folders for each project using the project's name.

Search Folders

The **Search Folders** panel is new to FCP5. There isn't much to see except two buttons, one of which lets you set a specific drive, partition, or folder to search for offline media. We'll see this again in the next lesson when we need to reconnect media.

Memory & Cache

The **Memory & Cache** panel allows you to control memory allocation to Final Cut Pro (Figure 1.9). Normally the application takes all memory available when it's the active application. However, if you have a lot of RAM available and you want other applications to do work in the background, you can reduce the amount of RAM dedicated to FCP, giving some to other uses. You can also control the percentage of memory allocated to working with still images. You may want to raise the number if you're working with very large still files for animation.

1.9   Memory & Cache Panel

The **Still Cache** size works at the default setting for most users. If you're working with a lot of large size, large format still images, you might want to raise this value depending on how much RAM you have and what it assigns as the default amount. A couple of hundred megabits should be sufficient for most needs.

The **Thumbnail Caches** work fine at the default settings unless you like to work in large icon view in the **Browser** or with thumbnails turned on.

Playback Control

This gives you access to real-time playback controls (Figure 1.10). Most of the primary functions are available directly in the **Timeline** from the small **RT** popup in the upper left corner (Figure 1.11), where they're more usefully accessed.

In this panel you can set **RT** to **Safe** or **Unlimited**. **Safe** will give you assured playback without dropped frames, your system and drives permitting, while **Unlimited** allows you to play back more real-time but with the possibility of dropped frames.

1.10   Playback Control Panel

Video Quality can be set to **Dynamic** (the default), **High**, **Medium**, or **Low**. The lower the settings, the poorer the image quality, but the greater the real-time playback capabilities. In almost all instances using **Dynamic** will be the preferred choice as the application automatically adjusts the playback quality to maintain as much real-time playback as possible.

1.11   Timeline RT Popup

Frame Rate can also be set here to help maintain real-time play-back even when compositing multiple layers with effects. This defaults to **Full** frame rate, but can also be easily changed to **Dynamic** if your system is struggling to maintain real-time capabilities;

Pulldown Pattern is the one function not available from the **RT** button in the **Timeline**. This allows you to set the real-time pull-down playback when working with film shot at 24fps dubbed to tape at 29.97fps, or shot on a 24 frame capable camera that actually records at 29.97fps.

Gamma Correction defaults to **Accurate**. This setting processes the display on the computer screen so that it more accurately represents that of a video monitor. It does, however, take some processor power to do this. On slower systems it might be better to set the popup to **Approximate**, which will leave the midtones unchanged and brighter on the computer screen than they will appear on a video display. Even if you're using the **Accurate** setting, it's better to edit with a video monitor connected to your system than to rely on the computer screen alone.

Frame Offset lets you compensate for the delay in digital to analog conversion. A four-frame offset will leave your **Canvas** display in sync with your output video going through DV conversion.

Record lets you set output to either **Full Quality** or **Use Playback Settings**. This feature allows you to record out to tape at low resolution for a quick dub as an edit check—for client approval, for instance.

External Editors

Next is the **External Editors** tab. Here you can define which applications are used to work on different types of files outside of FCP (Figure 1.12).

1.12   External Editors Tab

This allows you to launch an application to alter a clip from either the **Browser** or the **Timeline**. Select a clip and hold down the **Control** key, and from the shortcut menu choose **Open in Editor**.

This will launch the application that you specify in this preferences panel. After you edit the clip—such as a still image in Photoshop—those changes will be reflected in FCP.

You can set **External Editors** for stills, video, and for audio. Be aware, though, that if you set the QuickTime Player as your editor for video files, choose Soundtrack Pro as your editor for audio files, and then select **External Editor** for the audio portion of a sync sound clip, FCP will open the QuickTime Player, not Soundtrack Pro. FCP thinks of the audio track as part of a single video clip and so uses the QT Player. Single audio files, even if the creator type is QuickTime, will still open with the separate audio editor, such as STP.

🐁 *Note*_____

Changes in Photoshop: Sometimes changes made to a file in Photoshop, particularly to the layer structure and opacity, will cause the file to appear to be offline, bringing up the **Offline** dialog in Figure 1.13. Select **Reconnect** and navigate to the PS file on your hard drive. If the dialog does not come up and the file still appears to be offline, select it in the **Browser**, and from the shortcut menu chose **Reconnect Media**.

1.13 Offline dialog

Effect Handling

The **Effect Handling** panel (Figure 1.14) allows you to set other codecs to handle effects recording for various settings. Some third-party codecs can be used for specific formats. This lets you set third-party hardware cards to process effects in real time.

Audio/Video Settings

The key to setting up your **Audio/Video Settings** correctly is to start with the tape or other medium that was used to record your material. To capture your material from tape, you have to make sure that the **Capture Presets** in the **Audio/Video Settings** preferences you use match exactly the tape you're capturing from. If the material is DV shot in the North American television standard of NTSC with an audio sampling rate of 48kHz in the widescreen format, then your capture preset should be **DV-NTSC 48kHz Anamorphic**. If the material is analog and you're using a digitizing card like an Aurora Igniter, or if it's digital video that needs to be captured via SDI (Serial Digital Interface) using a board like a Black Magic DeckLink, then you would use the capture presets that come with that hardware. After the capture presets are fixed, you should make the **Sequences Settings** match your capture presets. When all these components are right, you're ready to begin capturing.

Scratch Disks	Search Folders	Memory & Cache	Playback Control	External Editors	Effect Handling
DV/DVCPRO – NTSC		effects handled by:	Final Cut Pro		
DV – PAL		effects handled by:	Final Cut Pro		
DVCPRO – PAL		effects handled by:	Final Cut Pro		
DVCPRO50 – NTSC		effects handled by:	Final Cut Pro		
DVCPRO50 – PAL		effects handled by:	Final Cut Pro		
Photo – JPEG		effects handled by:	Final Cut Pro		
Uncompressed 8-bit 4:2:2		effects handled by:	Final Cut Pro		
Uncompressed 10-bit 4:2:2		effects handled by:	Final Cut Pro		
DVCPRO HD 720p60		effects handled by:	Final Cut Pro		
DVCPRO HD 1080i50		effects handled by:	Final Cut Pro		
DVCPRO HD 1080i60		effects handled by:	Final Cut Pro		

1.14 Effect Handling (above)

1.15 Audio/Video Summary Tab (right)

The **Audio/Video Settings** are called up from the **Final Cut Pro** menu or by using the keyboard shortcut (**Command-Option-Q**). This brings up the **Summary** tab (Figure 1.15).

As the name indicates, this window summarizes the other four tabbed windows. Each popup gives the settings for that window, settings you define in the other windows. The names you assign appear here, and you can change easily from one preset to another. After you've made your selections, press the **Easy Setup** button at the bottom of the panel. These preferences are saved in the *Custom Settings* folder in your system's *Library*, inside *Application Support*, inside *Final Cut Pro System Support*. You can evoke **Easy Setup** quickly from the **Final Cut Pro** menu or with the keyboard shortcut **Control-Q**. The dialog box it brings up is basically the same one that you see when you launch the application for the very first time. In it you can choose any of your presets to switch quickly from one to another.

Sequence Presets

Sequence Presets offers you a whole list of setups for a great many different video formats, from DV, HDV, on to different format High Definition (HD) sizes. In Figure 1.16 you see only a few of the available options. If you want to use a preset other than what you have from Apple, you can create your own. Hardware manufacturers often create their own presets, which may be installed for you when you install the software that goes with your specific hardware.

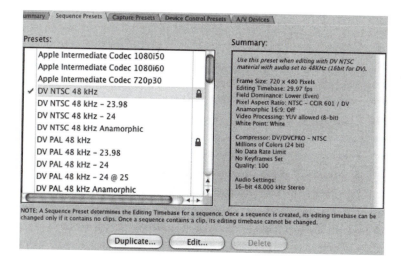

1.16 Sequence Presets Panel

If you're working in DV material, you'll probably want to base your sequence preset on one of the DV presets. If all your material was shot with the audio at a different sampling rate from the default 48kHz, you'll want to create a sequence preset with that sampling rate.

To create your own custom preset, start off by duplicating either the existing DV-NTSC or the DV-PAL preset. When the preset has been duplicated, the preset editor opens up. (Figure 1.17). As it opens, the **Name** panel is highlighted for you to rename your preset. You can also edit the description for the **Summary** panel.

Here are controls for all the possible audio and video parameters to set up a sequence exactly the way you need it to be.

Notice the tab for **Video Processing** that appears behind the **General** tab. This is important because it sets a number of default values. Figure 1.18 shows the **Video Processing** tab. Most of the settings can be left as they are, especially if you're working in DV.

Capture Presets

The next tab in the **Audio/Video** panel is **Capture Presets**, which opens with a set of options similar to those in the **Sequence Preset** panel. For DV you should use one of the DV presets, either **DV NTSC 48kHz** or **DV PAL 48kHz**, unless your material was shot at 32kHz, what camera manufacturers call 12-bit audio. If your camera was shooting at 12-bit, you need to create a new preset using a sampling rate of 32kHz.

1.17 Sequence Preset Editor

Sequence Preset Editor

Name: DV NTSC 48 kHz Copy

Description: Use this preset when editing with DV NTSC material with audio set to 48KHz (16bit for DV).

General | Video Processing

Frame Size: 720 x 480 Width Height Aspect Ratio NTSC DV (3:2)

Pixel Aspect Ratio: NTSC – CCIR 601 / DV (...   ☐ Anamorphic 16:9

Field Dominance: Lower (Even)

Editing Timebase: 29.97

Timecode Rate: Same As Editing Timebase

QuickTime Video Settings
Compressor: DV/DVCPRO – NTSC
Quality: ◄————————▷ 100 %
Advanced...

Audio Settings
Rate: 48 kHz
Depth: 16–bit
Config: Default

1.18 Video Processing Tab

General | Video Processing

○ Always Render in RGB
◉ Render in 8–bit YUV
○ Render 10-bit material in high-precision YUV
○ Render all YUV material in high-precision YUV

Codecs which do not support YCbCr (also known as YUV) can only use RGB rendering; RGB rendering may be chosen for YUV-capable codecs, but may cause intensity or color shifts in rendered material.

High-precision YUV rendering provides higher quality results when applying multiple effects, or when the original material had more than 8 bits of precision, but takes longer to render.

Process Maximum White as: White

This selects how RGB colors are mapped into YCrCb image processing. This option can be set to match cameras which produce "brighter than standard" white (also known as super-white).

Motion Filtering Quality:
Best
Normal
Fastest (linear)

This selects the filtering quality used when performing motion tab motion effects.

There are choices for capturing with HDV or for capturing using the Apple Intermediate Codec. If you're working in HDV and your computer is fast enough, at least a G4/1G with 1G of RAM, you should capture in HDV. This format is more processor intensive, both during capture and while you're editing. On slower systems you might want to look at capturing using the Apple Intermediate Codec, which takes less processor power and is easier to edit. It does take up more drive space, though. The files can be three times larger than native HDV files.

Again, if you want something other than the standard presets, you're best off to start by duplicating one of the locked items (probably the **DV-NTSC** preset) and opening the **Capture Preset Editor** (Figure 1.19).

Like in the **Sequence Preset**, you can give a name and description to your new settings, and you can set the parameters to match

1.19   Capture Preset Editor

those of your tape and the frame size, as well as flag whether your material is in 16:9 (widescreen) format. There are **Video** and **Audio** sections where you can set the capture codec as well as the audio sampling rate.

In this version of FCP, using the capabilities introduced in Quick-Time 7, you can for the first time capture multiple tracks of audio simultaneously if your material supports that.

To change to 32kHz, use the **Format** popup in the **QuickTime Audio Settings** portion of the panel.

Device Control

This panel opens with another set of options (Figure 1.20). Most users will want to have device control, which is pretty simple to set up. Notice FCP5's new control presets for HD and HDV, with separate controls for **HDV** and **Sony HDV**. These need to be selected if you're using one of those formats.

If you are capturing from an analog deck like VHS through a converter box, you should set the preset to **Non-Controllable Device**.

If you're working in DV you want to use either **FireWire** or **FireWire Basic**, unless you're using a professional deck controlled by a different protocol such as RS-422. All Sony cameras use the FireWire protocol, while all Canon cameras use **FireWire Basic**.

1.20 Device Controls Preset

1.21 Device Control Preset Editor

Other manufacturers use a mix, some models using one, others the other.

To set up a new device control preference, again start by duplicating one of the locked presets. Duplicating the **FireWire** preset will bring up the window in Figure 1.21.

Here you use a number of popups to define the type of device control you're using and how you're connecting to your deck. You also have a popup where you can set **Audio Mapping**, which controls how the audio from your timeline will be sent out to a device that is capable of assemble or inserting multiple tracks of audio simultaneous. You can send out up to eight tracks to a record deck such as Digital Betacam that can handle eight audio channels.

The sixth popup is for **Default Timecode**. Normally this is set to **Drop Frame** because this is the standard for DV. Here you can set either **Drop Frame** or **Non-Drop Frame**, depending on what was shot. Though Final Cut will automatically sense whether the timecode is drop or non-drop, it may take it a few moments playback to do so. If you know what format of timecode your source material is using, it's safer to set it here.

Capture Offset and **Playback Offset** allow you to calibrate the accuracy of your deck. This only works if the deck is consistently ahead or behind the capture point or edit point you specify. This is used to calibrate frame-accurate decks.

Note the **Autorecord and PTV** box that allows you to automatically put your deck in Record mode when using **Print to Video**. It

1.22   A/V Devices   1.23   Log and Capture Window

will automatically start your recording device, such as a camcorder, and record after a specified number of seconds.

A/V Devices

The last tab in **Audio Video Settings**, **A/V Devices** (Figure 1.22), gives you a group of popups that let you set the way you view material during playback and while recording. If you're working in DV, select the default **FireWire** option. If you're working in other formats with a third-party board, other options will also appear here.

Once this last window is done, your preferences are set. Go back to the **Summary** window and see what your settings look like. If everything is okay, save it as an **Easy Setup** setting in your *Custom Settings* folder of the system, *Library/Application Support/Final Cut Pro System Support/Custom Settings*.

Log and Capture

Once you have your preferences set, you are ready to capture your material. Go to **File>Log and Capture (Command-8)**. This brings up the **Log and Capture** window (Figure 1.23).

The window is divided in two. On the left is a viewer that lets you look at the video on your tape deck or camera as it plays back. The **Viewer** has controls at the bottom for playing the tape (Figure 1.24), a play button, buttons for fast forward and rewind, as well as a jog wheel on the left to inch your tape and a shuttle slider on the right to control forward and backward motion.

1.24 Log Viewer Controls

There is also a display that tells you the status of your deck. **VTR OK** indicates that the tape is loaded and that the **Capture** window is reading it correctly. The display will also indicate if the capture function is not communicating with the deck or camcorder properly. **No Communication** will appear if the deck is not recognized or if you're using a noncontrollable device for capturer such as a converter box.

Keyboard Shortcuts

The buttons aren't the only way to control the tape. You also have the keyboard, which is usually the most efficient way to work in FCP. Press the spacebar to play the tape. To pause, press the spacebar again. Spacebar to start, spacebar to stop.

Another common way to play the tape is with the **L** key.

- **L** is play forward.
- **K** is pause.
- **J** is play backwards.

On your keyboard they're clustered together, but you're probably thinking, Why not comma, period, and slash? There is reason to the madness. **J**, **K**, and **L** were chosen because they're directly below **I** and **O**. **I** and **O** are used to mark the In and Out points on your tape. Marking the In point defines where you will begin capturing material on your tape. Marking the Out point defines where the capture will end. They are probably the most commonly used keys on the editing keyboard. Hence **J**, **K**, and **L**, positioned conveniently for the fingers of your right hand with the **I** and **O** keys directly above them.

You can view your video at other speeds. You can play your clip fast forward by repeatedly hitting the **L** key. The more times you hit **L**, the faster the clip will play. Similarly, hitting the **J** key a few times will make the clip play backwards at high speed.

In addition to your keyboard shortcuts for **Mark In** and **Mark Out**, you also have buttons and timecode displays at the bottom of the **Viewer** for these functions.

The two inner buttons mark the In and Out points, **In** on the left, **Out** on the right. The timecode window on the bottom left displays the In point, while the timecode window on the bottom right shows the Out point. Of the buttons on the far outside, the left one will take the tape deck to the assigned In point, and the far right one to the assigned Out point.

At the top of the **Viewer** are two other timecode displays (Figure 1.25). The timecode in the upper right of the **Viewer** is the current timecode on your tape, and the timecode display on the upper left is the duration you set between your In and Out points as you mark the tape. Note the display that shows you your available drive space as well as equivalent amount of time for video and audio captured at your current settings.

On the right of the **Log and Capture** window is a tabbed window. The farthest tab on the right is the **Capture Settings** tab (Figure 1.26). Two popups and a button access the preference settings you have already created. **Device Control** and **Capture Settings** let you set the preferences based on the settings available to you. The **Scratch Disks** button takes you directly to the **Scratch Disks preferences** window so that you can change the assigned drives if you wish. The **Capture Settings** function in the **HDV Log and Capture** window only has a **Scratch Disk** button.

Let's now take a look at the middle tab in the window, **Clip Settings** (Figure 1.27).

> **✎ Tip**
>
> **Dragging Timecode:** A useful feature allows you to drag timecode values from any of the value boxes to any other value box. This is handy if you need to relog material and change timecode numbers. Hold the **Option** key and drag the timecode from any other timecode window, including the **Browser**, into the timecode box you want.

1.25 **Top of the Log & Capture Viewer**

1.26 **Capture Settings Panel (above)**

1.27 **Clip Settings Panel (right)**

1.28   Waveform Monitor and
        Vectorscope (left)

1.29   Mono Capture vs. Stereo Pair
        (below)

At the top are buttons that let you call up FCP's **Waveform Monitor and Vectorscope** (Figure 1.28), which allow you to ensure that your video levels are correctly set. There is also a button to reset to default values used by your digitizing card.

Below that the tab is divided in two sections, **Video** and **Audio** (Figure 1.27). The top part of the panel allows you to control the parameters of your video, letting you alter the **Hue**, **Saturation**, **Brightness**, **Contrast**, **Black Level**, and **White Level** of your clip as it is being digitized. This gives you useful control for images that have not been shot well or shot under less than ideal conditions. Fixing the levels here means that you won't have to fix them later and consequently have to render all your material.

However, if you are working in DV or other digital formats, this entire top part of the window will be grayed out. Why? Because your material was digitized when the camera was recording. All you can do now is capture your material, which is basically copying the digital information off the tape and onto your hard drive. You are making a clone of your tape material, and if you don't process it any further with effects and record it back into the tape, it will be an exact copy of the original material.

Below the **Video** controls is the **Audio** portion of the tab. There is volume level slider that allows you to control the audio levels of your material. As with digital video, the slider is not functional for data transfer. Notice the dimmed **Preview** checkbox, which allows you to monitor your audio through your computer from the **Log and Capture** window. The button position on the left in Figure 1.29 shows FCP set to capture two mono channels, while the button position on the right shows the stereo pair setting.

Below that is a popup that lets you set the number of audio tracks to ingest simultaneously, up to 24 tracks. Changing the popup will affect how many track meters appear in the area below. The button to the left of each pair of track meters lets you toggle the audio for those tracks between capturing as a stereo pair or as discrete mono tracks. There are new icons in FCP5 for this, rather than the popup in previous versions.

The green audibility buttons allow you to switch off specific tracks. They are useful if you have recorded audio on a single track only, which is very common on many camcorders when recording with a separate, external microphone. The audibility button allows you to switch off the track so that you don't capture a blank, mute track.

To switch off all video or audio—for instance, if you have a narration track and only want to capture the audio—toggle off the video (Figure 1.30) or audio checkboxes as needed.

Strategies for Capturing

There are basically three strategies for capturing or digitizing material, and you choose the one you want to use with the buttons at the bottom of the **Logging** window (Figure 1.31).

The options you have are:

- Clip
- Now
- Batch

Whichever way you decide to work, it is critical that you properly number your tape reels and enter the assigned number into the reel number panel of the **Log and Capture** window. The reel number becomes part of the data in the QuickTime media file together with the timecode. This is the only way you'll be able to recapture material, should you ever need to. Every clip must have a reel number assigned to it. This is so important that FCP starts with a reel assigned as 001. Every time you change a tape in a device-controlled deck, the application will sense it and put up the warning in Figure 1.32.

Capture Now

This is the simplest way to work, but it gives you least control. It also requires that your material be properly shot without video breaks. These can cause havoc with any capture, particularly a **Now** capture. FCP5 can capture around timecode breaks, but it will still lose audio/video synchronization if it comes across a section of unstable video or a section of tape with no video at all, even if timecode is present.

1.30   Video Checkbox

1.31   Capture Buttons

1.32   Reel Change Warning

Final Cut Pro has a user preference that allows you to set how the application treats timecode breaks. You have the option to abort capture on timecode breaks. You can also set it to create new clips whenever it encounters a break. If there a timecode break on the tape but the timecode continues getting higher, a new clip will start at the break, but the same reel number will be maintained. If the timecode resets to zero at the break, FCP will change and increment the reel number, as well as make a new clip. This will treat each portion of the tape where the timecode resets to zero as a separate tape. Avoid having breaks in your timecode if you can. It will make your life much easier.

Capturing large chunks of video with **Now** is a common work strategy. Before you initiate the capture, you first need to name the clip. Enter a name in the **Description** box of the **Logging** window as well as any other information in the **Shot/Take** box, the **Angle** box, or the other note areas. In FCP5 you have to name the clip first, before you initiate capture, because after capture it immediately appears in the **Browser** with the designated name. If no name has been given before, the clip is called *Untitled*, which will also be the name of the media file on your hard drive.

To use **Capture Now**, put the deck in play and click the **Now** button. A **Capture** screen comes up and begins recording as soon as it finds a video signal from your camera or deck.

FCP records the clip on your designated scratch disk until one of three events occur:

- It runs out of hard drive space.
- It hits your preference time limit.
- You hit the **Escape** key and stop the process.

Unlike previous versions of FCP, **Capture Now** starts almost instantaneously. A QT file is created immediately that FCP fills as the material is captured. In fact, if you're working on a system powered by a shared storage system, other users can open the file and start editing it while it is still being captured.

With the **Capture Now** method, you bring all your video material into your computer for editing into smaller subclips rather than using your deck to select clips.

Camcorders and FireWire-controlled DV decks are not very responsive to the control commands—start, stop, fast forward, rewind—nor are many of these devices really designed to shuttle and jog tape. This places great wear and tear on your deck's drive mechanisms, and if you're working off DV with a camcorder, you're putting a lot of strain on these tiny tapes and small mechanisms. They wear out quickly under this heavy use. What tape can't do quickly, i.e., move large amounts of data, computers are specifically designed to do. With **Capture Now** you're working to the computer's strength, using nonlinear, nondestructive editing to its fullest.

FCP has a wonderful tool for those working in DV with the **Capture Now** option. This is the ability to automatically mark up shot changes with **DV Start/Stop Detect**. We'll look at it on page 39 in the next lesson. This function has been built right into the **HDV Capture** window. It automatically breaks your material into master clips every time the camera was stopped and started.

Batch Capture

For a variety of reasons—because it's a traditional work method, because of available drive space—a still-commonly used work method is the batch capture strategy. This involves logging your tape and selecting the shots you want to capture. To the right of the **Viewer** in the **Log and Capture** window is the **Logging** tab (Figure 1.33), where you can enter a whole array of information about your clip.

The clip name is made up of a number of elements that you can choose with the **Prompt** checkboxes. Any checked item will be added to the name. You can make up a name that includes a label, a scene number, a shot/take number, and (new in FCP5) an angle name or number, which may be useful for multicam work, though it's more common to use the reel number to designate the various camera angles. These description values are the standard feature film format for logging film clips. Much of FCP's interface draws from that model. Of course, you can name the clip anything that's useful to you.

⇝ Tip _____
No Forward Slashes: Do not under any circumstances include a forward slash (/) in any naming convention you use. The forward slash in Unix, upon which OS X is based, is used to designate a file path. So if there is a / in the file name, the system will look for a folder name with the first part of the name, as in LS/Bridges/Trestle. It will look inside your *Capture Scratch* folder for a folder named *LS*, inside which is supposed to be a folder named *Bridges*, where the shot *Trestle* resides, none of which will be found.

⇝ Tip _____
Relogging Clips: If you ever need to relog a clip, use this simple method. Drag the original clip from the **Browser** into the **Log and Capture** window. This will load the clip's In and Out points into the window. Change the In and Out points to whatever you want. You can also use the **Go To** buttons to take you to the **In** or **Out** button on the tape, making it easier to reset the values.

1.33 Logging Tab

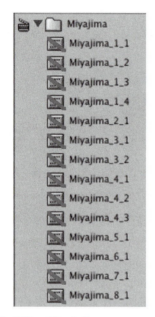

1.34 Offline Clips in Browser

✎Tip _____

Logging in the Browser: If you
have logging notes on paper that
were taken during the shoot, you
can create logging clips directly in
the **Browser**, using File > New >
Offline Clip. This will create an
uncaptured clip in the **Browser** in
which you can enter timecode values for In and Out points. If you
need to do a lot of these, you might
want to create a keyboard shortcut
for yourself. We'll see how to do
that in the next lesson.

You can also add notes and **Mark Good,** another film term, which refers to marking the takes that looked good to the director. In the **Logging** window, you can even add markers and marker comments before your material is captured.

After you've set an In and Out point for your clip and entered the logging information, you then press the **Log Clip** button. The clip immediately appears in your **Browser** or a designated bin with a bright red diagonal line through it. The red line indicates that the clip has not been captured.

✎ Tip_____
Logging Bin: To assign a bin in your **Browser** as your **Logging** bin, **Con-**
trol-click on the bin you want to log into and from the shortcut menu
choose **Set Logging Bin**. A little clapperboard icon will appear next to
the designated bin.

Rather than hitting the **Log Clip** button, you could also press **F2**. If the tape is rolling while you're playing—that is, you entered the Out point on the fly—something interesting happens. The deck stops, and you get a dialog box to confirm the clip name, if the **Name Prompt** checkbox is on. As soon as you click **OK** to accept the dialog, the frame after the previous Out point will enter as the new In point, and the deck will be put into play. The clip will appear in your designated logging bin with a diagonal red line through it (Figure 1.34). The clip is, in FCP terminology, considered offline, ready to be batch captured. The **F2** method can be very fast and efficient for logging.

The problem with this method of working is that you're putting the onus of the work on the log and capture process. It doesn't take advantage of nonlinear editing's real strengths. I feel that using **Capture Now** makes the whole organizing process much quicker and simpler. The FCP manual on page 238 lists in detail the importance and benefit of logging your material. This cannot be overemphasized. However, you should be aware that your material does ***not*** have to be logged from the tape before capturing, and it is often more efficient and productive with less machine wear to log the material after it has been captured. As video moves away from tape-based recording to hard disk or memory card–based recordings, this advantage will become ever more apparent.

If you do use **Log and Capture** either to conserve hard drive space or because you prefer to work that way, you will then need to complete the process by batch capturing your material:

1. Select the clips in your bin with the red diagonal bar through them, or select the bin itself.

2. Press the **Batch** button, which brings up the window in Figure 1.35 *or*
   Select the clips and choose **Batch Capture** from the **File** menu (**Control-C**).

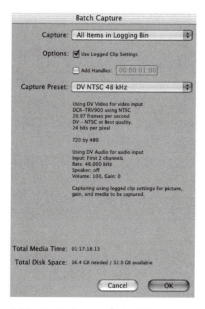

1.35 Batch Capture Dialog Window

The popup at the top allows you to select which clips you want to batch capture. There is also a window for setting handles and a checkbox for coalescing clips. Handles allow you to capture extra media beyond your marked In and out points. If you set handles, coalescing clips can save drive space and time. However, it's dangerous. It combines adjacent clips into one piece of media. You will now have created a single source file that supplies media for two or more clips. You may remove the source file and find you've unintentionally wiped out the media for a clip you still want. It's safest to leave **Coalesce** off.

Notice the **Total Media Time** and **Total Disk Space** needed information at the bottom of the box. It's useful to double-check your batch request to make sure you are capturing what you think you're capturing, as well as having the needed drive space. If something looks odd in the total time, check that you haven't selected more or fewer clips than you intended.

The popup in the middle of the **Batch Capture** dialog lets you select any one of your preset preferences. This is handy if you've captured at low resolution and want to quickly change to capture at high resolution. If you have these different preferences set up ahead of time, you can choose the preference in this popup.

Clicking **OK** will automatically set the deck off, capturing from your tape the clips you've logging into your **Browser**.

Another method I like is to use an abridged form of logging on tape before batch capture. It combines the benefits of **Capture Now** with the tape control of batch capturing. Here you quickly select In and Out points for large chunks of video on your tape, whole scenes or sections of material, dividing your tape up into four or five pieces, before you perform batch capture.

✏️**Tip** _____
Selecting for Batch Capture: You don't actually have to select each red-lined clip separately. You can just select the whole contents of the Browser for batch capture. FCP will then bring up a dialog box asking whether you want to capture all the clips, or just those offline. If you select offline clips only, it will batch capture all the material that is not already on your hard drive.

```
Filename: Temple
Duration: 00:01:39;24
Average Data Rate: 3700k/sec
Audio Shape: Stereo

Video Track 1 (342.5 MB)
   Duration: 00:01:39;24
   Frame Size: 720 x 480
   Color Depth: 24-bit Color
   Codec: DV/DVCPRO - NTSC at Most Quality
   Frame Rate: 29.97 fps
   Average Data Rate: 3512k/sec (117k/frame)

Audio Track 1 (Stereo, 18.3 MB)
   Duration: 00:01:39;24
   Average Data Rate: 188k/sec
   Format: 16-bit, Stereo
   Sampling Rate: 48.000 khz

Timecode Track Source TC
   Timecode: 00:21:38;10
   Reel: 005
```

1.36   Movie Analysis Window

Clip

The third option in the **Log and Capture** window is the **Clip** button. This functions in the same way as the **Batch** button, except it captures an individual clip. It's useful if you just need to capture a single shot or section of a tape. To use the **Clip** function you enter its In, Out, and naming information, and then press the **Clip** button to capture the one item. Many people use this as a controlled form of **Capture Now**.

1. Mark an In point near the beginning of the reel and then an Out point near the end.
2. Click **Clip** and let the deck and the computer do its thing.
3. After the clip is captured, it will appear in the **Browser** with your assigned name.

After you've set up your system and captured your material, you are ready to edit. Close the **Log and Capture** window before you start, however. Do not try to play video while **L&C** is open. **Log and Capture** is trying to suck in through the FireWire cable while the **Viewer** is trying to feed out through the same cable.

Once you've captured your material, you'll notice that it appears in the **Browser** as a clip with a duration but with no In or Out points defined. **Capturing** only sets the media limit, and FCP assumes you will want to edit the material further, so no In or Out points are designated. The clip has the _de facto_ In and Out points marked by the limits of the media; they're not displayed in the **Browser** in the **In** and **Out** columns. If you capture with handles, however, the clips do come in with your designated In and Out points marked and the extra media beyond it.

Tools

FCP has some tools to help you after you've captured your material. After you've captured a few clips, it's a good idea to analyze them to make sure everything is all right. Select the clip, and from the **Tools** menu choose **Analyze>Clip**. If you choose **File**, you will get the navigation service dialog window to select a piece of media on your hard drive. **Analyze** will bring up a window that gives you the clip's technical details (frame size, data rate, video and audio track information, etc.) (Figure 1.36). If something seems amiss here—the data rate is too low, or you have odd audio sampling rates or odd frames rates—you'll know something is wrong with your captured material.

Occasionally when FCP is capturing or digitizing, it produces a frame that is not the set duration and takes more time in the video stream than it should. FCP calls this a *long frame*. The application has a tool to find these long frames in clips. From the **Tools** menu, select **Long Frames>Mark**. This will scan the clips and place a marker at each long frame. If there are no long frames, you'll see the message in Figure 1.37. In the **Tools** menu, there is also an item that will remove the long frame markers for you, **Long Frames>Clear.**

1.37 **No Long Frames Detected**

If there are long frames in your clip, you can twirl open the clip in the **Browser** and see exactly where the long frames are.

The Long Marks on the clip will have timecode In and Out points and a duration for how many frames the long frame extends. It is possible with care to cut these out to patch together your video. You'll also have to adjust the audio to keep it in sync with the picture, which may be more problematic and not always possible. It's usually better to recapture the media.

Importing Music

In addition to capturing or digitizing material to bring it into FCP, you can also import material: video, audio, and still images. We'll look at importing these in the next lesson on page 32. Importing from a music CD is a somewhat different process. This is because audio files on music CDs are AIFF sound files but not at the same sampling rate as that used by digital video. The audio CD format uses a sampling rate of 44.1kHz, while digital video is either 32kHz or, more commonly, 48kHz.

While FCP can deal with resampling the audio while it plays it back, this requires processor power and may limit your ability to do real-time effects or to play back video without dropping frames, i.e., the video stuttering. Though FCP allows you to render at the item level, which we'll see in Lesson 5, I nonetheless still recommend resampling the audio to the correct sampling rate you want to use before importing it into FCP.

There are a number of ways to do this. One way is to use iTunes, which probably will launch anyway when you load a CD. This requires you changing your iTunes preferences, both your importing preferences and the location where your music is stored. As more and more people use iTunes as their personal jukebox, even in edit suites, it seems impractical to be constantly changing these preference settings.

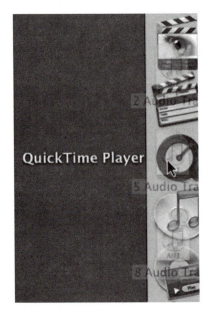

1.38   Audio Tracks to QuickTime Pro
       Player

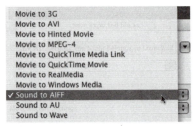

1.39   Export Popup

1.40   AIFF Options

There is a simple way to resample using the QuickTime Pro Player. Your serial number for FCP5 should automatically upgrade you to the QuickTime 7 Pro Player.

1. Load the CD and drag the track or tracks you want to convert from the CD to the **QuickTime** icon in the **Dock** (as shown in Figure 1.38) to launch the QuickTime Pro Player.

2. When the track or tracks have opened, go to **File>Export** or use **Command-E**.

3. Change the **Export** popup to **Sound to AIFF** (Figure 1.39).

4. Click the **Options** button and set the **Rate** to **32.000** or **48.000**, whichever you need. Make sure **Format** is set to **Linear PCM**, **Channels** to **Stereo**, and **Sample Size** to **16**, and as in Figure 1.40.

5. When you are finished with the **Options** window, set your media drive as the location to copy the track onto your computer.

6. Press the **Save** button.

The QuickTime Pro Player will then copy the track from the CD to your designated hard drive location and will resample and convert it to the correct format as it does so.

Back in Final Cut, when you drag the track into your **Browser** or use **Command-I** to import it, the track will appear in the **Browser** appended with the suffix *.aif* and will also be in the correct sampling rate that you changed it to. Your system will be happy that you did this.

Another way that I like to convert audio files to the correct format is to use Compressor, which is one of the applications that come with Final Cut Pro. You use the Compressor application to create Droplets, which act as tiny applications for running Compressor tasks. You can leave the Droplets on your desktop ready to be used at any time.

To make a Compressor Droplet, begin by launching Compressor.

1. When the application is open, in the **Presets** window go to the **Settings** tab and open the **Apple** presets. Go to **Audio Formats** and chose the format you want, probably **AIFF 48/16**, as in Figure 1.41.

2. Select the item, and click on the **Droplet** button (Figure 1.42).

To use your **Droplet** to convert an audio file:

1. Drag the audio files you want to convert onto the **Droplet** icon.

1.41 Compressor Preset (above)

1.42 Droplet Button (left)

1.43 Droplet Window (right)

The application will launch, and the items will appear in the **Source File** window (Figure 1.43).

2. Press the **Submit** button, which will open the **Batch Monitor** application, where you can watch the progress of your material being converted.

3. Finally, you'll want to drag the converted files onto your media drive before importing them in FCP.

Summary

Lesson 1 covers the opening the application and a quick tour of the interface, its windows, and their arrangements. We looked at setting up your system and audio/video settings, and the process of getting your material captured or digitized into Final Cut Pro, as well as importing audio files from CD using the QuickTime Pro Player and Compressor Droplets. Next we'll look at how to work with your clips in the **Viewer** and in the **Browser** and how to organize all the material you've brought into Final Cut Pro.

Lesson 2

Cutting Up Those Shots

One of the primary functions of the editor is selection, choosing which shot to use, selecting this shot, but not that shot. Whether you begin the selection process as part of logging and capturing your material, or you wait until your material is captured before beginning to make your selections, you have to begin at some point to make the decisions that will keep some material and reject others. Part of selection process, particularly if you're doing it on the computer, is to organize your material; so this lesson is about selection, and more than that it's about organization. Without organization you can edit a simple 10-minute video, or you can assemble long pieces of a home movies to make a video, but if you want to make a video of a greater length or greater complexity, you and your material have to be organized. That's the subject of this lesson.

Loading the Lesson

There are a number of different ways of working with your material and a few different ways to cut it up. I'll show you a variety of ways that seem to work well in Final Cut Pro 5. Let's begin by loading the material we need for this lesson.

1. Start by loading the DVD that came with this book into your DVD drive. Open the DVD.

You'll see a number of folders, one called *Lesson 2 Media* and another called *Projects*. Inside *Lesson 2 Media* is a QuickTime file, and inside *Projects* are numbered Final Cut project files.

2.   Drag the folder called *Lesson 2 Media* onto your media drive.

You should have a separate, fast hard drive dedicated to holding just your media, while your operating system, applications, and project files are on another.

The *Lesson 2 Media* folder contains some of the video material used in this book. When you begin any lesson that needs material from the DVD, the first step you should take is to drag the media folder onto the media drive of your computer. The footage included there will play much better and more smoothly from your high-speed drive than from any DVD drive.

3.   After you've copied the media folder, drag the *Projects* folder from the DVD onto the system hard drive of your computer. You should probably place it in the *Documents* folder inside your *Home* folder.

4.   Before you open any of the files you copied onto your computer be sure to eject the DVD and put it away.

5.   Open the *Projects* folder from your system hard drive and double-click on the file *Lesson 2*, which will launch the Final Cut Pro 5 application.

The project is empty except for one sequence that is also blank.

Where to Work

The Browser

To get started we need to import some material.

1.   Use **File>Import** (**Command-I**) to import the file called *Temple* from the inside the *Lesson 2 Media* folder on your media hard drive. Or, with the **Browser** as the active window, you could also drag the clip directly from the folder on your hard drive into your **Browser**.

This is a *master clip*. Every time you import a clip or capture a clip or bring a new clip into the **Browser**, the first instance of that clip is always a master clip. The **Browser** has a check column that will show you whether or not a clip is a master clip. You can also see this in a clip's **Item Properties**.

A master clip can be cut up into smaller clips called *affiliate clips*. Any copy or portion of a master clip has an affiliate relationship to the master. Master clips and affiliate clips must have certain things in common. They must have the same timecode; if you change the timecode on either the master or affiliate the other instances will change as well. They must have the same label; change the colored label on one and the others change as well. They also must have the same name; changing the name of the master or any of its affiliates will change the names of all the other items associated with it. So how do you work with your long master clips in FCP? There are a number of different ways of working to accommodate the way the application handles the media. We'll look at these a bit later, beginning on page 38.

The **Browser** gives you a great deal of information about your clips, their duration, In and Out points, **Media Start** and **Media End** times, as well as information about the type of video, the type of audio, stereo configuration, frame size, and frame rate (in the case of this clip, 29.97 frames per second, the standard frame rate for all NTSC video), plus a host of other useful information about your material.

As you scroll right along the window, you get more columns where you can type information such as **Description**, as well as the **Scene**, **Shot/Take**, **Angle**, and **Master Comments**. You will also see **Offline** and **Last Modified**, and new to FCP5, **Film Safe**, for those who would need to conform their material back to a film negative.

Only the **Name** column cannot be moved. It stays displayed on the left side of the window. All of the other columns can be grabbed by the header at the top of the column and pulled left or right to wherever you want the column to appear.

Using Shortcut Menus

Even more information can be displayed in the **Browser** columns by using the **Control** key, one of the most powerful tools in the application. Throughout Final Cut Pro, the **Control** key gives you access to shortcut menus. Even better than the **Control** key would be to get yourself a two- or three-button mouse, with left and right clickers and a scroll wheel. Any movable window or slider can be activated by moving the cursor over the item and using the scroll wheel. Any shortcut menu can be evoked by right-clicking with the mouse rather than using the **Control** key.

Hide Column
Edit Heading
Save Column Layout...
Load Column Layout...

✓ Standard Columns
Logging Columns

Show TC Rate
Show Aux 1 Reel
Show Aux 2 Reel
Show Speed
Show Frame Blending
Show Type
Show Creator
Show TC
Show Aux TC 1
Show Aux TC 2
Show Master Comment 3
Show Master Comment 4
Show Length
Show Capture
Show Source
Show Size
Show Thumbnail
Show Film Slate
Show Camera Roll
Show Lab Roll
Show Film Standard
Show TK Speed
Show Key Number
Show Ink Number
Show Daily Roll
Show Take Note
Show Shot Note
Show Scene Note
Show Media Start
Show Media End
Show Tracks
Show Good
Show Log Note
Show Label
Show Label 2
Show Audio
Show Frame Size
Show Vid Rate
Show Compressor
Show Data Rate
Show Aud Rate
Show Aud Format
Show Alpha
Show Reverse Alpha
Show Composite
Show Pixel Aspect
Show Anamorphic
Show Field Dominance
Show Description
Show Scene
Show Shot/Take
Show Angle
Show Reel
Show Master Comment 1
Show Master Comment 2
Show Comment A
Show Comment B
Show Master Clip
Show Offline
Show Last Modified
Show Film Safe
Show Out
Show In

2.1   List of Browser Column Items

Whenever I say "**Control**-click" in this book, you can right-click to bring up the shortcut menu. These menus are context sensitive and change according to where your cursor is. If your cursor is above the column headers in the **Browser** and you **Control**-click, you get a shortcut menu (Figure 2.1), a list of just some of the available items in columns, those items that are not already displayed in the **Browser**.

Notice in the shortcut menu that you can save and restore column settings similar to the way you can save and load window arrangements. These will be saved in a separate folder of your *~/Library/Preferences/Final Cut Pro User Data* folder called *Column Layouts*. You can also call up saved column arrangements directly from the shortcut menu.

The shortcut menu in the **Browser** header lets you hide a column. It also lets you add even more columns to your **Browser**. You can change the columns from the default **Standard** columns to **Logging** columns, prebuilt sets of columns that you can alter to your personal preferences. Column ordering is one of the only preferences in FCP that is project specific and cannot be restored by deleting your preferences files.

Another item hidden in the contextual menu is **Show Thumbnail**. This cool feature brings up a thumbnail that normally shows the first frame of the video. Grab the thumbnail and drag the mouse. This is called *scrubbing*, and what you're doing is dragging through the video clip itself so you can actually see what's in it. Viewing media like this in the **Browser** can save time. You can quickly scan through a shot to see if it's really the one you're looking for (Figure 2.2).

2.2   Show Thumbnail

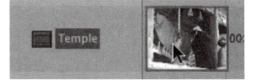

You can also change the Poster frame, the frame that appears in the thumbnail. The default is the first frame of the video (or the In point), but if you scrub through the video and find a new frame you would like to set as the thumbnail, press the **Control** key and release the mouse. A new Poster frame has been set. If you change the Poster frame for a clip here or in any other **Browser** window, the frame will change for each instance of that clip anywhere in the **Browser** and will also display as the Poster frame when the **Browser** is set to Icon view.

There is also a shortcut menu in the **Browser** window itself (Figure 2.3), which accesses a number of features, including a really useful one introduced in FCP5. This is the ability to change the display size of the text in the **Browser** from the default **Small** to **Medium** or **Large**. As computer screens getting bigger, with higher resolution, this becomes an important feature.

There is also a context-sensitive shortcut menu for any item in the **Browser**. Figure 2.4 shows the shortcut menu for a clip. Notice the new feature in FCP5 for **Reveal in Finder**, which will take you to the media file wherever it's located on your hard drives. Also notice the new **Multiclip** functions for use with material from multicamera shoots, which we'll look at in Lesson 7 on page 185.

2.3 Browser Shortcut Menu

The Viewer

After you've imported your clip, double-click *Temple* in your **Browser** to open it in a **Viewer**. The **Viewer** is similar to the viewer in the **Log and Capture** window that we saw in the last lesson. Here the **Viewer** is looking at the media on your computer's hard drive rather than at your tape. In Figure 2.5 you see the top of the **Viewer** display. Notice the time display in the upper left corner that gives the duration of the clip as 1:39;24. That's one minute, 39 seconds, and 24 frames. The timecode display on the upper right is the current timecode display. The section of video starts at 21:38;10, a little bit more than 21 and one-half minutes into the tape from which it was captured. We'll be working with this short piece of material in this lesson.

Playing Clips

There are a number of different ways of playing a clip to look at your video very much like the **Log and Capture** window. The most obvious is the big **Play** button in the middle of the **Viewer** controls (Figure 2.6). Here the shuttle slider is on the left and the jog wheel is on the right. If you like working with the mouse, these will be for you, but it is not the most efficient way to work by any means. I'd recommend learning to use the keyboard. It's your friend, and it's really a much simpler, easier way to control your editing than the mouse.

2.4 Clip Shortcut Menu

2.5 Top of the Viewer

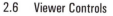

2.6 Viewer Controls

Tip

Open Sequence: Should your project ever open and you don't see any **Canvas** or **Timeline**, it means that there is no sequence open. There needs to be at least one sequence in a project. Double-click the sequence in the **Browser**, and it will open the **Timeline** together with its **Canvas**.

Tip

Shortcut Help: If trying to remember all the keyboard shortcuts is shorting out your brain, you can get color-coded special keyboards with keys that display the shortcuts. A great tool, I find, is Loren Miller's KeyGuide, which you can get from Loren's web site http://lormiller. home.mindspring.com. No FCP editor should be without one. He makes them for a number of applications as well as Final Cut.

Spacebar

As in the **Log and Capture** window, the simplest way to play your clip is just to press the spacebar. To pause, press the spacebar again. To play the clip backwards, press **Shift**-spacebar.

This method is much quicker and keeps your hands on the keyboard and off the mouse. Using the keyboard, you can play and manipulate clips in the **Viewer** with great efficiency.

As the clip plays, the playhead moves through the *scrubber bar.* The scrubber bar is the white area just below the picture in the **Viewer.** If you mouse down in this area, you can move forward and backward through the shot by moving the mouse left and right. This moves the playhead, which is the vertical line in the scrubber bar with a small yellow triangle on top of it. There are playheads scattered throughout Final Cut Pro. You can see one in the **Canvas** and another in the **Timeline**. These two are linked together.

Keyboard Shortcuts

As with the **Log and Capture** window, the best way to control your media is with the J, K, and L keys, L to play forward, K to pause, and J to play backwards. These are your VCR controls. As in the **L&C** window, tapping L multiple times will play forward fast, and tapping J multiple times will play backward fast. These keyboard controls on a fast computer are very responsive. Here too the **I** key will mark the In point, and the **O** key will mark the Out point. There are other useful keyboard shortcuts for working with your media. To play a clip one frame at a time, tap the **Right** arrow key. To play it slowly, hold down the key. To play slowly backwards, hold down the **Left** arrow key. Pressing **K** and **L** together will give you slow forward, and **K** and **J** together, slow backwards (see Table 2.1).

To go back to the previous edit—the cut prior to the point where you are currently—use the **Up** arrow key. To go to the next edit event, use the **Down** arrow key. To go to the beginning of the clip, press the **Home** key; to go to the end press the **End** key.

Custom Keyboard Layouts and Buttons

FCP has the ability to customize the keyboard to suit your needs and also to make buttons out of any of over 900 functions within

Table 2.1   Some Principal Keyboard Shortcuts

Play	**L**
Pause	**K**
Play backwards	**J**
Fast forward	**Repeat L**
Slow forward	**L + K**
Fast backwards	**Repeat J**
Slow backwards	**J + K**
Go to previous edit	**Up Arrow**
Go to next edit	**Down Arrow**
Go to beginning	**Home**
Go to end	**End**
Mark the In point	**I**
Mark the Out point	**O**
Go to In point	**Shift-I**
Go to Out point	**Shift-O**
Play Around Current Point	****
Play from In point to Out point	**Shift-**
Play from current position to Out	**Shift-P**
Match Frame	**F**
Reveal Master Clip	**Shift-F**
Mark Clip	**X**
Add Marker	**M**

the application. To customize the keyboard, go to the menu **Tools>Keyboard Layout>Customize (Option-H)**. This brings up the window in Figure 2.7. Unlock the keyboard with the button in the lower left, scroll through the list on the right, and drag the function onto the key of your choice. To find a function, start to type its name in the query box at the top of the list.

2.7 Custom Keyboard Window

✏ Tip

New Button and Keyboard Pre-
sets: FCP5 has new preset **Button**
Layouts available under the **Tools**
menu. There are presets for **Audio**
Editing, **Media Logging**, and **Multi-**
clip. There is also a special keyboard
layout under the **Tools** menu for
Multicamera Editing.

Notice the tabs at the top that give you access to all the modifier
key combinations. In the **Keyboard Layout** menu, you can also
Export and **Import** custom keyboards. If you want to entirely
redo the keyboard, use the **Clear** button in the lower right corner.
Fortunately, there is also a **Reset** button to return it to its default
condition.

FCP also has the ability to create buttons which you can place in
various windows of the interface. To create a new button, drag
whatever function or functions you want to any one of the little
coffee bean-like holders in the upper right of any of FCP's windows. The little holder can be further customized by adding colors to the buttons, and spacers to group button. You can even
color the spacers. Also in the button holder shortcut menu, you
can save your button configurations for all your windows
(Figure 2.8). To remove a button, drag it out of the bean. It will
disappear, like an item from the **Dock**, in a puff of smoke.

Button bars and keyboard layouts are normally saved in folders
inside ~/*Library/Preferences/Final Cut Pro User Data*, but they
can be saved anywhere. They can also be loaded from anywhere,
from another computer over a network, or from a CD or key-
chain drive. That way you can carry your own configurations
with you wherever you go.

Creating Subclips

Look through the video. It was shot in the tiny Japanese moun-
tain village of Damine (pronounced Dameenay). Often wreathed

2.8   Button Holder Shortcut Menu

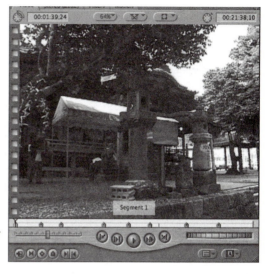

2.9   Master Clips with Segments in Viewer

in blue wood smoke in winter months, the village is famous for a number of things: its Shinto temple to the goddess Kanon; its ancient annual rice festival, *Dengaku*, held in February; and *kabuki*. The village has the only children's *kabuki* troupe in the world. This short video section shows a few shots of the village and the temple. More and more video editors are working with long sections of material that have not been logged or captured as single shots. Working with single shots may be efficient when capturing narrative material or any carefully controlled and scripted shoot, but for documentary, news, wedding videos, or any other production that's shot quickly without careful slating and marking between shots, it's usually more efficient to do your logging after the material has been captured. FCP affords you some excellent tools to do this.

If you're working in DV, you have the benefit of **DV Start/Stop Detect**, which will automatically segment you material into separate clips at each shot change. This is based on the system detecting the sudden change in time in the metadata that holds the date/time stamp. For this to work, you have to have set the clock in your camera. If you haven't, you won't be able to use **DV Start/Stop Detect**. To use this feature in FCP, select the clip in the **Browser** or the clip in the active **Viewer** window, and from the menus choose **Mark>DV Start/Stop Detect**. This process will add markers at every shot change based on that date/time stamp. If the clip isn't in the **Viewer**, double-clicking on it will open it in the **Viewer** with all its segments (Figure 2.9).

40   Lesson 2: Cutting Up Those Shots

2.10   Marquee-Dragging Before Making Subclips

★**Tip**

Moving Shots Out of Bins:
To move a shot out of the bin back to the top level of the **Browser**, drag the shot out of the bin and pull it onto the **Name** column header. That puts it at the top level of the project window.

★**Tip**

Command-D: This keyboard shortcut is not used in FCP5. I use the custom keyboard feature to assign the DV Start/Stop Detect function to it.

★**Tip**

Shortcuts: You can easily move between segments with keyboard shortcuts.
Shift-M (or **Shift-Down** arrow) takes you to the next marker.
Option-M (or **Shift-Up** arrow) takes you to the previous marker.
Option-` to extend the marker.
Command-` or the **Delete** button in the **Marker** dialog box deletes the marker you're positioned on.
Control-` to delete all markers.

Once the material has been segmented, you can twirl open the disclosure triangle in the **Browser** and marquee-drag through all the markers, as shown in Figure 2.10. Then select from the menus **Modify>Make Subclip** or use the keyboard shortcut **Command-U**. Before I do that, I often move the master clip—in this case, *Temple*—into a bin appropriate for its content. To create a new bin, either **Control**-click in the **Browser** and from the shortcut menu choose **New Bin**, or use the keyboard shortcut **Command-B**. I do this so that when I make the subclips from *Temple*, they're already placed in the right bin. Notice in Figure 2.10 that each of the segments has an In point marked, but no duration.

Once your material has been segmented, you can rename the subclips and move them to appropriate bins or organize them however you want. You can do this because subclips are master clips, and though they share the same material as the clip they were segmented from, they do not have a master/affiliate relationship with that clip.

★**Tip**

Ordering Columns: If you organize your reels in the **Browser** by **Media Start**, all the shots will get jumbled up from different reels. To get around this, click first in the column header for **Reel**, which will order the **Browser** based on the reel numbers. Then **Shift**-click on the **Media Start** column header to create secondary ordering. Now the clips will be sorted based first on reel number and then on timecode number. And if the reels were properly numbered, you'll see the material exactly in the order in which it was shot.

☞ *Tip*
_____

Make Offline: To delete a clip from the **Browser**, select it and hit the **Delete** key. This, however, will leave the clip on your drive. If you really want to delete the clip both from your project and from your hard drive, select the clip and **Control**-click on it, choosing from the shortcut menu **Make Offline**. This will bring up the dialog box in Figure 2.11, which offers three options, each more final than the next.

Important: If you make a subclip offline, you will delete all the media associated with that clip and all the subclips, master clips, and affiliate clips that share the same media file.

2.11 Make Offline Dialog

After you've created your subclips, you can marquee-drag to select the segment markers inside the master *Temple* clip and hit the **Delete** key to remove them, if you wish.

In Figure 2.12 you can see the renamed subclips in the bin. Notice that the clips are not in alphabetical order. They are sorted according to their **Media Start** time, so they appear in the order they were in the master clip *Temple*. The **Duration** column shows the length of each subclip, based on the length of the segment between markers.

At this stage you're breaking down your material, organizing it, arranging it in bins, renaming clips, adding notes, and so on. This is critical if you're working on a project that's longer than 10 minutes or so or a project with a lot of material, regardless of its finished length. This process of viewing, logging, and organizing should not be skimped, rushed, or dismissed as drudge work; it is crucial to the editing process.

In addition to naming your clips, the **Browser** has many more columns where you can enter information about your material. One simple way to access these is to use the clips' **Item Properties**.

Name	Media Start ▼	Duration
Temple	00:21:38;10	00:01:39;24
wide shot temple grounds	00:21:38;10	00:00:10;16
store	00:21:48;26	00:00:08;14
bowing at incense bowl	00:21:57;10	00:00:17;23
man leaving temple	00:22:15;05	00:00:10;10
wide temple bell	00:22:25;15	00:00:09;08
woman through incense bowl	00:22:34;23	00:00:15;09
woman through incense 2	00:22:50;02	00:00:13;17
woman praying	00:23:03;21	00:00:14;15

2.12 Renamed Subclips in Bin

☞ *Tip*
_____

Renaming Clips: Though you can rename your clips and subclips anything you want, be aware that the underlying media that remains on your hard drive is unchanged in any way. Most importantly, its name is not changed. So if you ever need to reconnect the media or recapture it, FCP will want to do it under its original naming convention.

2.13 Logging Tab

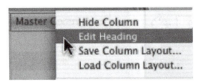

2.14 Editing Comment Column

Either **Control**-click on a clip and select **Item Properties>Logging** or use the keyboard shortcut **Command-9**. The third tab of **Item Properties** is the **Logging** panel, where information can be called up as needed. I set my own keyboard shortcut for this, **Command-Shift-L**. It takes me directly to the **Logging** panel of a clip's **Item Properties** (Figure 2.13).

The **Tab** key will take you from one description text entry panel to the next. Notice that two items that should be **Master Comment 1** and **Master Comment 2** have been renamed **Camera** and **Sound**. You can change names by **Control**-clicking in the **Master Comment** column header in the **Browser** and choosing **Edit Heading**, as shown in Figure 2.14.

Cutting Up Master Clips

If you're working in a format other than DV, you can still cut up your material using subclips. There are a few different ways to do this.

Markers

One way I like is using *markers*. Open your long capture into the **Viewer**, and add markers as you play the clip—on the fly if you like—by tapping the **M** key or the ` (grave accent) key. You can create markers with more precision, of course, as well as set up extended markers to segment the material. Try this with *Temple*.

1. Double-click on *Temple* to open it into the **Viewer**.

2. Set a marker at the beginning of the clip. Do this by moving the playhead to the beginning of the clip with the **Home** key and pressing either the **M** key or the ` (grave accent) key. That will add a marker to the clip, just like the segment markers that **DV Start/Stop Detect** creates.

3. If you wish, you can label the marker. Press the **M** (or `) key again while sitting over the marker. This brings up the dialog window in Figure 2.15.

4. Change the name of the marker if you wish.

This name will carry over into the name of the subclip. In this case, the subclip would be called *WS with memorials from "Temple"* subclip. You can add something to the **Comment** panel, but this will not carry over when the clip is made into a subclip. However, the comment information will remain with the original clip.

Notice also in Figure 2.15 how the marker information displays in the **Viewer**. This stays with *Temple* and will appear whenever the playhead is over the marker, unless the marker is deleted, of course.

5. Play through the clip either with the spacebar or by scrubbing in the scrubber bar until you find the shot change. Use the **Left** and **Right** arrow keys to find the first frame of the next shot at 21:48;26.

6. Add another marker.

You can work your way through the clip, adding markers at each shot change. As with **DV Start/Stop Detect**, the markers can be turned quickly into subclips.

7. Marquee-drag to select the markers from *Temple* in List view and press **Command-U**.

If you're working on narrative film or tightly scripted material, *extended markers* might be useful. When you capture large sections of material, there are often unnecessary pieces: clapperboards, director's instructions, setting the camera, bad takes. You can avoid adding these into your subclips by extending a marker.

1. Start by finding where you'd like the subclip to begin.

2. Add the marker with the **M** or ` key.

3. Play through the shot until the director shouts, "Cut!" or you find the end of the piece you want to make into a subclip.

4. Now extend the marker from the menus by going to **Mark>Markers>Extend**, or by using the keyboard shortcut **Option-`** (grave accent mark).

You can go through your video by markings and extending markers so that the scrubber bar in the **Viewer** might look something like Figure 2.16. The nice thing about this technique is that when you create your subclips by selecting them and hitting **Command-U** or using the **Modify** menu to **Modify>Make Subclip**, the subclips are only for the duration of the extended marker. By extending the markers you've defined the limits of the media available for each shot, basically defined rough In and Out points.

In the *Temple* clip, for instance, there are some camera bobbles, such as right at the end of the second shot, the glass-fronted hut. The start of the third shot also has a reframing zoom. By using extended markers, you can cut these areas out so that they don't appear unexpectedly during a transition. You might also not want

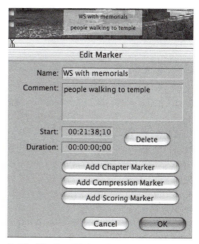

2.15 Marker Dialog Window

> **Tip**
>
> **Edit Marker:** If you Shift-click the Marker button in either the Canvas or the Viewer, it not only sets a marker but also opens the Edit Marker dialog, where you can enter information. You can also use Command-Option-M to open the Edit window for the nearest marker before the current position of the playhead.

2.16 Extended Markers in the Viewer

to subclip a shot, for instance, the fourth shot in *Temple*. Extend the previous marker to the end of the third shot, and don't add a marker for the fourth shot. This is why there are only seven markers or extended markers in Figure 2.16.

Do not extend markers or define subclips too tightly. This should only be a rough cut covering the entire portion of usable media.

FCP will treat the limits of the subclip as the limits of its media and will not allow you to extend the shot farther, so always make the ends of the subclips, the limits of the media, as far as you can without going into another shot or into some rough material, like a swish pan or a quick zoom that you don't want on the screen.

Markers are an excellent tool for entering information about clips, even if you're not using the markers to actually edit your material. Here you can add comments, as well as create *chapter markers* and *compression markers* to use with iDVD or DVD Studio Pro and *scoring markers* to carry over to Soundtrack Pro. It's important to note that these specialized markers should always be added only to the **Timeline** itself. None of these markers, if added to clips, will carry over into other applications. Markers are also searchable within a sequence, as we shall see.

Using In and Out Points

Another method of working with media without **DV Start/Stop Detect** is to open the original master clip into the **Viewer** and then mark your shots with In and Out points.

1. If you have placed any markers in *Temple*, delete them so that you have only the long clip itself. Marquee-drag through the markers and press the **Delete** key.

2. Next open *Temple* into the **Viewer** by double-clicking on it, or dragging it into the **Viewer.**

3. Mark an In point at the beginning of the clip with the **I** key.

4. Play through the clip or scrub through it until you find the last frame of the video. Use the **Left** and **Right** arrow keys to find the frame at 21:48;25.

5. Mark an Out point with the **O** key.

Tip
Removing Subclip Limits: Creating a subclip limits the available media to the length of the shot. If you ever need the rest of the captured material within the original shot, select the clip or clips in either the **Browser** or the **Timeline** and use **Modify > Remove Subclip Limits.** You'll then be able to open the shot in the **Viewer** and access the whole length of the clip's media that is on your hard drive.

2.17 Viewer with In and Out Points Marked

Your **Viewer** will look like Figure 2.17. Note the Out point mark in the picture, indicating that the playhead is at the Out point.

6. To make this shot a subclip, press **Command-U** or use **Modify>Make Subclip**. The clip will immediately appear in the **Browser** with its name highlighted, ready to be renamed.

7. Type in a name.

Switch back to **Viewer**, and you're ready to mark new In and Out points to the master clip to make the next subclip.

Slicing Up Master Clips

All of the methods described previously—using **DV Start/Stop Detect**, working with markers to define sections of your long clips, or cutting up the long clip by defining In and Out points—use the **Make Subclip** feature of Final Cut Pro, but there are a couple of other ways to work in FCP that allow you to cut up and organize your material without actually creating subclips. I call

✦ Tip

Window Commands: There are four handy keyboard shortcuts to navigate your principal windows: Command-1 is the Viewer. Command-2 is the Canvas. Command-3 is the Timeline. Command-4 is the Browser. These commands will allow you to make that the selected window the active window. And the Q key will quickly toggle you to the **Viewer** and between the **Viewer** and the Canvas.

Edit Points

A note on where edit points occur. The shot change between edits actually takes place between the frames. That is, you see one frame, and the next frame you see is the first frame of a different shot. So when you're marking In and Out points, you should know where the shot change is actually taking place. If you mark the In point for a frame that you're looking at in the **Viewer**, that will be the first frame of the new clip. The edit will take place in the space before that frame. If you mark the frame you're looking at as an Out point, that will be the last frame in the clip, and the edit will take place **after the frame you're looking at**.

these methods the Slice methods: slicing up your material, while keeping the entire contents of your long clips. There are a several ways to do this.

Slice 1

The first Slice method is in the **Viewer**. Here we're marking In and Out points but not creating subclips of the material.

1. First open *Temple* from the **Browser** into the **Viewer**.

It will probably have an In and Out point marked. We need to clear those.

2. **Control**-click on the scrubber bar at the bottom of the **Viewer** to evoke a shortcut menu.

3. Select **Clear In and Out**. This will—surprise, surprise—clear the In and Out points (Figure 2.18).

4. Let's begin with the second shot in the *Temple*. Find the shot change at 21:48;26.

5. Mark an In point by hitting the **I** key.

6. Press the spacebar to play *Temple*. Use and the **Left** and **Right** arrow keys to find the end of the shot, the last frame of the shot of statue at 21:57;09.

7. Create a new bin in the **Browser** (**Command-B**) and name it *Clips*.

8. Drag the sliced clip of *Temple* from the **Viewer** and drop it into the *Clips* bin. Do not rename this clip; this would rename *Temple*. The new clip still has an affiliate clip relationship to the master clip.

✈**Tip**
Clearing from the Browser: If you've opened a clip from the **Browser** and want to clear its In and Out points, you can use the keyboard shortcut **Option-X**. You can also use this shortcut to clear In and Out points marked in the **Timeline**. You can't, however, clear the In and Out from a clip that's been opened from the **Timeline**. A clip that's in a **Timeline** must, by definition, have an In and Out point, a start and end frame, even if it's the first and last frame of the clip.

2.18 Viewer Shortcut Menu

9. Go back to the **Viewer** and repeat the process, marking In and Out points for each shot and dragging them into the *Clips* bin.

As we saw earlier, these clips cannot be renamed because they are all affiliate clips of the master clip *Temple*. However, there is a feature that gets around this problem.

10. Select all the clips you've created in the *Clips* bin by marquee-dragging through them or by double-clicking on the bin to open it and using **Command-A** to **Select All**.

11. With the clips selected from the **Modify** menu, use **Modify>Make Master Clip**.

This will turn all of the clips into master clips, allowing you to rename them and organize your material.

Slice 2

The second Slice method is in the **Timeline**. This is where you really are slicing with a digital razor blade.

1. First open *Temple* from the **Browser** into the **Viewer.**

It will probably have an In and Out point marked. We need to clear those.

2. **Control**-click on the scrubber bar at the bottom of the **Viewer** and choose **Clear In and Out** from the shortcut menu or use the keyboard shortcut **Option-X**.

3. If it's not open already, open the empty **Timeline** by double-clicking on *Sequence 1* in the **Browser** and drag *Temple* into it, dropping the clip on **V1**.

When you place a clip in the **Timeline**, the playhead automatically jumps to the end of the clip, ready for you to place another clip in position. In this case, we don't want to do that.

4. Click in the **Timeline** window to make it active (or use **Command-3**), and then press the **Home** key to take you back to the beginning of the **Timeline** (Figure 2.19).

5. Press the spacebar to play *Temple*. The video plays in the **Canvas.**

6. Again use the spacebar to stop and the **Left** and **Right** arrow keys to find the first frame of the shot of the glass-fronted hut at 01:00:10;16.

> ✎ *Tip*
>
> *Opening a Clip:* Another way to open a clip into the **Viewer** is to select it and press the **Return** key. Normally the **Enter** key will do the same thing as the **Return** key, but if you select a clip in the **Browser**, this is the only instance in which it will not. With the clip selected, the **Enter** key is used to highlight and select the name so that the clip can be renamed.

2.19   Timeline Window

Razor Blade Tool - b

2.20 Blade Tool

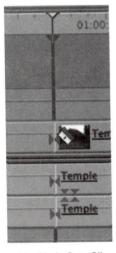

2.21 Blade Cuts Clip

7. Take the **Blade** tool from the **Tools** palette (Figure 2.20) or call it up with the keyboard shortcut **B**.

8. Bring the **Blade** to the playhead so that it snaps to it. Click on the clip (Figure 2.21).

9. Go back to the **Selection** tool from the top of the **Tools** palette, or bring it back with the keyboard shortcut **A** (*A* for *arrow*).

Tip

Snapping: Snapping can be toggled on and off with the **N** key or by clicking on the **Snapping** button in the upper left corner of the **Timeline** window (Figure 2.22). When the button is green, snapping is on; when it's black, snapping is off.

This will cut the video and audio on the clip as though you were cutting it with a knife or a razor blade, which is what was formerly used to cut film, audio tape, and even videotape when it was first edited. What you are doing is the digital metaphor for the same process. When you make the edit, notice the little red triangular marks that appear. They indicate where there is a cut between two shots with contiguous time code. These are *Through Edit* marks that can be switched on and off in the **Timeline Options** panel of the **Sequence Settings** (**Sequence>Settings** menu or **Command-0** [zero]).

The **Timeline Options** functions are available directly from a tiny triangle in the bottom left of the **Timeline** window that acts as a popup menu (Figure 2.23). Here you also toggle on and off the Through Edit marks. This popup also allows you to set track heights as well as save and restore track layout arrangements. Track heights are customizable by dragging between the tracks in the track header, as shown in Figure 2.24.

Snapping - n

2.22   Snapping Button (above)

2.23   Timeline Options Popup Menu (middle)

2.24   Adjusting Track Heights (right)

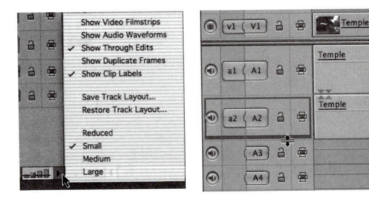

2.25 Clip Cut in the Timeline

1. Now that you've made one cut, find the next shot. Its first frame starts with the quick zoom at 01:00:19;00. This time rather than using the **Blade** tool, use **Control-V** to cut the shot.

2. Go through the **Timeline** and slice more clips by using **Control-V** to cut at the first frame of every new shot. (Figure 2.25).

3. After you've cut out the clips you want from the long shot in the **Timeline**, go to the **Browser** and select *Sequence 1*.

4. From the **Modify** menu, select **Modify>Make Sequence Clips Independent**.

5. Drag the clips into a bin in the **Browser**. These clips are all master clips and can be renamed, reedited, and organized.

Another method would be not to make the sequence clips independent first, but simply to drag the clips back into the **Browser**, and with the clips selected there, use **Modify>Make Master Clip**.

Deleting Clips

This process of going through your material to cut it up can also be used to make selections, keeping just the shots you want to work with and throwing away those you don't need.

1. To remove a shot from the edited sequence in the **Timeline**, select the shot and press **Delete**, the large **Delete** key next to the equals sign (=).

Edit Points Redux

We talked about where the cut takes place when you're editing, that the In point cuts the space before the frame you're looking at, and the Out point cuts after the frame you're looking at. The **Blade** always cuts on the gap in front of the frame you're seeing in the **Canvas**. So to put the edit after the last frame of the first shot in *Temple* when cutting in the **Timeline**, you have to be looking at the first frame of the shot after it. If you do **Control-V** on the last frame of the first shot, the next shot will have one frame of the previous shot at its head.

⭐Tip
Ripple Delete: In addition to the keyboard shortcut **Shift-Delete** for for removing a shot and rippling the sequence, on extended keyboards you can also use the **Forward Delete** key to do this. This is the small **Delete** key next to the **End** key.

This will remove the clip from the timeline, but it will also leave a gap.

2. So let's undo that with **Command-Z**.

The undo will make the shot reappear in the hole in the timeline. Instead of deleting it, we will do what's called a *ripple delete*.

3. Select the clip, hold down the **Shift** key, and press **Delete**.

In addition to removing the clip, the ripple delete also pulls up all the other material in the timeline, shortening the sequence.

4. Double-click one of your newly created independent clips, either from the sequence or from the ones you dragged into the **Browser**.

Notice that this *Temple* shot comes in with an In and Out point marked, and notice also that the clip contains all the video that's in the original master shot called *Temple*. The upside of this is obvious. Because a sliced clip is a copy of the master clip, you can now access any shot in the reel from inside any sliced clip.

That's the upside; the downside is scrubbing. The master clip is made up of a long length of material, perhaps even a whole reel of film or a roll of videotape, though I would advise against this. It's now difficult to scrub in the **Viewer** because even a tiny movement will move the playhead a long way up and down the scrubber bar.

Slice 3

With the Slice 2 method, you're cutting the pieces you want to keep and moving them into the **Browser**. Let's look at another method of working in the **Timeline**. Here we'll cut away the pieces we don't want to use and leave the good material in the **Timeline**. This method works especially well for narrative fiction or for material that's heavily scripted, material that has rough sections that need to be edited out even before it's organized into bins. It also works very well for news and other material with a quick turn around, material you don't have to store, organize, or log carefully.

1. Begin by deleting everything in *Sequence 1*. **Command-A** will **Select All**, and the **Delete** key will remove everything.

2. Next make sure there aren't any In and Out points marked in the master clip *Temple*. Bring a fresh copy into the sequence by dragging it into the **Timeline.**

3. Press the **Home** key to return to the start of the sequence.

4. Play forward until you reach the beginning of the second shot at 01:00:10;16. We want to remove the second shot from the sequence because we don't need it. Make sure the clip isn't selected.

🐾 *Note*

Important: It is critical that you have nothing selected in the sequence when you use this technique. Anything that is selected—clip, audio, title, anything—will be ripple deleted instead of the marked In and Out section. The simplest way to avoid this is to press **Command-Shift-A** for **Deselect All**. This drops anything that's been selected. A good habit to get into before you execute this technique is to always make the **Timeline** the active window and press **Command-Shift-A**, or if you really like the menus, **Edit** > **Deselect All**, the opposite of **Command-A**, **Select All**. Also note that if there is anything selected in the sequence, the autoselect function will not work, and you will not see the highlighting in the sequence.

5. Mark an In point in the sequence by pressing the **I** key.

6. Play forward through the second shot and through the zoom at the beginning of the third shot, until about 01:00:21;02. This is all the material we want to cut out, the glass-fronted hut section. We will cut out everything from the first frame of the second shot to and including the frame where the playhead is parked just like we mark In and Out points in the **Viewer.**

7. Press the **O** key to enter an Out point in the **Timeline**, which should look like Figure 2.26.

Notice the highlighted area in the tracks. This is the **Autoselect** feature. Tracks can have their selection toggled on and off with the buttons circled on the left in Figure 2.26. This allows you to select some tracks while not selecting others.

2.26 Timeline Selection

8. Now press **Shift-Delete** to execute a ripple delete, removing that section of the video.

👍 *Tip*

Autoselect Shortcuts: There is a collection of keyboard shortcuts using the keypad of the extended keyboard to toggle off and on the autoselect functions. **Command-1, 2, 3**, and so on will toggle tracks **V1, V2, V3**, and so on. **Option-1, 2, 3, 4**, and so on will toggle audio tracks **A1, A2, A3, A4**, and so on.

This method is a fast, efficient way to cut material quickly. You end up with the shots you want to keep in the timeline. If you do want to organize and rename your material again, running **Modify>Make Sequence Clips Independent** will now separate the clips in the **Timeline** from their master/affiliate relationship. Now you can pull them into bins and rename them if you wish.

Slicing, whether in the **Viewer** or the **Timeline**, has the advantage of quickly and easily accessing all your material while still cutting it up into shots for editing. It has a couple of disadvantages:

- The problem of not being able to scrub easily in the **Viewer**, as we discussed earlier on page 50.
- The problem with transitions of accidentally running into material from another shot.

🦋 *Note*_____

Browser and Timeline Clips: This is a good point to explain a bit about the relationship between the clips in the Browser and the clips in **Timeline**. Quite simply, there is no relationship—no direct, linked relationship anyway, other than their master/affiliate relationship. Apart from that relationship, which forces them to have the same name and label, they are two separate and distinct items. They may be copies of each other, but they are quite separate clips that share the same media. When you drag the master clip from the **Browser** and place it in a **Timeline**, you are placing an affiliate copy of the master clip. So when you razor blade and ripple delete the clip in the **Timeline**, you are not in any way affecting the master clip that remains untouched in your **Browser**.

Comparison

2.27 Subclip in the Viewer

Let's see how making subclips is different from slicing. Open one of the subclips you created earlier using **DV Start/Stop Detect**. Unlike a sliced clip with its In and Out marking a small portion of the master clip, in the subclips the In point and Out point do not appear at all (Figure 2.27).

The subclip is treated as a separate piece of media, though in reality it's not. Notice the film sprocket holes on the left side of the frame in Figure 2.27. These holes on the left or right edge of the frame indicate that you're at the limit of the media for that clip. Though the subclip is only a portion of the piece of the *Temple* media on your hard drive, it's treated in FCP as a complete, self-contained piece of media. Hence the film sprocket indicator. The advantage to working in the subclip method is that it's easy to scrub the clip, running the mouse along the length of the media.

If you need to access more of the media within that subclip, you can use **Remove Subclip Limits** from the **Modify** menu. When you do this, the clip, if it's in the **Viewer**, will suddenly disappear, and a slug will be loaded in its place. The application has always done that, and I'm not sure why it still does. If you again open that clip after the subclip limits are removed, the clip will revert to its whole length, without In or Out points.

You can also remove subclip limits from a shot or a whole bin of shots directly in the **Browser.** Just select the bin and pull down **Remove Subclip Limits** from the **Modify** menu. All the subclips will revert to full-length clips.

👍 *Tip*

Keeping Ins and Outs: If you want subclips to retain their In and Out points after the subclip limits are removed, you need to set In and Out points for them. The simplest way is to hit the **X** key. This will mark and In and Out points at the beginning and end of the subclip in the **Viewer.** Now when the subclip limits are removed the In and Out will be retained.

The simplest way to do this for a whole group of subclips in the **Browser** is to drag them all into a sequence first. Dragging the subclips into a timeline will immediately define In and Out points for the clips. If you then delete the original subclips in the **Browser** and drag the clips from the sequence back into the **Browser,** the In and Out points for these clips will remain. With **Remove Subclip Limits,** the clips will behave as sliced clips, with Ins and Outs defined, but with whole lengths of the media available on either side.

The fact that you can't normally exceed the limits of the subclip is also an advantage, while being a problem with the slice method described earlier. The issue is transitions. These take extra media, extending the shot to create space for themselves. Transitions will take any available media. In the slice method, that media may include sudden zooms, garbage frames, or bits of another shot. These appear as a sudden flash during a transition, barely noticeable, but disconcerting.

Because subclips can't extend the media beyond their duration, this will never happen with a subclip. The trick to using subclips is to make sure that you include in your subclip not just the really good bit of the shot you want to use, but as much extra material as you safely can without including any garbage or spurious frames. This means then when you edit down the subclips there will be room for the transition to extend the material.

Range Clipping

Another technique for slicing or making subclips is to use the **Range** tool in the **Timeline.** Some people prefer this method because it offers a visual display of the In and Out points as you work. Let's try this.

2.28 Range Tool

2.29 Range Tool in the Timeline

2.30 Range Selection Two-Up Display
in the Canvas

1. Again, make sure there are no In and Out points in the master clip *Temple* before dragging it into an empty timeline.

2. Select the **Range** tool from the tools. It's under the second icon from the top (Figure 2.28). You can also call it up by hitting **GGG** (the letter **G** three times).

3. Position the playhead in the **Timeline** where you want the clip selection to begin.

4. With the **Range** tool, stroke one section of the clip (Figure 2.29).

Unfortunately the **Range** tool, unlike the **Blade**, does not respond to snapping, but the crosshairs let you position the **Range** selector very precisely. As you stroke the clip to make the selection, the **Canvas** will give you a two-up display that shows you the start and end frames as well as the timecode (Figure 2.30).

5. Now grab the selection from the **Timeline** and drag it to the **Viewer**, where it will load as a sliced clip.

6. To turn the range selected portion of the clip into a subclip, you have to drag it into the **Browser**, where it can be converted into a new subclip.

Organizing the Clips

Once you've got your material cut up, you should spend some time getting it put away so that you can find it again. There are no firm rules about this, and I find each project tends to dictate its own organizational structure. Usually I begin with one bin that holds all the master shots. These are usually pretty big chunks of video: 10, 20, 30 minutes, usually not smaller. This master bin holds all the reels of material. I don't like to capture whole reels, though occasionally I do. I usually capture in 15–20 minute blocks, depending on how it was shot and where a natural break occurs. These get stored in the master bin as clip *001a, 001b,*

002a, 002b, 002c, 003a, and so on, the number being the reel number and the letter suffix a piece of that reel.

From the master shots, clips are separated out into bins. Keeping the master shots has the advantage that you can go back to the material in bulk to look through it again. As the project nears completion, I like to do this to see if I overlooked or discarded anything, which can be useful in light of the way the material gets cut together.

The separate bins can be organized in a variety of ways. Tightly scripted projects like some corporate videos and narrative film projects that have numbered scenes tend to have material broken down in scene bins, with sub-bins for different types of shots or characters, depending on how complex the scene. So for a narrative project, you may have a number of scene bins in addition to your master bin, as shown in Figure 2.31.

The figure shows the beginning development of one method of scene organization. In the **Browser** is a *Masters* bin that holds the three master reels captured so far. Three scenes have been shot, and there are three corresponding bins *Scene 7, Scene 8,* and *Scene 10.* The *Scene 7* bin is open and has been subdivided into two bins, *Frank* and *Anna.* In each of those bins would be single shots, probably close-ups, of Frank and Anna with their take numbers. Also in the *Scene 7* bin are three takes of the wide shot and a sequence called *Scene 7,* in which the scene is actually edited together from the wide, cover shots and the close-ups.

In the **Browser** you'll also see a bin for *Scene 8,* probably a short bridging scene, with just two takes. It has no sequence of its own.

Scene 10, the open bin at the bottom of the figure, is a more complex scene with a number of bins for characters, covers, cutaways, and for a sub-scene between two characters. There are also two sequences called *Scene 10* and *Scene 10a,* which are the main scene together with a subscene between two characters that may be edited separately and embedded (or ***nested*** as it's called in Final Cut Pro) within the sequence *Scene 10.*

These edited sequences *Scene 7* and *Scene 10* together with the bridging shot for *Scene 8* and eventually *Scene 9,* when it's shot and captured, will all be placed in the sequence called *Final,* which you see at the very top of the **Browser** window.

2.31 Narrative Film Organization

2.32 Documentary Organization

Documentary projects tend to break the material down into subject matter: a bin for the tree shots, another for river scenes, another for snow scenes, another for all the interviews, another for narration tracks, another for music, another for graphics as in Figure 2.32, which shows part of a documentary organization. There are no hard and fast rules on how material is organized; the organization is usually determined by the subject matter.

Notice that the *Interviews* bin, in addition to having the capturing interview material, also has sequences in which the interviews are edited down into the key soundbites. These are the pieces of the interview that might be used in the *Final* sequence.

Notice also the open bin *Trees*, inside of which is a sequence also called *Trees*. I like to work with a sequence within the bin. Inside the sequence will be all the shots that are in that bin. In this way I can either look at individual shots that can be searched by FCP's **Finder**, which we'll see in a moment, or I can quickly look through all the shots by scrubbing through the sequence or playing through it at double speed. By putting it in a sequence you get to see what all your choices are, rather than just relying on the find command to locate particular pieces of material. For similar reasons, I like to keep master reels as long clips in separate bins. It allows me to look through the material again in shoot order, as it was the day the cameraperson shot it.

The real trick in organizing your material is to break it down into enough bins so that the material in your **Browser** has a logical structure, but not so many bins that it becomes difficult to find material. As you move clips into bins, add notes—lots of them. The more information you include on the clips, the easier it will be to find them.

FCP provides ways to help you organize your material. Principally you have bins, and bins within bins. But at the most visible level you have color-coded and user-definable labels. **Control**-click on a clip or bin to call up a shortcut menu from which you can select from label colors and names (Figure 2.33). You can set the names however you like in the **Labels** panel of **User Preferences**.

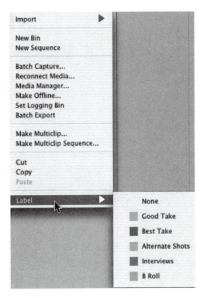

2.33 Shortcut Menu Labels

☞ *Tip*
___
Moving Between Sequences: Keeping a sequence of shots available
for a subject allows you to drag a shot from one sequence into a final
sequence. A second computer monitor is useful for this to give yourself enough screen real estate. You can also copy shots that are in one
sequence and paste them into another. One thing I like about keeping a
subject material sequence is that as shots get copied and used in the
final sequence, they can be deleted from the sequence to avoid the
danger of reusing a shot unintentionally. Or, often better, is to mark the
shot as *used.* Go to **Item Properties** (**Command-9**) and add an asterisk
to the name. By marking it used, you don't remove it from the
sequence, so if later on you find a place where that particular shot will
serve you better, it's still an available shot in your choices, though you
may want to replace its earlier use. **Dupe Detection**, which we'll see
on page 100, is a big help in finding that other usage of the shot.
___

The **Browser** or the **Logging** panel of **Item Properties** both give
you all the information boxes we saw earlier. Use them. Do not
overlook or hurry through the note-taking and entering process.
All editors have their own ways of organizing material, loading
information into the computer, and keeping it consistent. However you do it, it opens up to you one of computer-based editing's
great boons, the computer's ability to search through huge
amounts of data almost instantly. But you have to enter the information first. You can enter it either directly in the **Browser** fields,
or by **Control**-clicking the clip and selecting **Item Properties>Log-
ging Info.**

What is entered in the **Logging** panel also appears in the **Browser**
columns and will be searchable with FCP's search engine.

All these tools are a great help to editors, but nothing helps an
editor in long form more than a good visual and aural memory.
Simply being able to remember material over perhaps hundreds of
reels is a real gift, but even without this talent, looking closely at
all your material, making good notes, and having a decent search
engine will go a long way toward making your life a lot easier.

Final Cut has an excellent search tool, which is why adding the
notes is so important. You can call up Final Cut's **Finder** with the

2.34 Find Dialog

2.35 Finder Results

keyboard shortcut **Command-F** (Figure 2.34). The first popup in the **Find** window lets you search:

- The open project
- All open projects
- The *Effects* folder

The second popup selects **All Media** or a choice of **Used** or **Unused Media,** while the third popup lets you replace or add to existing results. The two popups at the bottom define parameters. The left one sets where it's going to look, while the right sets the search options.

Unless you have pretty good idea where the information is—for instance, if you're looking for a specific type of file—just leave it on the default **Any Column.**

If you press the **Find All button** rather than the default **Find Next,** the requested clips appear in a new **Browser** window (Figure 2.35). It found these clips because I had typed the word *temple* in the **Scene** name in the **Logging** panel for each shot. Notice also that it found *Sequence 1,* which contains a shot with that scene name.

The two buttons at the bottom let you:

- Show a selected item in the regular **Browser** bins
- Remove selected items from project

This **Remove** is not the powerful **Make Offline** tool we saw earlier on page 41, which lets you delete the media. This one deletes the clip in the **Browser** window.

The key to being able to find something with the search engine is to enter the data correctly to start with, to anticipate how you'll be searching for the material, by subject matter, by type of shot, by words spoken. By anticipating the questions you might want to ask of the material you'll be able to input the right data into the logging columns. With the right data loaded, searching through your material becomes a breeze.

Note

Search Engine: This is the Browser's search engine, so unfortunately FCP cannot at this time search through marker screen information. It would be very useful if it could, but as of this writing, it has not been implemented. If you use the search feature in a specific sequence, you will get a more limited search engine, but one that does look for text in the marker screen information (Figure 2.36).

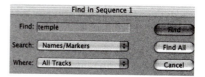

2.36 Sequence Search Window

Look Before You Cut

However you work your video into clips or subclips, what you're really doing is looking through your material. What you should watch for is relationships, shots that can easily be cut together. Getting familiar with the material is an important part of the editing process, learning what you have to work with and looking for cutting points. I think this is one reason why many editors still like to use the batch capture method. It allows them the first opportunity to look at the available material. Many editors still like to look through their material carefully after its been captured, putting the shots into a sequence to look through it.

Look through the master shot *Temple*. It's quite short but it shows a few shots that have obvious relationships. The same woman, in the white woolen hat, appears in four of them:

- In the third shot, as she bows before an incense bowl
- The shot from behind her that looks a little blue, in which she is walking up the stairs
- Another, in quick succession to the previous one, also from behind as she goes up the steps
- In medium shot from the side as she bows and prays

These shots can obviously be cut together to make a little sequence. You might want to put in a cutaway between the shot of her bowing at the bowl and her from behind walking up the steps or at the top of the steps already. From either of those two shots, a direct cut to her bowing would work without problem.

Searching for these relationships between shots is critical as you look through your material. Some editors like to immediately create small sequences and group them together, not finely honed, but roughly laid out, so that important first impression is preserved. You may not use it in your final project, but assembling related shots quickly into a sequence is an efficient way to make notes about your material. We'll look at assembling material into sequences in our next lesson.

Duplicating Sequences

✪Tip
Sequence Settings: Sequences
require precise settings to be com-
patible with the material placed in
them. Rather than creating a new
sequence, it might be simpler for
these lessons to duplicate an existing sequence, which duplicates its
settings as well.

1. Select the sequence called *Sequence 1* that appeared in the **Browser** when you opened *Lesson 2*.

2. Then go to the **Edit** menu and select **Duplicate**, or use the keyboard shortcut **Option-D**. This duplicates everything currently in that sequence and automatically names it *Sequence 1 Copy*.

3. Rename this sequence something appropriate.

4. Open it by double-clicking on it, press **Command-A** to select everything that may be in the **Timeline**, and press the **Delete** key.

✪Tip
Pulling Windows: To separate the
timelines, just grab the tab and tear
one timeline away from the other.
You can always stick them back
together again by pushing one tab
back next to the other. Any tabbed
window call be pulled apart like this.
All the elements of the **Viewer** can
be in separate windows as can the
contents of the **Browser**. Bins can
be opened separately and tabbed
together into clusters. It can be a
very useful tool.

Everything's gone, and you now have a brand new, pristine, empty timeline that you're sure has the right settings for your work.

You can have multiple sequences open at the same time. Timelines normally tab together into one **Timeline** window, but you can pull the timelines apart so that you have two sequences open on the screen at the same time. You can pull shots from one sequence into another. By doing this, you're actually copying the shot from one sequence into the new sequence.

While you edit, you just put together the shots you want to work with—edit them, rearrange them, shorten and lengthen them—how you like. You can just park your edited sequence to be used later, either as an edited group of shots or just as a holding bin for a group of shots, but unlike a simple bin, here the shots are laid out in the specific order you have arranged.

There are many different ways to work, perhaps as many different ways as there are editors. The longer the project, the more variations in work flow. How you organize your material is critical in long-form production. Many people like to work in organized bins; some prefer to work with multiple sequences with very few bins. The final scene is then made up by selecting shots from multiple open timelines and moving them to the final sequence. This way of working is best with very large computer monitors.

Others prefer to work with multiple bins, all of them open at once, all in Icon view. A second computer monitor is almost a prerequisite for working like this. Others prefer to work with toggled open bins set in list view with the **Comments** and **Log Notes** columns pulled over next to the **Name** column. Others like to use the **Find** tool, leaving found multiple lists open at the same time.

As you become more experienced, you'll find yourself working with some methods more than others. You'll probably also find that on different projects, you work in different ways. Some material lends itself to working with multiple sequences; other material might not. Some work flows are faster than others. Laying out clips in bins that you trim in the **Viewer** and then rearrange as a storyboard might sound good, but cutting up and rearranging material entirely in a timeline is probably a lot quicker for small amounts of material.

Media Manager

At some stage in the editing process, you may want to remove all the excess material from your hard drive and just keep the core material that your project needs. You may do this housekeeping more than once in the course of creating a longer project. You may do it fairly early once you've gleaned out the good material, and you may do it toward the end of the project as you're finalizing it. Or maybe at the very end of the project after everything is edited and reduced to one sequence and its media for archiving purposes. Whenever you decide, in Final Cut Pro you should try to use **Media Manager** (Figure 2.37).

You select **Media Manager** from the **File** menu. You can apply **Media Manager** to single or multiple sequences or multiple clips or bins. Whatever you select, **Media Manager** will only include those items in the consolidation.

2.37 Media Manager Window (right)

2.38 Media Manager Popup (below)

Because of FCP's master/affiliate architecture, if you wish to Media Manage the contents of a sequence or group of sequences, there is an important procedure you should follow.

1. Select the sequence or sequences to be Media Managed and duplicate them. This is purely for protection. It may not be necessary if you're in the final stages of your project.

2. With the sequences selected, choose **Modify>Make Sequence Clips Independent**.

This separates the clips within the sequences from their master affiliation. With the clips separated, **Media Manager** can deal with the material without needing all the master clip material.

The **Media Manager** window (Figure 2.37) itself is pretty self-explanatory. It lists your options and what the system will do with them. The summary information at the top of the window explains what your options are doing, below that the bar graphs show the amount of media involved, how long it is, and how much your media management will produce.

The **Media** popup offers a number of options (Figure 2.38). The default copies the media to a new location, which is picked from the **Browse** button at the bottom of the window. With the **Copy** process, the media is copied and the unused media deleted or not, as requested, and a new project is created. The new project opens immediately into FCP.

Make sure that you uncheck the box for **Include affiliate clips outside selection** if you do not want the additional affiliated clips associated with that media. Notice also the **Include nonactive multiclip angles** checkbox. Use this feature with multicamera sequences. It defaults to being checked, but if you're finished with your edit and want to consolidate your material, you'll probably want to uncheck this box.

If the clips in a sequence have the same name, which often happens, the names are incremented with a suffix to distinguish them from each other. Notice that **Media Manager** gives you the choice to **Base file names on** either the **existing file names** or **clip names** (Figure 2.39). If you choose file names, FCP will use the names given to the media on the hard drive. If you use clip names, the names for the new media will be that given by you within the application.

The **Move** option actually moves the media to the new location. When moving to a different drive or partition, the media will have to copy over, and after the operation is completed, the original media will disappear from the original location. If you use the **Move** option and other clips are associated with the media, a dialog box appears (Figure 2.40).

Selecting **Add** will maintain the link to clips in other projects. Choosing **Continue** will break the link. Because this is undoable, choosing either **Add** or **Continue** will bring up a further warning before you can execute the action.

When media is moved, it's transferred to the designated place and put in a folder named after the project. This folder, in turn, is inside another folder called *Media*. Though the filing system seems convoluted, the process is efficient. In the **Move** option, unlike the **Copy** option, a new project is not created; the media is moved to a new location specified with the **Browser** button.

2.39 Base Files Names on Popup (above)

2.40 Moving Dialog (right)

Additional Items Found

29 items outside of your current selection have been found to reference media about to be processed during this operation.

If you add these items to your selection, an additional 1.8 GB of disk space will be required for an additional 00:08:24;24 of media referenced by these items.

If you select Continue, these items will not be added to your selection, and they might be taken offline.

Add   Continue   Abort

2.41 Recompress to Photo JPEG   2.42 Create Offline to DV NTSC

The **Recompress** function is useful, for instance, if you want to take your existing project and edit it on a PowerBook using **OfflineRT**. You can use **Recompress** as in Figure 2.41 to convert your material to 320×240 using Photo-JPEG or whatever presets you have available. After editing in the Photo-JPEG format, you'd need to use the **Create Offline** function of **Media Manager** and recapture your material at full resolution, perhaps back in the DV format you started in, as in Figure 2.42.

The **Use Existing** option is really the opposite of the **Move** option. While **Move** transfers the material but does nothing to the project, **Use Existing** creates a new project with whatever is included in **Media Manager**. If you have **Delete Unused** selected, it will immediately delete the unneeded portions from your hard drive and replace them with only the media required for the new project. This is fatal and final. I would recommend using this option only if you are pressed for drive space. If you have the space available, use **Copy** or **Move**.

The **Create Offline** option makes a new project with sequences and/or clips as requested in **Media Manager**, but leaves all the clips marked **Offline**, with the red diagonal line through them, ready to be recpatured.

Media Manager defaults to no handles and not moving render files. I would recommend making some handles, especially for **Create Offline**. One second is usually good. Probably dumping the render files is a good idea, unless the project is render intensive. Then it might be worthwhile preserving them to save time later.

Summary

In this lesson we've covered the master/affiliate relationship in FCP, as well as cutting up media, creating subclips, organizing your material so that you can work efficiently, and consolidating with the **Media Manager**. In the next lesson we'll look at editing sequences.

Lesson 3

Building Your Sequence

Now that you've brought your material into Final Cut Pro and have cut it up, we're ready to begin putting it all together. There is no right way to edit a scene or a sequence or even a whole film or video; there are only bad ways, good ways, and better ways. In this lesson we're going to look at some video and edit it.

Loading the Lesson

As in the previous lesson, start by loading the DVD into your DVD drive. When you begin any lesson that needs material from the DVD, you should first drag the needed folders onto the media drive of your computer. The sound and video clips included there will play much better and more smoothly from your computer's high-speed media drive than from any DVD drive. For this lesson you'll also need the folders called *Lesson 3 Media* as well as the project file called *Lesson 3*, which is inside the *Projects* folder on the DVD.

1. If you haven't already done it, drag the *Projects* folder to your internal system drive. Again, probably the best place for it is in your *Documents* folder.

2. Drag the *Lesson 3 Media* folder onto your media drive.

3.1 **Offline Files Dialog Box (above)**

3.2 **Reconnect Dialog Box (right)**

3. Before opening anything, eject the DVD from your computer.

4. Double-click on the *Lesson 3* project file inside your *Projects* folder on your hard drive to launch the application.

When the application finishes launching, you'll be greeted with FCP5's new **Offline Files** dialog box (Figure 3.1).

5. Do *not* click the default button, or press **Return** or **Enter**. Instead click on the **Reconnect** button.

You will then get FCP5's newly revised **Reconnect Dialog** box (Figure 3.2). Notice in this version you have the ability to limit the search to specific drives or partitions, which can be useful if you are working on a shared area network or any system with a great deal of storage.

6. Click on the **Search** button to have FCP search either a specified area or all available resources. If the application cannot find the files, use the **Locate** button to navigate to them.

The computer will look for the first file in the list—in this case, the QuickTime movie called *Food*. When the file is found, you'll get a dialog box that looks similar to the one in Figure 3.3. This is the Tiger (Mac OS X 10.4) navigation services dialog box.

3.3   Reconnect Selection Window

7.   If that is the correct file on your media drive, click **Choose**.

The files will then appear in the bottom portion of the **Reconnect Dialog** box, where you press the **Reconnect** button to reestablish the link between the clips and the media in its new location.

Working with Clips

Inside the **Browser** of your copy of *Lesson 3*, you'll see a couple of sequences:

- *Sequence 1*
- *Food Sequence*

Sequence 1 is empty. We'll look at *Food Sequence* in a moment. In the **Browser** there is also the master clip, *Food*, a bin called *Clips*, and an audio file called *Music.aif*. Open the *Clips* bin and you'll see the shots from *Food* cut up into subclips.

These are the clips we're going to work with in this lesson. Take a quick look at *Food Sequence*. This is where we're going. To begin, let's look at where we're coming from, the material we have to work with.

1. Double-click on the clip called *Food*, which will bring it into the **Viewer**. The material is one minute and 17 seconds long.

2. Play through the material.

3. Open the *Clips* bin and double-click on the shot called *Food 1*, which is 6:01 long, six seconds and one frame.

4. Play the shot, let it pan from left to right across the trays of food, let the pan end, give it a beat, and then stop.

5. Enter an Out point.

This is probably around 1:37;01, making the shot about four and one-half seconds in length.

Try it a few times until you get the pacing of the movement down. You might find that the more times you try it, the more you're shaving off the shot. Perhaps you'll feel that the front needs to be shortened as well. Instead of beginning right at the start of the shot, enter an In point just before the camera pans right. When you have it the way you want it, you're ready to move it into the

3.4   Dragging into the Timeline

Timeline.

3.5   Edit Buttons

3.6   Canvas Edit Overlay (CEO)

There are five ways to get material from the **Viewer** to the **Timeline**:

- Drag it there. Grab the image from the **Viewer** and pull it directly into the **Timeline**, dropping it onto **V1** as in Figure 3.4.

- The second way is to press the little red button, the middle button, in the group of three at the bottom left of the **Canvas** (Figure 3.5).

- The third way is use the keyboard shortcut **F10**.

- The fourth method is to drag the clip from the **Viewer** to the **Canvas**, and the visual dialog box in Figure 3.6 appears immediately.

- The final way, which I wouldn't recommend to anybody, is to drag the clip onto one of the edit buttons.

Exposé allows you to temporarily see all your open windows at once, so you can easily click on any window to bring it to the front. You can set a Dashboard shortcut to show or hide the Dashboard.

3.7   Dashboard and Exposé Controls in System Preferences

👉 ***Tip***_____

Exposé and Dashboard: Mac OS X 10.3 introduced Exposé and 10.4 introduced Dashboard. These features use the **F** key keyboard shortcuts, which interfere with FCP's and other applications' shortcut functions. I would recommend reassigning the keyboard shortcuts for these applications inside your **System Preferences**. Go to your Dashboard and Exposé controls and change the Exposé shortcuts to **Option-F9, F10, F11** for Exposé (Figure 3.7) and Dashboard to **Option-F1**. I suggest these as they are not already assigned in FCP, but if you prefer, you can simply switch them off or use other ones to your taste.

🐾 ***Note*** _____

Poor Playback: One of the most common causes of poor playback (especially frustrating for new users of FCP) is caused by the viewing window not fitting the video. If you look at your DV video in a small frame while the material is set to full size, you're expecting the computer to display only a portion of the video while playing it back. This will inevitably cause stuttering video on your computer monitor and usually cut off playback output to your FireWire connection. You can tell if the image is too large for the viewing window when you see scroll bars on the sides, as in Figure 3.8. To correct this, select **Fit to Window** from the **Viewer Size** popup or use the keyboard shortcut **Shift-Z**.

3.8   Due To Scrollbars Showing, Image is Too Large

Fit to Window works on all windows. It is one of my favorite shortcuts because it will fit the contents of a sequence into the **Timeline** window, a useful feature because the playhead and the sequence window do not track together while you're playing back your edited material.

Overwrite

Let's look at the **Canvas Edit Overlay** (**CEO**). It offers a number of different editing options. The most commonly used is the **Overwrite** command.

1. Drag the clip from the **Viewer** until the box marked **Overwrite** highlights.

2. Drop the clip.

It will overwrite whatever is in the **Timeline** beginning at the point where the playhead is parked.

When you drag a clip onto the **CEO**, or use a button or a keyboard shortcut to execute an edit, the clip is placed in the **Timeline** on the designated destination tracks, in this case **V1** and **A2/A2**. These are the default destination tracks set in the patch panel at the head of the **Timeline** (Figure 3.9).

3.9   Patch Panel (above left)

3.10   Patch Panel with Stereo Music (above right)

The number of tracks and the types available as destination tracks are controlled by what is loaded in the **Viewer**. For instance, if you have a still image in the **Viewer**, only one destination track for video will be available. Similarly, if you have a piece of stereo music loaded in the **Viewer**, only two tracks of audio will be available as destinations and no video tracks, as in Figure 3.10. In FCP you can have one track of video combined with up to 24 tracks of audio. If you load a clip like the one shown in the **Viewer**, you'll have options for setting destinations for each one of the 24 audio tracks.

The FCP patch panel has a number of distinct functions. One of them, **Destination Track** selection, controls how material gets placed into your sequence. **Autoselect** is similar. It controls how edits—like an **Add** edit with the **Blade** tool or **Control-V** as we did in the last lesson—are executed, which items are copied, where they are pasted, and a number of other functions.

By marking In and Out points in a clip and editing it into a sequence, you have created what's called a three-point edit. In a three-point edit you're defining three elements required to execute the edit function:

*   Where you want the clip to start (by marking an In point)

*   Where you want the clip to end (by marking the Out point)

*   Where you want to place the clip (by the position of the playhead)

Note

Different In Point: You can also define the In point in the **Timeline** to be a different point from the playhead. Go to the **Canvas** or the **Timeline** window and press the I key to mark an In point (Figure 3.11). This will be the In point for the next edit, and when you drag the clip from **Viewer** to **Canvas** or hit **F10** or the red **Overwrite** button, the clip will drop at the marked In point and not at the playhead's current position.

So that we can look at the functionality offered in the **CEO**, let's quickly drag a few shots into the **Timeline** to see how they work.

Note

Overwrite Constraint: Note that F10 does not overwrite directly from the **Browser**. F10 only works when overwriting from the **Viewer**. If the **Viewer** is closed, F10 will put in a slug, a long section of black with a stereo audio track.

3.11   In Point Mark in the Timeline

1. If you haven't already done it, drag *Food1* from the **Viewer** and drop it on **Overwrite**.

2. Then select clips *Food2* and *Food3* in the **Browser** and drag them directly to the **Overwrite** box in the **CEO**.

The clips will appear in the **Timeline** following *Food1* in their bin order. Note that every time you place a clip in the **Timeline**, the playhead automatically leaps to end of the clip, ready for the next edit event, and the **Canvas** displays the last frame of the sequence. Also notice that in the **Timeline**, *Food2* and *Food3* will appear with **Through Edit** markings. This happens because the shots have contiguous timecode.

Insert

If **Overwrite** is the most commonly used of the **CEO** features, then the next most used must be **Insert**. This is where an NLE system shows its power over a linear editing system.

1. Move the playhead to the edit between *Food1* and *Food2*.

As you move the playhead onto the edit point, it should snap strongly to the join and display on the tracks the marks in Figure 3.12. If you don't see the snap marks, **Snapping** is turned off.

2. Press the **N** key. Try it several times, toggling the **Snapping** function on and off.

3.12   Snap Markings

The Magic Frame

If the playhead moves to the end of the last clip in a sequence, the **Canvas** displays the last frame of the last clip with a blue bar down the right side. This is the Magic Frame, because the playhead is actually sitting on the next frame of video—the blank, empty frame—but the display shows the previous frame, **the frame in front of the playhead.** This is the only time the application does this. Otherwise it always displays the frame after the playhead. Let's try it.

3.13 **The Magic Frame**

1. Place a clip in an empty sequence and use the **Up** and **Down** arrow keys to move back and forth between the beginning and the end of the clip. You see the first and last frames of the clip.

2. Now, leaving a gap in the **Timeline**, place another clip in the sequence.

This time when you use the **Up** and **Down** keys to **move back and forth**, at the beginning **of the first shot** you see the first frame of the video, but at the end **of the first shot,** you see the first frame of black, the empty **gap in the Timeline.** This is important to remember that the playhead is always sitting at the start of the video frame, despite what the Magic Frame shows you.

The **N** key may become one of your most often-used keys in Final Cut Pro. You'll find as you work with the application that you'll be constantly changing from one mode to the other.

Now with snapping on, you should have the playhead parked between the clips.

3. Grab *Food5* directly from the **Browser** and drag into across to the **Canvas,** calling up the **CEO.**

4. Drop it on **Overwrite** to see what happens.

Food5 wipes out all of *Food2* and some of *Food3.*

5. Quickly undo that with **Command-Z.**

6. This time, instead of dragging *Food5* onto **Overwrite,** drag it onto **Insert.**

Immediately the **Timeline** rearranges itself. *Food5* drops into the **Timeline,** appears between *Food1* and *Food2,* and pushes everything further down in the **Timeline,** as shown in Figure 3.14.

Food1	Food5	Food2	Food3
Food1	Food5	Food2	Food3
Food1	Food5	Food2	Food3

3.14 The Insert Edit

Insert will move everything down the track regardless of a clip's position. So if you insert into the middle of the clip, the clip will be cut, and everything on all the tracks will be pushed out of the way. This applies to all tracks, including music or narration, which you may not want to cut.

Track locks are useful in these circumstances. For instance, to prevent an Insert edit from slicing into a music track, lock the track or tracks. All the other tracks will move, but the locked tracks will remain stationary.

Let's try this and see what happens.

1. Undo the Insert edit you did when moving *Food5* into the **Timeline**.

2. In the **Browser**, grab the icon for the audio file called *Music.aif*.

3. Drag it directly into the **Timeline** and place it right at the beginning of tracks **A3** and **A4**. It's a stereo pair of music tracks.

4. Move the playhead back between *Food1* and *Food 2*.

5. Execute the Insert edit with *Food5*.

You'll notice that immediately not only is the video and audio for *Food5* being inserted into the sequence, but the music track is actually being cut with the Insert edit.

6. Undo this edit with **Command-Z**.

7. Just click on the track locks (Figure 3.15) at the head of each track. (Remember to lock and unlock both tracks of a stereo pair.)

8. Redo the Insert edit, and you'll see that the video moves to accommodate the clip; the music track now does not.

9. Before we go any further, let's undo the Insert edit and remove the audio on **A3** and **A4**, bringing the **Timeline** back to just the three clips, *Food1*, *Food2*, and *Food3*.

3.15 Track Locks

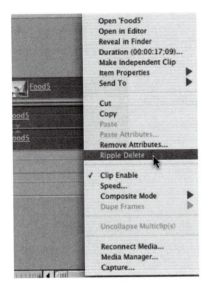

3.16   Shortcut Menu > Ripple Delete

You could use the **Control** key and the shortcut menu to do a ripple delete of *Food5* (Figure 3.16), or just ripple delete with **Shift-Delete**. You can also ripple delete using the **Forward Delete** key, sometimes marked as **Del**, on an extended keyboard.

👍 *Tip*

Keyboard Shortcuts: As usual in FCP, there are keyboard shortcuts for locking and unlocking tracks. To lock a video track, press **F4** and the track number. To lock an audio track, press **F5** and the track number. If you want to lock all the video tracks, use **Shift-F4**. For all the audio tracks, **Shift-F5**. These key commands are toggles: unlocked tracks will lock, and locked tracks will unlock.

Sometimes it's handy to lock all the video or audio tracks except one. Use **Option**-click on the lock, and that track will remain unlocked while all the other tracks of that type, video or audio, will lock. Do **Option**-click on the track again to unlock everything.

Alternative Overwrite and Insert

Overwrite and **Insert** are the primary functions in the **CEO**, but let's look at another way to do them.

Drag *Food5* directly from the **Browser** to the **Timeline**. As you drag it onto the edit point between *Food1* and *Food2*, a little arrow appears, indicating how the edit will be performed. If the arrow is pointing downward as in Figure 3.17, the edit will overwrite. If the little arrow is pointing to the right as in Figure 3.18, you will be doing an Insert edit, which will push the material out of the way.

You'll notice that in addition to the arrow indicators, the colors change. In **Overwrite**, the track color changes to the highlighted brown color. In **Insert**, the track has an outline box.

We'll skip **Overwrite with Transition** and **Insert with Transition** for a later lesson and look at:

- **Replace**
- **Fit to Fill**
- **Superimpose**

3.17   Overwrite Arrow (right)

3.18   Insert Arrow (far right)

Replace

Replace is remarkably sophisticated in the way it works. It will replace a clip in the **Timeline** with another clip either from the **Viewer** or dragged from the **Browser** to the **CEO**. The trick to understanding how **Replace** works is to understand that it works precisely from the point at which the playhead is positioned.

Let's do a Replace edit.

1. Start with your base three shots in the **Timeline**, *Food1*, *Food2*, and *Food3*.

2. Place the playhead at the edit point between *Food1* and *Food2*, right at the beginning of *Food2*.

3. Open *Food5* into the **Viewer** and make sure the playhead there is close to the beginning of the clip.

4. Drag the clip from the **Viewer** into **Replace** in the **Canvas**, or use the keyboard shortcut **F11**. *Food5* will immediately replace *Food2*.

The **Viewer** and the **Canvas** will show the same frame because Final Cut has taken what was in the **Viewer** and placed it in exactly the same frame position as the shot it's replacing in the **Timeline**. It's extending the shot that was in the **Viewer** forward and backward from the point where the playhead was to fill exactly the duration of the shot it's replacing.

Take a look at the clips in Figure 3.19. The clip in the **Timeline**, *Food2*, has the playhead parked near the end of the shot. I want to replace it with the clip *Food5*. In the **Viewer** *Food5* has the playhead near the beginning of the shot. The current position of the playhead in *Food5* is indicated. I won't be able to replace *Food2* with *Food5* even though the new clip is much longer than the clip it's replacing. Why? Because FCP calculates the Replace edit from the position of the playhead. There just aren't enough frames in front of the current position of the playhead in *Food5* to replace all the frames in front of the current position of the playhead in *Food2*.

If you tried to do a Replace edit now, you would get an error message saying *Insufficient content for edit*. Whenever you see this message, it means that FCP cannot execute the edit or function the way you asked it to, usually because there isn't enough media available to perform the function.

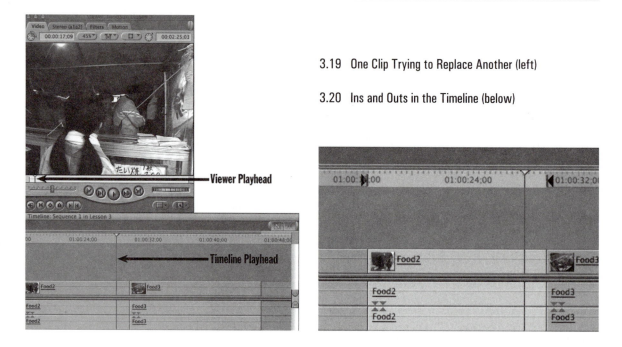

3.19   One Clip Trying to Replace Another (left)

3.20   Ins and Outs in the Timeline (below)

If you're having trouble doing a Replace edit, try this simple way to get the clips to line up. Take both clips, the one in the **Timeline** and the one in the **Viewer**, back to their In points and do a replace from there.

Another way is to use **Overwrite** after first defining the limits of the shot you want to replace. That's easy to do in FCP. With the playhead parked over the shot, press the **X** key. This sets In and Out points on the timeline that are exactly the length of the clip, as in Figure 3.20. If you now do an Overwrite edit, it will effectively replace the shot in the **Timeline**.

Fit to Fill

Fit to Fill functions similarly to **Replace** except that it's never hampered by lack of media. **Fit to Fill** adjusts the speed of the clip to match the area it needs to occupy. This is a great tool for putting into the **Timeline** still images or titles that you want to be a specific length. Because stills aren't real video, FCP can produce the frames very accurately and quickly. It's a little more problematic when using it with video, where it can raise some serious problems.

Food1	Food6 (45%)		Food6 (45%)	Food2
Food1	Food6 (45%)		Food6 (45%)	Food2
Food1	Food6 (45%)		Food6 (45%)	Food2

3.21 Slow Motion Clip in the Timeline

1. To see how this functions, first undo the last edit so that you're back to having just *Food1*, *Food2*, and *Food3* in the **Timeline**.

2. Insert *Food5* into the **Timeline** between *Food1* and *Food2*.

3. Open the clip *Food6* in the **Viewer**.

You can see by the duration in the upper left corner of the **Viewer** that *Food6* is quite a bit shorter than *Food5*. *Food6* is 7;23, while *Food5* is 17;09.

4. With the playhead parked over the middle of *Food5* in the **Timeline**, drag the *Food6* from the **Viewer** and drop it on the **Fit to Fill** box, or use the keyboard shortcut **Shift-F11**.

The clip will immediately drop into the **Timeline**. Unless it is exactly the same size as the clip it's replacing, a colored bar will appear at the top of the **Timeline** above the clip, red if your system is not capable of playing back a speed change in real time and green if it is. The red or green line indicates that the section of the **Timeline** needs to be rendered at some point before output. If the line is red, the clip will have to be rendered immediately to be viewed; if it's green, you will have real-time preview. This section needs to be rendered because of the speed change to *Food6*, which is now in slow motion to accommodate the **Fit to Fill** edit. The clip in the **Timeline** also shows the speed change, in this case, 45% of real speed—pretty slow (Figure 3.21).

Notice also the dark green bar that appears inside the audio portion of the clip. This indicates that the audio will also need to be rendered as well before final output. The audio too is slowed down together with the video.

Let's check the speed.

5. Select the clip in the **Timeline** and hit **Command-J**, which calls up the **Speed** dialog box (Figure 3.22).

The speed displayed in the **Timeline** isn't quite accurate. The real speed of this clip is 44.89%.

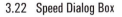

Speed

Constant Speed

Duration: 00:00:17;09

Speed: 44.89 percent

☐ Reverse
☑ Frame Blending

Cancel   OK

3.22 Speed Dialog Box

✎ Tip

Changing to SloMo: When a speed change is done to a shot already in a sequence, a ripple edit is performed, i.e., the contents of the Timeline shift, based on the new length of the clip. This is usually good, but sometimes you just don't want that to happen. If you want to slow down the material, the easiest way is to go to the head of the clip in the Timeline and mark the shot with the **X** key. Then press the **Command-Option-F**, which will match back not to the clip in the Browser, but a new copy of the media from your hard drive. Mark an In point in the new clip that appears in the Viewer. Use **Command-J** to call up the **Speed Change** dialog; change the speed, for example, to 50%; and then **Overwrite** back into the Timeline. It will cut back into the Timeline for the same duration as the original clip, except that portion of the shot will now be in slow motion.

Modify>Speed (**Command-J**) is where constant clip speed changes are made, to make a clip in slow motion as **Fit to Fill** is doing here, or to speed the clip up. The real problem with speed changes is that it is difficult to create smooth motion, particularly at odd speeds such as 44.89%. This may not be always be noticeable, but you can often get some nasty stuttering effects, particularly if the clips are speeded up. In slow motion we get some unpleasant-looking artifacts because it becomes difficult for the application to make sensible intermediate frames. The program needs to extrapolate and create frames that don't exist and blend them together at the correct frame rate of 29.97fps. It's better if you want to do slow or fast motion to use simple multiples: 50%, 150%, 25%, or 200%. These are much easier to calculate and generally produce better results. **Fit to Fill** calculates an absolute number and, as you can see, usually a bizarre one.

Frame blending can help, but it will slow down render time. The default is to have **Frame Blending** turned on. With **Frame Blending** off, FCP merely duplicates or drops frames as necessary to make up the right speed. For slow motion you usually want to have **Frame Blending** turned on, but for clips being speeded up, it works better to have it switched off.

Rather than using **Fit to Fill**, if you do want to slow down or speed up a shot to fit a gap in your sequence, use the procedure in the *Changing to SloMo* tip. I think this will make the smoothest Fit to Fill, especially for interlaced video.

Superimpose

Superimpose is used primarily to place titles on the track above a piece of video. It works a bit like **Replace**. The clip you're superimposing takes its duration from the clip below. Drag the clip from the **Viewer** to **Superimpose**, and it will be placed above the clip where the playhead sits.

Let's ripple delete the **Fit to Fill** shot in the **Timeline** so that we're left with only *Food1*, *Food2*, and *Food3*.

1. Place the playhead somewhere over the middle of the *Food2*.

2. Drag *Food5* from the **Browser** to the **Canvas** and drop it on the **Superimpose** box, or use the keyboard shortcut **F12**.

	Food5		
Food1	Food2		Food3
Food1	Food2		Food3
Food1	Food2		Food3
	Food5		
	Food5		

3.23 Superimpose Clip

The clip appears in the **Timeline** directly above the destination track (Figure 3.23), while the audio goes below the destination audio tracks onto **A3** and **A**.

Making a Sequence

Now that we've gone through the principal means of going from **Viewer** to **Canvas**, let's edit in the **Timeline** itself, trimming and adjusting the clips. We'll edit together a quickly paced sequence of shots.

Note
Superimpose: There is often some misunderstanding about the term superimpose. In FCP it means placing a clip on the track above the current destination track. It does not mean what many people expect in the sense that the superimposed image will appear partially transparent and the underlying image will still be visible beneath it.

Tip
Finding Buttons: If you like using the buttons at the bottom of the Canvas, you are not limited to the three normally visible. You can also have Superimpose, Fit to Fill, and the transition edits. Mouse down on the Replace button, and the others will appear as in Figure 3.24.

Rather than working on the clips in the **Timeline**, let's start afresh with the first clip.

1. Delete everything in the **Timeline**. With the **Timeline** window active, press **Command-A** to **Select All** and then use the **Delete** key to remove everything from the sequence.

3.24 All the Edit Buttons

Storyboarding

Some editors like to build storyboards in bins. Working in Large or Medium Icon mode, you can:

- Trim and set the clips
- Set the Poster frame
- Arrange the layout order of the shots in the **Timeline**.

To set the Poster frame of a clip when you're in Icon view, either:

- Open the clip into the **Viewer**, find the frame, and use **Marks > Set Poster Frame (Control-P)**, or
- Hold down **Control-Shift** on the icon in the bin. This will let you scrub the clip. Hold down the modifier keys to scrub through the clip and release the mouse on the frame you want to set as the Poster frame.

Storyboarding is a fast, easy way to move the shot order around, to try different arrangements and ordering. You can make a quick arrangement of your shots, marquee-drag through them to select them, and then drag them into the **Timeline** (Figure 3.25).

The shots will appear in the sequence in the order they are in the bin. Notice the shots in the **Timeline** in Figure 3.25 follow the order of the shots as they're laid out: left to right, top to bottom. Be careful with the row heights: clips that are placed higher up in the bin will appear earlier in the sequence.

3.25 Storyboarded Bin and Shots in the Timeline

2. Double-click on *Food1* in the **Browser** to open it into the **Viewer.**

3. Scrub through to the point where the camera starts moving from left to right.

4. Find the beginning of the movement and mark the In point.

5. Now find the end of the movement and mark the Out point. We can leave the shots a little loose at this stage.

6. After you've marked the In and Out points, drag the clip to **Overwrite**, or press **F10.**

I'm not sure which part of the second shot, *Food2*, I'll use at this stage, but I'll probably use something.

1. Take *Food2* from just before the zoom starts and let it run almost to the end, including the hands turning the skewers.

2. Again **Overwrite** to the **Timeline.**

Food3 is a little more complex. I want to use more than one part of the shot.

1. Start by marking the In at the beginning of the shot.

2. Mark the Out just before the small pull back.

3. **Overwrite.**

Because the shot in the **Viewer** was loaded from the **Browser**, it is not the shot that I just placed in the **Timeline**. By putting the shot in the **Timeline**, I made a copy of the shot that's in the **Viewer**. So now I can set new Ins and Outs in the **Viewer** without affecting what I've already done to the shot in the sequence.

Marking Edit Points

Many editors like to mark their Out points on the fly. This has the advantage of allowing you to judge the pace of the shot and of the sequence, to do it almost tactilely, to feel the rhythm of the shot. After a few tries you'll probably find you're hitting the Out point consistently on the same frame. If you're not, perhaps it isn't the right shot to be using, or perhaps you should look again at the pace the sequence is imposing on you. It's possible the shot doesn't work where it is.

Marking the In point is a little different because usually you want to mark the edit point before an action begins, but judging how far in front of the action to begin on the fly is difficult. Some editors like to mark the In point while the video is playing backwards. By playing it backwards, you see where the action begins, and you get to judge the pace of how far before the action you want the edit to occur. Sometimes you want the edit to happen in the middle of the action. Then you might make the In point cut while playing forwards. We'll look at cutting on action in Lesson 7 on page 210.

⭐Tip

Timecode Location: To go to a specific timecode point in either the Canvas, the Viewer, or the Timeline, tap out the number on your keypad—for instance, *21023*—and press Enter. The colons and semicolons are not needed. The playhead will immediately move to that point.

1. Set a new In point just before the pan left begins.

2. Let the shot carry over to the steaming kettle, until about the 2:00;02 mark. Put in an Out point.

3. Add that to the **Timeline**.

Let's take a third section from that clip.

1. Mark an In point just before the camera tilts up.

2. Put the Out point shortly before the shot ends.

3. Edit that into the sequence on the end.

Food4 might fit nicely before the close-up of the steaming tray.

1. Position the playhead in the **Timeline** between *Food2* and *Food3*.

2. Mark an In point at the beginning of *Food4* and an Out point just before the pan to the right, around 2:10;23.

3. Drag the clip to **Insert**, or use the shortcut **F9**.

We might be able to get another piece out of *Food4*.

1. Mark an In point around 2:13;03, just before the static portion of the shot of the man hunched over his soup.

2. Mark an Out point just before the camera pans left around 2:17;11.

3. Move the playhead in the **Timeline** in front of the first portion of *Food4*, to the edit point that separates *Food2* and *Food4*.

4. Execute an Insert edit to move the shot from the **Viewer** into the **Timeline**.

Let's look at *Food5*. It's the most human part of the material, the little girl at the food stall. My thought is to use it as bookends: the little girl at the beginning of the sequence and at the end.

1. Make the first part of the shot one clip, basically until after she hands the vendor her money.

2. Mark an In point near the beginning of the shot and an Out point around 2:30;19.

3. Make sure the playhead is at the start of the **Timeline**, then drag to **Insert**.

4. Make the second part of *Food5* begin shortly before the vendor reaches for the biscuit, around 2:32;18. Mark an In point there and let it go until just before the end.

5. Move the playhead to the end of the **Timeline** with the **End key.**

6. Drag the second half of *Food5* from the **Viewer** to **Overwrite**, or use **F10.**

We want *Food6* before the last shot.

1. Open up *Food6* in the **Viewer** and play it.

2. Start it with an In point near the beginning.

3. End it with an Out point after the move with the biscuits, around 2:45;13.

4. In the **Timeline** the playhead is probably at the end of the material. Use the **Up** arrow to move backwards one edit.

5. Now drag the clip from **Viewer** to **Insert**, or use **F9.**

The total duration of this little sequence should be roughly about 45 seconds, depending on how tightly you cut the shots. Looking through it, it's obvious it needs to be tightened up as well as have the order rearranged.

Swap Edit

There are three pieces of *Food3* in the sequence. Let's begin by moving *Food1*, which is now the second shot in sequence, between the first two pieces of *Food3* in the **Timeline**. This is called a *Swap edit*. Figure 3.26 shows the sequence of shots before the Swap edit.

1. Grab the shot and pull it along the **Timeline** to the edit point between the first and second portions of *Food3*.

2. Before you release the clip, hold down the **Option** key.

A downward hooked arrow appears on the clip (Figure 3.27). You'll also see a number displayed. This tells you how far in the sequence you have moved the clip.

3. With the clip on the edit point, release the mouse and then release the **Option** key.

3.28 After the Swap Edit

Note

Swap Edit Limit: The Swap Edit function that lets you move clips will only work on one clip at a time. Unfortunately, you can't grab a couple of clips or a small section of clips and do the same thing. It also works best if you have **Snapping** turned on to avoid slicing off a little bit of a shot by accident.

Figure 3.28 shows the sequence after the Swap edit. In the **Timeline** window, you'll see that you've done an Insert edit as well a Ripple Delete. You've removed the clip from one point in the sequence, placed it somewhere else in the timeline, and pushed everything out of the way to make room for it. I use this great hidden tool often.

You can only move one shot at a time when you do a Swap, but there is a handy way to move groups of clips. Look at the two pieces of *Food4* followed by the first part of *Food3*. These should be moved together right after *Food5* at the head of the **Timeline**. This would make them the second, third, and fourth shots in the sequence. I could just move *Food2* after them, but let me show you a way to move groups of clips.

1. Start by selecting the clips.

2. Cut them out not with the usual **Command-X**, but with **Shift-X.**

Shift-X performs a Ripple Cut instead of a simple Lift edit that leaves a gap in the track. This not only cuts the clips out of the timeline, but also closes the gap the missing clips leave behind.

3. Now go to the edit at the end of *Food5*, between *Food5* and *Food2*. You want to place the clips and use **Shift-V**, which will paste the clips as a Paste Insert edit. **Command-V** would also paste, but as an Overwrite edit. Your timeline should be laid out like Figure 3.29.

The sequence is getting better, but there are still a few edits I don't like and quite a few shots that need trimming. We'll get to trimming in a moment, but let's rearrange a few more shots.

In the first shot, I like the way the camera moves around the girl at the beginning, and I like the way she hands over her money

3.29 Timeline after Paste Insert

with her fingers splayed out. I don't care for the hesitation in the middle. What I'd like to do is move *Food2* right into the middle of that first shot. I know *Food2* is too long; we'll get to trimming it shortly.

✊ *Tip*

Gaps and Syncing: FCP defines a gap as a space in the **Timeline** that extends across all tracks. So if you have a music track on **A3** and **A4**, for instance, FCP will not see the space between the shots on the video tracks as a gap. This is where the ability to lock tracks helps. If you lock those music tracks, you can then close the gap. Or use **Option**-lock to lock all other tracks, and again you can close the gap.

Besides the shortcut menu, there are two other ways to close a gap in the track:

1. With the playhead over the gap, press **Control-G**.
2. Click on it to select the gap and then press the **Delete** key.

Be careful, though, with closing gaps like this. It can throw shots out of sync with elements on other tracks like music or narration tracks.

---

1. Scrub or play through the beginning of the timeline to find the point just after the camera finishes moving around the girl, around 2;17 into the sequence.

2. Use **Control-V** to slice the clip in the sequence.

3. Play or scrub forward in the timeline to find the point just before the vendor reaches his hand out for the money, around 2;28.

4. Press **Control-V** again. You have now isolated a short section to cut out.

5. Ripple delete it either by **Control**-clicking to call up the shortcut menu or by selecting it and pressing **Shift-Delete**.

✊ *Tip*

Moving the Playhead: Shift-Left or **Right** arrow will move the playhead forward or backward in one-second increments.

3.30 Range Tool Selection in the Timeline

You could also have done this by marking an In and Out point in the **Timeline** and ripple deleting the short section.

A third way to do this would be to use the **Range** tool (**GGG**), which we saw in the previous lesson. Here, instead of using it to select a portion of the clip to save, you can also use it to select a portion of the clip to ripple delete (Figure 3.30). You may have to switch off **Snapping** to make such a short edit. While you're dragging with the **Range** tool, you'll see a two-up display in the **Canvas** showing you the start and end points of the edit (Figure 3.31). After making the selection, ripple delete it.

There is obviously now a jump cut in that first shot between the two pieces. So let's take *Food2* from further down in the sequence

3.31 Two-Up Canvas Display

and do a Swap edit to move it in between the two cut pieces in *Food5*.

The arrangement is almost right, but I don't care for the very last shot. Just after the vendor puts the biscuit in the bag, the camera jiggles. I'd like to remove this. So let's do this in the **Timeline**.

1. Scrub or play the timeline to the frame when the biscuit just disappears into the bag behind the counter.

2. Mark an In point in the timeline.

Right after this the camera is jostled.

3. Move further down the timeline to where the vendor is about to reach forward with the bag, as his hands separate, and mark an Out point here with the **O** key.

4. To make sure nothing is selected in the sequence press **Command-Shift-A** (**Deselect All**), and then use **Shift-Delete** to ripple delete the middle portion of the shot.

Now we have the same problem we had in the first shot.

Jump Cuts

The sequence as we've laid it out so far has the most obvious form of jump cut, which is any abrupt edit that jars the viewer. **Editors usually** consider this a **mortal sin**. The most common cause is placing side-by-side shots, such as the two halves of *Food5*, that are very similar, but not the same. You get this disconcerting little jump, as though you blacked out for a fraction of a second. It suddenly pulls the **viewers away** from the content of the video as they say to themselves, or perhaps even out loud, "What was that?" You can also get a jump cut if you put together two very different shots, such as the shot of a long street with a small figure of a person in the distance, cutting to a tight close-up. It's disorienting because the viewer has no reference that the close-up belongs to the person seen in the far distance in the previous shot. These are jump cuts. The general rule is to avoid them if you can. Or use them so often that it becomes your style. Then it's art.

This time we're going to move the last portion of *Food3* from its earlier position. This is the shot of the tilt up from the kettle.

5. Drag *Food3* with **Option** and drop it between the two halves of *Food5* that you just split to do a Swap edit.

6. I also cut out from the sequence the second portion of *Food3*, the pan from the steam tray to the kettle.

7. Your timeline should look like Figure 3.32.

If you look through the sequence, you'll see that the shots are in the order we want, but we still need to tighten it up quite a bit, trimming the shots to make them faster paced, which we'll look at next.

3.32 Timeline after Last Edit

👆 *Tip*

Timeline Scaling: You can change the scale of the Timeline to zoom in and out with the tabbed slider at the bottom of the window. Pulling either end of the tab will change the scale of the **Timeline** window. At the bottom left is a little slider that will adjust the scale (Figure 3.33).

3.33 Scaling Slider and Tabbed Slider

My personal favorite is to use the keyboard shortcuts **Option- =** (think **Option- +**) to zoom in and **Option- –** (that's **Option minus**) to zoom out. What's nice about using the keyboard shortcuts is that if nothing is selected in the sequence, it leaves the playhead centered in the **Timeline** as you zoom in and out. If a clip is selected in the **Timeline**, the scaling will then take place around that rather than around the playhead. You can use **Command- +** or **Command- –** to scale in any other active window, but **Option- +** and **Option- —** will scale the **Timeline** regardless of which window is active.

Trimming Your Sequence

The trim tools—**Roll** and **Ripple, Slip** and **Slide**—are clustered in the fourth and fifth buttons (Figure 3.34).

The first two trim tools, **Ripple** and **Roll**, change the duration of clips, while the second two, **Slip** and **Slide**, leave the clip duration intact.

A *ripple* edit moves an edit point up and down the timeline by pushing or pulling all the material on the track, shortening or lengthening the whole sequence. In a ripple edit, only one clip changes duration, getting longer or shorter. Everything else that comes after it in the track adjusts to accommodate it. In Figure 3.35 the edit is being rippled to the left, and everything after it moves to accompany it, just as in a ripple delete.

A *roll* edit moves an edit point up and down the timeline between two adjacent shots. Only those two shots have their durations changed. While one gets longer, the adjacent shot gets shorter to accommodate it. The overall length of the track remains unchanged. In Figure 3.36 the edit point itself can be moved either left or right.

A *slip* edit changes the In and Out points of a single clip. The duration of the clip remains the same, and all the clips around it remain the same. Only the In and Out of the slipped clip change. If more frames are added on the front, the same amount are cut off the end, and vice versa, if some are added to the end, an equal amount are taken off the beginning. In Figure 3.37 the contents change by changing the clip's In and Out points, but neither its position in the timeline nor either of the adjacent shots are affected.

A *slide* edit moves a clip forward or backward along the timeline. The clip itself, its duration, and In and Out points remain unchanged. Only its position on the timeline, earlier or later, shortens and lengthens the adjacent shots as it slides up and down the track. In Figure 3.38 the central clip *Food4* can slide up and down the timeline. The shot itself isn't altered; only the two adjacent shots are.

3.34   Trim Tools

3.35   Ripple Edit Left

3.36   Roll Edit Directions

3.37 Slip Edit Directions

3.38 Slide Edit Directions

The Ripple Tool

We're first going to work with the **Ripple** tool. Press the fourth button and extend the popout to select the tool as in Figure 3.39. You can also call it up by pressing **RR**; that's the **R** key twice.

Let's use it on some of the shots we want to work on. Start with the first edit between shots *Food5* and *Food2*. Take the tool and place it near the edit. Notice it changes direction as you move it across the edit as in Figures 3.40 and 3.41.

When the tool is on the right side, it will ripple the second shot; when it's on the left side, it will ripple the first shot.

In this case, we want to ripple the second shot. As you grab the clip on the right side of the edit point, you will get a small two-up display in the **Canvas**, as shown in Figure 3.42. Pull the shot until you have trimmed off the beginning zoom, all the way until just before the hands come into the frame to turn the skewers. You might want to trim some off the end as well, rippling the left side and pulling the shot a bit until just as the hands leave the frame. It might be easier to do this if you toggle **Snapping** off, which you can do with the **N** key.

A word of caution about rippling: If you're working with material that's cut to narration or music, rippling will easily upset the timing of the sequence, because it's pulling and pushing the entire track and its sync sound. So what's working for you at this moment in the edit may be ruining something else further down the timeline. In these cases, the **Roll** tool may work better for you.

3.39 The Ripple Tool

3.40 Ripple Tool Right

3.41 Ripple Tool Left

3.42 Ripple Canvas Display

3.43 The Roll Tool

The Roll Tool

The **Roll** tool is also under the fourth button in the tools as in Figure 3.43. It can be evoked with the **R** key. Like the **Ripple** tool, it can be used in the **Timeline**, as shown in Figure 3.44.

The **Roll** tool acts on both shots, extending one shot while shortening the other. While the **Ripple** tool changes the enter length of the sequence by moving everything up and down the line, the **Roll** tool only affects the two adjacent shots.

A good candidate to try with the **Roll** tool is the edit towards the end of the sequence between *Food6* and *Food5*. As you roll to the left, a two-up display will again appear in the **Canvas** as in Figure 3.45. I rolled the shot back a little to the point in *Food5* just before the girl looks up at the vendor.

Using **Roll** and **Ripple**, tighten up some of the shots in the sequence.

👉 **Tip**
Ripple and Roll Shortcuts: You can also use the Ripple and Roll tools incrementally with keyboard shortcuts in the **Timeline**. Select the edit point by moving the playhead over it and pressing the **V** key. Now, by using the **U** key, you can toggle through **Ripple Right**, **Ripple Left**, and **Roll**. Whichever edit you have selected, you can now move incrementally with the less-than bracket < and the greater-than bracket >. (Actually, it's the comma and period, but most people think of them as < and >.) Each tap will move the edit one frame left or right in the direction the bracket is pointed. **Shift-<** and **Shift->** will move the edit for the duration you have set for **Multi-Frame Trimming** in your **User Preferences**. This also works if you select a clip in the **Timeline** and choose either the **Slip** or **Slide** tools. The [and] keys, together with **Shift-[** and **Shift-]** are set to work in exactly the same way.

3.44 The Roll Tool in the Timeline

3.45 Roll Canvas Display

Extend Edit

Final Cut's **Extend Edit** is another nice way to perform a roll edit. It's a simple way to move an edit point, even one with a transition.

1. Choose an edit and click on it to select it.

2. Find your new edit point in the **Timeline** (or in the **Canvas**) and hit **E** or select **Sequence>Extend Edit**.

If the selection is dimmed or you hear a system warning, it's because you don't have enough media to perform the Extend Edit.

The Slip Tool

Let's look at **Slip** tool, which works in the **Timeline** and the **Viewer**. **Slip** is one of my favorite tools. You can select it from the fifth button in the **Tools**, as shown in Figure 3.46. You can also call up the **Slip** tool with the **S** key.

3.46   The Slip Tool

One shot that you might want to slip is the first of the two *Food4* shots in the sequence. Grab the clip in the sequence with the **Slip** tool and start moving it from side to side as in Figure 3.47. What you're doing is slipping the media for the clip up and down its length. The overall duration of the clip remains unchanged but the section of media for that duration is adjusted. The **Canvas** shows you a two-up display. The frame on the left shows the In point, the first frame of the shot, while the frame on the right is the Out point, the last frame of the shot. The two-up display will help keep you from slipping the clip too far into some unwanted material.

It is also possible to slip in the **Viewer**, which can be especially beneficial when you're adjusting a clip before you bring it into the **Timeline**.

1. To slip in the **Viewer**, double-click the clip to load it into the **Viewer**.

3.47   The Slip Tool in the Timeline

2. Hold down the **Shift** key as you grab either the In point or the Out point and drag. This way you will drag both points together and maintain a constant duration.

You are slipping the In and Out points of the clip, and what you see in the display is the start frame in the **Viewer** and the end frame in the **Canvas** as in Figure 3.48. It doesn't matter which end you grab to pull. The display is always the same: start in the **Viewer**; end in the **Canvas**.

3.48 Slipping in the Viewer with the Canvas Display

3.49 The Slide Tool

The Slide Tool

Let's look at the last trimming tool, the **Slide** tool, also in the fifth **Tools** button (Figure 3.49). The **Slide** tool can be brought out with **SS** (S twice).

It works only in the **Timeline**, unlike the **Slip** tool. The **Slide** tool doesn't change anything in the clip you're working on; it grabs the clip and pulls it forward or backward along the **Timeline**, wiping out material on one side, extending the material on the other side, as shown in Figure 3.50.

You're not moving just one clip. You're also affecting the two adjacent clips. That's why they're highlighted with boxes in Figure 3.50.

The two-up display in the **Canvas** (Figure 3.51) shows you the two adjacent shots that you're displacing. On the left, the end of the shot before the one you're moving. On the right, the beginning of the shot after the one you're moving.

3.50 The Slide Tool in the Timeline (above)

3.51 The Slide Tool Canvas Display (right)

You are limited in how far you can slide a clip by the amount of media available in the adjacent shots.

The Trim Edit Window

If you're going to be doing a lot of trimming, you can call up a separate **Trim Edit** window (Figure 3.52) where you can work with the **Ripple** and **Roll** tools as well as still having access to the **Slip** tool.

1. You open the **Trim Edit** window by moving the playhead to an edit point and using the menu **Sequence>Trim Edit** or the keyboard shortcut **Command-7**, or by double-clicking on an edit point.

Notice the bars on the top of the windows in Figure 3.52. They're colored green in the application. The green bars indicate what mode you're in. When a green bar appears over both sides, as in Figure 3.53, you're in Roll mode. By clicking on one side or the other, you can either ripple the outgoing shot as in Figure 3.54 or the incoming shot in Figure 3.55. To get back to rolling the edit point, click on the space between the two frames. You can also toggle between the **Ripple** and **Roll** tools in the **Trim Edit** window

3.52 Trim Edit Window

3.53 Roll Edit Indication

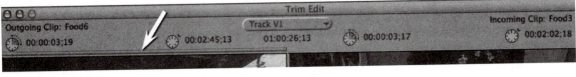

3.54 Ripple Left Indicator

3.55 Ripple Right Indicator

with the **U** key. This is very handy but can be slightly deceptive because the cursor doesn't change, just the marking on the clip.

There's a lot of useful timecode information at the top of the **Trim Edit** window (Figure 3.56):

- The number to the far left is the duration of the outgoing shot (*A* in Figure 3.56).
- The next timecode number is the Out point of the outgoing shot (*B* in Figure 3.56).
- The center number under the track indicator is the current time in the sequence starting at one hour (*C* in Figure 3.56).
- The next number displayed is duration of the incoming shot (*D* in Figure 3.56).
- On the far right of the window, the number is the current In point of the incoming shot (*E* in Figure 3.56).

3.56 Time Displays in the Trim Edit

A   B   C   D   E

You can play either side of the **Trim Edit** window with the J, K, and L keys. Which side plays is partially determined by the green bars. When you're in Ripple mode, the side that plays is determined by which side is selected. When you're in Roll mode with both sides selected, the side that plays will be the one the cursor is over. If the cursor is hovering over the left side, the outgoing clip will play. If the cursor is hovering over the right side, the incoming clip will play.

The spacebar serves an interesting function in the **Trim Edit Window**. It acts in looped play-around mode. It will play around the edit point again and again so that you can view it repeatedly. To play either side slowly, hold down the K key together with the L key. The amount of play-around, how much before the edit and how far after the edit, is controlled in **User Preferences** under **Preview Pre-Roll** and **Preview Post-Roll**. The default is five seconds before the edit and two seconds after. I usually set it down to two or three seconds before and two after.

To trim an edit, enter a new In or Out point, press the O key on the outgoing side to change the Out point, or press the I key on the ingoing side to change the In point. You can also use the little plus (**+**) and minus (**–**) buttons at the bottom of the window to make incremental edits on either side of the **Trim Edit** window. This is also a user-defined function controlled in **Preferences** under **Multi-Frame Trim Size**. You can set it as high at 99 frames if you want.

Final Cut Pro has the ability to do *dynamic trimming* in the **Trim Edit** window. You'll see a little checkbox at the bottom of the window that activates this function, which can also be turned on in **User Preferences**. This allows you to play in the **Trim Edit** window using the J, K, and L keys. Whenever you press the K key to pause, the edit will automatically execute. This will work in any edit mode: Roll, Ripple Left, or Ripple Right. As soon as you press the pause key, the edit will be executed. Try it. It's pretty slick.

Fine tune the edits as much as you can, tightening them so that the shots move quickly and flow smoothly through the short scene.

How Long is Long Enough?

A static shot, either close-up or medium shot, needs to be on the screen a shorter time than a long shot in which the audience has a lot to look at **or one in which they**'re following a movement. While a close-up can be on the screen quite briefly, a long shot will often contain a great deal of information and needs to be held longer so that your viewer has time for his or her eye to rove around it. A moving shot, such as a pan, you can often hold longer because the audience is basically looking at two shots, one at the beginning and the other at the end. If the movement is well shot, a fairly brisk move, no more than about five seconds, you can also cut it quite tightly. All you need to show is a brief glimpse of the static shot, the movement, and then cut out as soon as the camera settles at the end of the move. **A shot that has been seen before, a repeat, can be on the screen quite briefly for the audience to get the information. Though there is no hard and fast rule, generally shots without dialog remain on the screen no more than six or eight seconds on television with its relatively small screen. In feature films shots can be held for quite a bit longer because the viewer's eye has a lot more traveling to do to take in the full scope of the image. This is probably why movies seem much slower on the television screen than they do in the theatre.**

🐾 Note

Trim Edit Shortcut: In the Trim Edit window, in addition to the trim buttons, you can use the keyboard shortcuts < and > or [and] to trim plus or minus one frame and Shift-< and Shift-> or Shift-[and Shift-] to trim plus or minus the multiframe trim size. Like the buttons, these will work on the fly while you're in looped play-around mode.

Look at your finished sequence. It should look something like *Food Sequence* in the **Browser**. I'm still not happy with the piece, principally because the audio is so abrupt and choppy, marking each cut. The audio needs to be smoothed out, perhaps extending sound from a single clip or adding some constant underlying sound from somewhere else. But that's for the next lesson.

Summary

You've learned how to use the **Canvas** editing tools:

- **Overwrite**
- **Insert**
- **Fit to Fill**
- **Replace**
- **Superimpose**

You've learned how to use the various sequence editing tools:

- **Roll** and **Ripple**
- **Slip** and **Slide**
- **Trim Edit window**

In the next lesson we're going to look at how to work with sound, how to get rid of some of those rough patches and smooth out the aural presentation of the sequence.

Lesson 4
==

Using Sound

Film and video are primarily visual media. Oddly enough, though, the moment an edit occurs is often driven as much by the sound as by the picture. So let's take a look at editing sound in Final Cut Pro. How sound is used, where it comes in, and how long it lasts are key to good editing. With few exceptions, sound almost never cuts with the picture. Sometimes the sound comes first and then the picture; sometimes the picture leads the sound. The principal reason video and audio are so often cut separately is that we see and hear quite differently. We see in cuts. I look from one person to another, from one object to another, from the keyboard to the monitor. Though my head turns or my eyes travel across the room, I really only see the objects I'm interested in looking at. We hear, on the other hand, in fades. I walk into a room, the door closes behind me, and the sound of the other room fades away. As a car approaches, the sound gets louder. Screams, gunshots, and doors slamming being exceptions, our aural perception is based on smooth transitions from one to another. Sounds, especially background sounds, generally need to overlap to smooth out the jarring abruptness of the hard cut. As we shall see, dialog poses a special, interesting problem for the editor when it comes to overlapping sound.

Loading the Lesson

This is going to sound familiar, but it's worth repeating. Begin by loading the material you need on the media hard drive of your computer.

1. If you don't already have it on your drive, drag the *Lesson 4 Media* folder from the DVD to your media drive.

2. Drag the *Projects* folder from the DVD into your home *Documents* folder if you have not already done so.

3. Eject the DVD and launch the *Lesson 4* project that's on your hard drive in the *Projects* folder.

4. As in earlier lessons, choose the **Reconnect** option to relink the media files when the **Offline Files** dialog appears.

Setting up the Project

You'll find in the project's **Browser** an empty sequence called *Sequence 1* and a number of other sequences that we'll look at during this lesson. There is also a master clip called *Backstage* and another folder called *Clips*, which contains the subclips pulled from the master.

Viewing Your Material

In this lesson we're going to look at backstage preparations for a kabuki performance. Before beginning the lesson, it might be a good idea to look through the material, which is about three and one-half minutes long. You can start by double-clicking the shot *Backstage* to open it in the **Viewer** and then playing through the material.

The Split Edit

A common method of editing is to begin by laying the shots in scene order entirely as straight cuts, as we did in the previous lesson. Take a look at the sequence called *Rough Cut*. This is the edited material cut as straight edits. What's most striking as you play it is how abruptly the audio changes at each shot. But audio and video seldom cut in parallel in a finished video, so you will have to offset them. Take a look at the sequence called *Final*. The three and one-half minutes that is *Backstage* has been cut down to one minute and 23 seconds for the *Final* sequence. This is where we're going. Notice how the audio overlaps and the way it fades in and out. When audio and video have separate In and Out points that aren't at the same time, the edit is called a *split edit, J-cut*, or *L-cut*. Whatever you call it, the effect is the same. There are many ways to create a split edit.

In the Timeline

Many instructors tell you to create split edits in the **Viewer**, but I think the **Viewer** is the least flexible place to perform this function. Let's set up a split edit inside the **Timeline**. It's a much more logical place to perform this type of work and very effective.

In making split edits, particularly in the **Timeline**, you will be frequently linking and unlinking clips, switching off the link between synced video and audio. You can do this with the little switch in the upper right corner of the **Timeline** window that toggles **Linked Selection** off and on (Figure 4.1), or you can use the keyboard shortcut **Shift-L**. When **Linked Selection** is turned on, the button is green; when it's off, the icon is black.

Before we begin working on the sequence, it would probably be a good idea to duplicate the *Rough Cut* sequence. Select it and use **Edit>Duplicate** or the keyboard shortcut **Option-D**. This way you can also refer back to the original *Rough Cut* should you ever need to.

⯈ Tip

Missing Buttons: If the Snapping and/or Linked Selection buttons are missing, **Control**-click on the button holder, and from the shortcut menu select Remove > All/Restore Default.

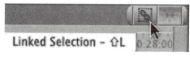

4.1   Linked Selection Button

Viewing Rushes

Old habits die hard. I can't get over the British term for overnight film processed material, *rushes*, rather than the American term, *dailies*. Whatever you call them—rushes, dailies, tape cassettes, reels—this is the raw material that editors work with. Watching this material for the first time, whether it's in a darkened screening room, on a tape deck in a room crowded with humming electronic equipment, in the viewfinder of your camcorder, or even in the **Viewer** in Final Cut Pro—that first moment has a magic of its own. Don't miss it. Use it to grasp your first impressions, to find those visceral moments that affect you. As you watch, think about the relationships between pictures, between moments in time. Think about and watch for those moments that repeat themselves in various forms. This first viewing and listening is crucial to editing. If a piece of dialog is difficult to understand the first time you hear it, then it probably will be for your audience as well. As you work, you'll be hearing it dozens of times more, and by then it will probably seem okay to you. You'll get it; but your audience, unless they're equipped with Replay or TiVo, have only one shot at it. Even with a Replay, they're not going to enjoy backtracking on the program very often.

Backstage01	Backstage06	Backsta	Backstage04		Backstage11	Backstage17	Backstage06
Backstage01	age06	Backsta	Backstage04		Backstage11	Backstage17	Backstage06
Backstage01	Backstage06	Backsta	Backstage04		Backstage11	Backstage17	Backstage06

4.2 Duplicated Clips in the Timeline

4.3 Timeline Window Options

Start by double-clicking the copy of *Rough Cut* and take a look at the **Timeline.** You may notice a couple of red lines at the base of two of the clips in the **Timeline,** on the second and the seventh shot, which are circled in Figure 4.2. These red lines indicate where portions of the shot *Backstage06* are duplicated. This function can be toggled on and off in the with the tiny triangle popup at the bottom left of the **Timeline** window (Figure 4.3). While **Dupe Detection** created performance problems in FCP4, its behavior has been much improved in the current version of the application. **Dupe Detection** will go through a number of other colors if clips are used more than once. You can control its functionality from the first panel of **User Preferences.** To remove the duplicate shot from the *Rough Cut copy* sequence, select it and press **Shift-Delete** to perform a ripple delete edit.

The trick to smoothing out the audio for this type of sequence—or any sequence with abrupt sound changes at the edit points—is to overlap sounds and create sounds beds that carry through

Tip

Find the Duplicate: To quickly find the other duplicate in the **Timeline,** Control-click on the **Dupe Detection** indicator. A shortcut menu will tell you where it is (Figure 4.4). If you select the item, it will move the playhead to its location in the sequence.

4.4 Shortcut Menu for Dupe Detection

4.5 Dragging Audio to Create Split Edit

other shots. Ideally, a wild track was shot on location, a long section of continuous sound from the scene, a couple of minutes or more, which can be used as a bed to which the sync sound is added as needed. Here there was no wild track as such, but some of the shots are lengthy enough to have a similar effect.

Making Split Edits

1. Play through the first three or four shots in the *Rough Cut copy* sequence. The change between the first and second shot is quite noticeable, even more so between the second and third.

2. Hold down the **Option** key and select the audio portion of the second shot, *Backstage06*.

3. With the **Option** key still pressed, tap the **Down** arrow twice. This will move the stereo pair of audio down two tracks. This can be done with any tracks, video or audio, as long as there is nothing in the way, like another clip, that prevents it.

4. Again holding down the **Option** key, drag the head of the audio edit point toward the beginning of the **Timeline** (Figure 4.5). While you drag it, a small box will appear. It gives you a time duration change for the edit you are making. If **Snapping** is turned on, it may be helpful to toggle it off with the **N** key.

5. Repeat the process on the other side of the audio. Holding down the **Option** key, drag out the audio so that your sequence looks like Figure 4.6.

You have now created two split edits for the clip *Backstage06*.

Note
Toggling Linking: Option-clicking the audio (or video) edit point will toggle off **Linked Selection**, if LS is turned on. If **Linked Selection** is off, Option-clicking the edit point will toggle it on.

Note
Linear or Logarithmic: FCP has two cross fades, the default +3dB as well as a 0dB transition. The +3dB cross fade that FCP calls an equal power cross fade is generally preferred because it gives a logarithmic roll of sound, which is the way sound really works. The 0dB cross fade is a linear fade. It will often produce an apparent dip in the audio level at the midpoint of the cross-over from one track to the other.

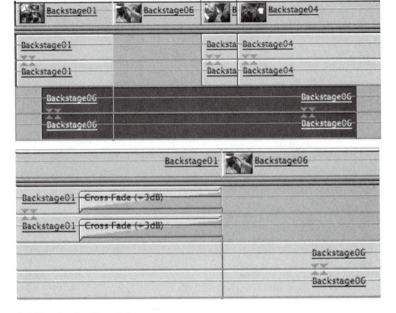

4.6   Timeline after Making Split Edits

4.7   Cross Fade Applied

Adding Audio Transitions

We want the sound of the first shot, *Background01*, to fade out before it ends. The simplest way to do this is to apply an audio cross fade.

1.   Select the edit point by clicking on it.

2.   To add the audio transition, either use the menu **Effects>Audio Transitions>Cross Fade (+3dB)**, or use the keyboard shortcut **Command-Option-T**.

Because the audio is not butted against anything, the application will by default create an end-on-edit transition, as shown in Figure 4.7. We'll look at transitions in much greater detail in the next lesson.

In the Viewer

You can also create a split edit in the Viewer. To do this we'll use a clip from the **Browser**.

1.   Find the clip *Backstage06* in the *Clips* bin in the **Browser**.

2.   Double-click on it to open it into the **Viewer**. Because we want to use all the audio, begin by marking a split audio In point at the beginning of the clip. With the playhead at the very start of the shot, either **Control**-click and from the shortcut menu choose **Mark Split>Audio In** (Figure 4.8), or use the keyboard shortcut **Command-Option-I**.

4.8   Marking Split Audio In

Slipping Out of Sync

Sometimes when you move an unlinked audio track it may accidentally slip out of sync with the video material. If that happens, you'll see time indicators in the **Timeline** tracks (Figure 4.9) showing you how far out of sync the clips have slipped. The time slippage shows in a red box. The minus number means that the audio is three frames ahead of the picture. A plus number indicates that the audio is later than the video.

4.9   Out of Sync Audio

4.10   Out of Sync Shortcut Menu

If the audio does slip out of sync, the easiest way to get it back is to simply undo, but sometimes you don't notice the right away, or it's occurred off the screen further down the track. Then the simplest way is to **Control**-click on the red box and choose from the options (Figure 4.10).

You could also nudge the clip back into sync. **Option**-click on the audio to select only the audio portion of the clip. If you just click on the audio, you'll normally select both video and audio even though they are out of sync. With only the audio selected, use the < and > keys to slide the clip forward or backwards.

As it moves, the time displays will update and finally disappear when the clip is back in sync. Every hit of the < or > keys nudges the clip one frame. Holding down the **Shift** key will nudge the clip the trim amount you selected in your **Multi-Frame Trim Size** in the **Editing** tab of **User Preferences**.

4.11   Typing in Numeric Value to Move Audio

You can also select the audio portion of the clip (or whichever portion has free track space around it) and type plus or minus the value in the red box as in Figure 4.11. Then press the **Enter** key to move the clip.

3. Play through the clip till you find the In point for the edit at about 1:23;14.
4. Instead of hitting **I** to enter the In point, use **Control-I**.
5. Play forward till you get to the Out point at 1:28;22.
6. Instead of hitting **O** to enter the Out point, use **Control-O**.

Note the markings in the **Viewer** scrubber bar and on screen in Figure 4.12 that indicate the split edit.

4.12   Split Edit in Viewer

4.13 Patch Panel Setting Destination Tracks

Viewer To Timeline

The simplest way to get the split edit from the **Viewer** to the Timeline is to drag and drop it.

1. Open the sequence called *Split Edit* by double-clicking on it.

2. Reset the destination tracks by clicking the **A4** button to bring the **a2** patch down to **A4**. Then click on the **A3** button, patching the **a1** button down to **A3**, as in Figure 4.13.

3. With the playhead at the end of the shot in the **Timeline**, drag the clip from the **Viewer** to the **Timeline**, as in Figure 4.14.

What will happen is that the edit will be performed as in Figure 4.15. This seems to be an anomaly in the software that has persisted through every version of the application. Grab the clip in the **Timeline** and slide it to butt up against the first shot, as shown in Figure 4.16.

Next we need to look at how to control the audio levels. This can be done either in the **Timeline** or in the **Viewer**. It's easier and quicker in the **Timeline**, but the **Viewer** controls afford a great deal more precision.

4.14 Dragging Split Edit to the Timeline

4.15 Displaced Split Edit in Timeline

4.16 Correctly Placed Split Edit

Controlling Levels

Next we need to look at how to control the audio levels. This can be done either in the **Timeline** or in the **Viewer**. It's easier and quicker in the **Timeline**, but the **Viewer** controls afford a great deal more precision.

In the Timeline

To work in the **Timeline**, let's return to the first *Rough Cut* duplicated sequence that still contains all the clips. To adjust the audio levels in the **Timeline**, you first need to turn on the **Clip Overlays** button in the lower left corner of the **Timeline** window (Figure 4.17) or use the keyboard shortcut **Option-W**.

4.17   Clip Overlay Button

When the **Clip Overlays** are turned on, a thin pink line appears through the middle of the audio portion of the clips. This is the audio level control for the clips. Notice also the thin black line that appears at the top of the video. This controls the opacity for the video portion. It's a good idea to leave the **Clip Overlays** turned off when you're not using them, because it's easy to accidentally shift the level line while trying to grab a clip to move it.

Play the audio for the third shot in the sequence, *Backstage05*. It's pretty low and adds nothing to the soundtrack except to muddy it a bit. To eliminate the audio, you could select the audio portion of the clip with the **Option** key and delete it. However, if you ever decide you want that audio or if you move the clip to a place where the audio is needed, it's a bit of a nuisance to get it back.

A simpler way is to reduce the audio level to zero. With **Clip Overlays** turned on, move the cursor over the line. It will change to the **Resizing** tool. Grab the line and pull it down to the bottom of the clip as shown in Figure 4.18.

4.18   Dragging the Level Line

Fading Levels in the Timeline

You usually don't want to reduce the overall levels. More often you'll want to reduce the levels of portions of the sound, raise other portions, or fade in or out. For a simple fade up, you could use the cross fade transition that we saw earlier, or you can do it by fading up the level line. To do this you can use the **Option** key, but if you're doing a lot of work on the audio. as we are here, it's simpler to use the **Pen** tool. There are a number of **Pen** tools available in the very last of the **Tools** (Figure 4.19). You can also call up it up with the **P** key.

4.19   Pen Tools

4.20 Pen Tool in the Timeline

4.21 Adding a Keyframe

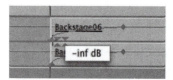

4.22 Lowering the Keyframe Level

4.23 Fade Out in the Timeline

Let's create a fade in at the beginning of the second shot, *Backstage06*, that's on **A3/A4**.

1. Move the **Pen** over the pink level line in the clip. The cursor will change to a pen nib (Figure 4.20), allowing you to click on the line to create an audio keyframe. This adds a tiny diamond to the level line. (Figure 4.21). Put a keyframe about one second from the beginning of the shot by clicking with the **Pen** tool on the level line.

2. As you move the cursor to the newly created keyframe it will change into a simple crosshairs cursor. This lets you grab the keyframe and move it up or down. Pull the keyframe down to about –7dB as in Figure 4.22. Notice that because there are no other keyframes on the level line, the volume for the entire clip is reduced.

3. With the **Pen** tool grab the very left end of the level line. Pull it down to create a curved fade up ramp (Figure 4.23).

✎ Note _____

Stereo Pair: Notice that as you lower the level, both tracks go down together. That's because these tracks are a *stereo pair* of audio tracks, indicated by the inward pointing pairs of triangles you see in the Timeline. Should you have separate tracks for **Mono (a1)** and **Mono (a2)** audio, you'll have to lower each track separately. Should you need to switch from **Mono (a1)**/**Mono (a2)** audio to a stereo pair or vice versa, select the clip and go to **Modify > Stereo Pair**, or use the keyboard shortcut **Option-L**.

✎ Tip _____
No Switching Necessary: If you don't want to switch to the **Pen** tool from the standard **Selector** tool, as you move the cursor to the level line and it changes to the **Resizing** tool, hold down the **Option** key. The cursor will automatically change to the **Pen** tool. If you are working with the **Pen** tool and you want to switch to the straight-level line-moving **Resizing** tool, hold down the **Command** key.

We haven't finished with *Backstage06* yet. We still need to bring the sound up to full level as the shot is introduced, and then fade it out at the end.

4. To bring the level back up, first add a keyframe at about the point where the cross fade begins on **A1/A2**.

5. Next, add another keyframe at about the point where the cross fade ends. Push the level line back up to 0dB (Figure 4.24). Because this is the last keyframe on the level line, everything after that point will come back up to full volume.

6. Finally, we want to fade out the audio at the end. With the **Pen** tool, add a keyframe to the level line about two seconds before the end of the clip. Go to the end of the clip, and pull the end of the line all the way down to create a slow fade out as in Figure 4.25.

4.24 Ramping Up the Audio (far left)

4.25 Slow Fade Out (left)

Controlling Track Levels

There may be occasions when you want to change the audio level for an entire track—say, of music—to give it a lower base level, especially CD music, which is often recorded and compressed at maximum audio levels, often too high for use with most digital video systems. You can do this by selecting the track you want with the **Track** tool, the third button in the **Tools** (Figure 4.26).

You can select a single track, multiple tracks forward and backward, a single track forward and backward, or a whole track of audio and adjust its level globally.

Select the items or the track with the **Track** tool (**T**). Once you have your track or clips selected, go to **Modify>Levels**, or use the keyboard shortcut **Command-Option-L**.

4.26 Track Tools

Waveform in the Timeline

When you're working in the **Timeline**, it may be beneficial to turn on the waveform display in **Timeline** window (Figure 4.27).

Do this by going to the **Timeline Options** popup on the lower left corner of the **Timeline** window, where we saw **Dupe Detection** earlier, and select **Show Audio Waveforms**, or use the keyboard shortcut **Command-Option-W**.

Because displaying the audio waveform in the **Timeline** takes a good deal of computer processing power (prereading the audio and then displaying it), the redraw ability and video playback capabilities of the computer are markedly slowed down. So it's a good idea to toggle the waveform display on and off as needed with that handy keyboard shortcut.

4.27 Waveform in Timeline

4.28 Levels Controls

4.29 Pasting Audio Attributes

This command calls up a dialog box that allows you to adjust the audio levels of the clips (Figure 4.28). The slider or the value box will change the gain setting for all the clips selected. The **Relative** and **Absolute** popup sets how the gain is affected. **Absolute** will make the level you set affect the whole of all the clips, eliminating any fades. Using the **Relative** setting will change the value of the levels relative to any current settings or fades. This global levels control not only works on audio, but also works on opacity as well on a title or on the video portion of a clip.

Another way to change the audio level of more than one clip is to change its attributes. You can copy an audio clip by selecting it and pressing **Command-C**. Select the clips you want by marquee-ing or **Command**-clicking, and then use **Paste Attributes** from the **Edit** menu or press **Option-V**. Then check the attributes you want to paste to the other clips' **Levels** or **Pan** values (Figure 4.29).

Notice the **Scale Attributes Over Time** checkbox at the top. It defaults to the on position. If you have keyframed the levels in the copied clips, that keyframing will be distributed proportionately onto the pasted clip, based on the relative durations of the clips. If the copied clip is shorter, the keyframing will be spread out; if it is longer, the keyframing will tighten up. If you want to paste the keyframes in the same duration as in the copied clip, uncheck **Scale Attributes Over Time**.

☞ *Tip*

Changing a Range of Keyframes: You can also change the relative or absolute levels of a group of audio keyframes. Use the **Range** tool (**GGG**) to select the area that includes the audio keyframes (Figure 4.30). If you then apply the **Levels** function, it will raise or lower the relative or absolute values of the keyframes in the selected area..

4.30 Range Selection of Audio Keyframes

More Fades

Before we look at how to control audio levels in the **Viewer**, let's do some more work on the *Rough Cut copy* sequence.

Take a look at the fifth shot in the sequence *Backstage11*. We need to overlap its audio underneath the adjacent clips.

4.31 Backstage11 Overlapping Clips

1. With the **Option** key pressed, select the audio portion of the clip. Still holding down the **Option** key, tap the **Down** arrow key twice to move the stereo pair onto **A3/A4**.

2. Holding down the **Option** key again, drag out the front and end of the audio portion of *Backstage11* so that it overlaps the adjacent clips as in Figure 4.31.

3. The next step is to add a fade out at the end of *Backstage04* on **A1/A2**. Select the edit point and use the keyboard shortcut **Command-Option-T** to put in the default audio transition.

Backstage17, which immediately follows *Backstage11*, is quite loud and has a pronounced music track. Like you did with *Backstage05* earlier in the sequence, suppress its sound completely by dragging the level line right down to the bottom.

For the next shot, *Backstage03*, I want to fade up the sound, but as so often when working with video, I want the fade to come up before the shot actually begins.

1. Use a roll edit or extend edit to move the audio portion of the shot earlier in the sequence.

2. To do this again, hold down the **Option** key and click on the edit point in the audio portion of the clip.

3. Either use the **Roll** tool to move that audio edit about a second earlier, or do an extend edit, moving the playhead about one second earlier and pressing the **E** key to create a split edit that looks like Figure 4.32.

4. To complete the fade, with the edit still selected, press **Command-Option-T** to add the cross fade.

I would like to fade in the overlapping *Backstage11* a little earlier. To do this I need to ripple the sequence to move the overlapping on **A3/A4** so that they butt up against each other. We'll do this with the **Ripple** tool.

4.32   Roll or Extend Audio Edit (above)

4.33   Multitrack Ripple Edit (right)

1. With the **Ripple** tool, select the left side of the edit between *Backstage04* and *Backstage11*.

2. Hold down the **Command** key and click just to the left of the audio portion of *Backstage11*, in the empty space between it and the previous shot (Figure 4.33). You'll now ripple the empty space together with *Backstage04*.

3. Pull the edit until the audio tracks collide on **A3/A4**.

In the Viewer

Let's add the fade at the beginning of *Background11* in the **Viewer**.

1. Hold down the **Option** key again and double-click on the audio portion of the clip. This opens the clip to the **Audio** tab in the **Viewer** (Figure 4.34). Here you see the clip's audio waveform.

2. Move the cursor over the mauve line in the center of the audio track. Notice that it changes to the **Resizing** tool we saw earlier, which allows you to raise and lower the audio level.

At the top of Figure 4.34 you'll notice the **Level** slider and the **Decibel Indicator** box. It's currently at 0, which is the level at which the audio was digitized or captured.

As you move the line up or down with the cursor, both the **Level** slider and the **Decibel Indicator** box at the top move. A small window appears in the waveform as well that shows the amount in decibels that you're changing the audio level (Figure 4.35).

3. To add a keyframe, either use the **Pen** tool or hold down the **Option** key as the cursor approaches the level line. The cursor then changes into the **Pen** tool.

4. Go about one second into the shot in the **Viewer** and add a keyframe.

Tip _____
Real Time Adjustment: You can adjust audio levels in real time while playing in the **Audio** tab of the Viewer. Press **Control- +** to raise the level and **Control- −** to lower the level plus or minus one decibel. You can also use **Control-[** or **Con-trol-]** to raise or lower the levels in plus or minus 3dB increments. After a small hesitation, the audio will continue to play. Unfortunately, you can't actually mix like this. These controls only affect the clip's overall level. They won't take audio key-framing into account. Though if you do this in the **Timeline** with the **Range Select** tool, as we saw, you can raise and lower a section of key-frames.

4.34   Audio Viewer (left)

4.35   Decibel Level Change Indicators

5. Go back to the beginning of the clip and pull the level line down so that the audio fades up from the beginning of the shot (Figure 4.36).

You can also add keyframes with the little diamond button next to **Level** slider.

1. Click the little button, which will turn green while adding a keyframe to the level line.

2. Go to a different point in time.

3. Pull the **Level** slider up or down to change the sound volume, and another keyframe will be added.

There are several ways to delete an audio keyframe:

*   Grab it and pull it down out of the audio timeline.

*   Hold down the **Option** key when you're over the keyframe. The cursor will change into the **Pen Delete** tool (Figure 4.37).

*   Use the shortcut menu, by **Control**-clicking on the keyframe and selecting **Clear**.

*   If the playhead is sitting on a keyframe, you can also remove it by clicking the little green keyframe diamond next to the **Levels** slider. This will turn the keyframe button gray and remove the keyframe in the **level** line.

To move the keyframe, grab it and slide it left, right along the line.

4.36   Audio Fade In

4.37   Pen Delete Tool

Fixing Soft Audio

Sometimes the audio is just too low to be as forceful as you'd like, even after you crank it up with FCP's level controls. A neat little trick is to double up the audio tracks. Just put another copy of the same sound on the track below. A simple way to do this is to hold the **Option** key to select just the audio. Hold the **Option** key and drag down to see the right-pointing **Insert** arrow. Now add the **Shift** key to constrain the direction, and change the arrow to the downward-pointing **Overwrite** arrow. Drop the audio on the tracks below. You will have created a duplicate. Now push that audio up as well. Double your pleasure.

A neat feature of FCP is the ability to merge up to 24 tracks of audio with a single track of video. Normally this is done in the **Browser**. In fact, when you're working in the **Timeline**, the **Merge Clips** function in the **Modify** menu is greyed out. But you can still do it in the **Timeline** to your audio-doubled clip. Select the clip, then **Command**-click the duplicate audio tracks to select them as well, and use **Modify > Link** or **Command-L** to link them all together as a single clip with four or more audio tracks.

Another way to increase really low audio levels is to use nesting. Turn the clip volume as far up as it will go, which is 12dB, select the clip, and use **Sequence > Nest Item(s)** or the keyboard shortcut **Option-C**. This will embed the clip in a sequence of its own. The audio for the nested sequence will be at the 0dB level, and you can raise that another 12dB to further boost the sound.

4.38 Reset Button and Grab Handle

To delete all the keyframes in the audio, click the **Reset** button, the button with the red **X** next to the grab handle at the top of the panel (Figure 4.38).

4.39 Zoom Tool in the Waveform with Audio Slice

> ★ *Tip*
> *Zoom a Marquee:* You can also use the **Zoom** tool to drag a marquee along a section of the waveform to zoom into just that portion of the display. This technique will work in the **Viewer**, the **Canvas**, as well as the **Timeline**.

One of the great features for editing sound in the **Viewer** is that you can do it with great precision, down to $^1/100$th of a second. To do this you have to zoom into the waveform, either with the scaling tab at the bottom of the **Viewer** window or with the **Zoom** tool (Figure 4.39), which you can call up with the **Z** key. To zoom out, hold down the **Option** key while you click in the waveform. You can also use **Command-+** to zoom in and **Command- –** to zoom out. The black band in Figure 4.39 represents one frame of video, and you can zoom in farther still. Notice the tiny slice of audio that has been cut out of the track, less than one video frame in length.

Middle of the Sequence

Let's finish off the *Rough Cut copy* sequence. There are only a few more levels to tweak. Further along in the **Timeline** is another portion of *Backstage05*. This time we do want to use the sound.

1. Again with the **Option** key, select the audio portion of the clip and move the stereo pair down to **A3/A4**.

2. Extend the front of the sound until it butts up against *Backstage11*, also on **A3/A4**.

3. Extend the end of the sound as far as it will go, which isn't that far.

Between *Backstage03* and *Backstage05* are two shots, *Backstage09* and *10*. Both of these shots are quite loud.

4. Marquee-drag or **Command**-click to select the pair of them, and use **Modify>Levels** or **Command-Option-L** to reduce their levels to −9dB.

5. To smooth the transition between *Backstage09* and *Backstage10*, add a cross fade transition between the pair.

Pan Values

4.40 Changing Spread Value

In addition to the mauve level line in the **Viewer**, there is also a purple pan line. In a stereo pair such as this material, the pan lines are defaulted to −1. This indicates that the left channel is going to the left speaker and the right channel to the right speaker. By moving the lines up toward zero as in Figure 4.40, the two tracks are centered between the speakers. Going to 1 will make the channels cross over and swap sides. You can also use the **Pan** slider or type in the value box at the top.

When you have a multitrack recording with **Mono (a1)** and **Mono (a2)** sound, the **Viewer** appears with separate tabs, one for each channel. **Level** and **Pan** values can then be set separately for each track, one set to −1 and the other to 1. This allows you to move the audio from one side of the stereo speakers to the other.

When you're working with separate channels using the pan line, you can shift the sound to come from either the left side or the right side. Moving the **Pan** slider to the left to −1 will move all the sound to the left speaker, and moving the **Pan** slider all the way to the right to 1 will move the sound to the right speaker. Like **Levels**, **Pan** values can be keyframed. The classic example is the racing car that approaches from the left with all the sound coming from the left speaker, roars by, and disappears to the right, while the sounds sweeps past to the right speaker.

A little trick to quickly get the channels between the speakers between the speakers is to select the clips in the **Timeline** and use the keyboard shortcut **Control- .** (period) to center the tracks to the zero value.

4.41   Middle Portion of the Completed Sequence

4.42   Selecting the Ripple Edits

6. Add a cross fade transition to the beginning of *Backstage13*, which follows *Backstage05*. Select the edit point at the beginning and press **Command-Option-T**.

7. With the **Pen** tool, add a slow fade out to the end of *Backstage13*. The middle portion of the sequence should now look like Figure 4.41.

End of the Sequence

There is an interesting little problem in the ending portion of the sequence that will again require a ripple edit of empty space.

1. Pull the audio tracks for *Backstage02* down onto **A3/A4** and extend them front and end as far as you can.

2. For *Backstage16*, which is the second to last shot, just add a cross fade at the edit point.

3. One more stereo pair to pull down onto **A3/A4**, the last shot *Background14*. Bring the audio down to **A3/A4** and extend the front until it meets *Backstage02* on **A3/A4**.

I want to put a cross fade transition between the two shots on **A3/A4**, but I can't because there isn't enough media available on the end of *Backstage02*. I need to ripple that shot back by 15 frames to create enough space for the overlap.

4. With the **Ripple** tool, select the edit at the end of *Backstage02*. Holding down the **Command** key, click just to the left of the beginning of *Backstage16* tracks on **A1/A2**, as shown in Figure 4.42.

4.43   Numerical Ripple Edit

5. Pull the edit point to the left so that it moves 15 frames, or edit it numerically. (Type *−15* and press the **Enter** key.) As you type, a little box will appear at the top of the **Timeline** window telling you that you're rippling the edit (Figure 4.43).

6. Finally, add the cross fade between the two audio clips on **A3/A4**.

4.44 Audio Mixer

Audio Mixer

Final Cut Pro has a nice audio track mixing console. One of the exciting new features of this mixer in FCP5 is its ability to interface using the Mackie MIDI protocol with a digital hardware mixer. This really makes this combination of software and hardware a very powerful tool.

You can call it up the mixer directly from the **Tools** menu or with the keyboard shortcut **Option-6**. Better still, from the **Windows** menu, select **Arrange>Audio Mixing**. This opens the **Audio Mixer** into FCP's **Tool Bench** (Figure 4.44).

The number of tracks that appear in the mixer is determined by the number of tracks in the active sequence. Switch sequences and the number of sliders changes to match the sequence.

When you're working with DV, only two output channels appear on the right edge. In other formats that allow more outputs, more channels will appear. You can output up to 24 channels, if you have the hardware to support it, and edit to tape up to eight channels of output. You can select the number of channels in your **Sequence>Settings** (**Command-zero**) in the **Audio Outputs** panel

4.45 Audio Outputs

4.46 Selecting Output Channels

(Figure 4.45). To set which track goes to which output channel, **Control**-click at the head of the track in the **Timeline**, and choose from the shortcut menu (Figure 4.46).

Though the standard level for digital audio is −12dB and the absolute volume that digital audio can reach is zero, notice that the output meters exceed zero. This isn't because you can go beyond zero as you can in analog audio; it's there to give you an indication of how far over zero your audio is being driven, which the regular audio meters in FCP do not do.

4.47 Patch Panel and View Buttons

For complex mixing you often don't want to have all the tracks visible at once. You can set which tracks are visible with the patch panel dots on the left edge of the mixer. The **View** buttons above that let you preset different groups of tracks. The patch panel and **View** buttons can be seen in Figure 4.47. **View 1** might be set to show all the tracks, while **View 2** would be only **A5/A6** and **A7/A8** as in Figure 4.47, while **View 3** was only **A1/A2** and **A3/A4**, whatever arrangement you want.

The horizontal sliders in Figure 4.47 are pan sliders, letting you control the spread of audio channels. Notice also the **Mute/ Solo** buttons, which let you mute individual tracks, or solo them so that only a single channel or combinations of channels are heard as you need. These **Mute/Solo** buttons are also available in the **Timeline**. You open them by clicking on the tiny speaker button in the far lower left corner of the **Timeline** window, which pops open the array of **Mute/Solo** buttons (Figure 4.48), just like the ones in the mixer. Notice the green **Visbility** (audibility) buttons at the head of the **Timeline**. The difference between these and the **Mute** buttons is that when audibility is switched off, that track will not play out to tape. If a track is muted, it will still output even though it can't be heard during playback in the **Timeline**.

4.48 Timeline Mute/Solo/Audibility Buttons

To control your levels with the mixer, move the sliders up and down as desired. If the audio is a stereo pair, moving one slider will move the pair. It's best to work this mixer by setting levels for individual tracks one at a time, or to connect it to a hardware mixer.

When you set the level with a slider, it sets the level for the whole track from when you mouse down up until you release the mouse. The default is for the sliders to work on the levels for the whole track, but you can automate your slider controls to create keyframes. To do this, you have to activate the **Keyframe** button in the upper right corner of the mixer (Figure 4.49), which can also be toggled on and off with the keyboard shortcut **Command-Shift-K**. When this is on, whatever you do with the sliders will be recorded and appear as keyframes in **Timeline**. There are three settings in the **User Preferences** for the amount of keyframes added to the track (Figure 4.50). The default **Reduced** is a good compromise. **All** can produce thousands of keyframes, while **Peaks Only** is too coarse and produces very long slow ramps.

Audio Peaks

FCP can analyze the audio levels of a clip or a sequence and place markers indicating where the sound exceeds acceptable levels. You can then either pull down the levels or keyframe the area around the overloaded audio and pull it down that way. It's simple to do.

Start by selecting the clip you want analyzed, either in the **Browser**, **Viewer**, or an active **Timeline** window. Then choose from the **Mark** menu **Audio Peaks>Mark**.

The application will quickly look through the clip or sequence and place a marker wherever it detects an audio peak. With sequence markers, the analysis is done quickly, and with waveforms displayed in the **Timeline**, it's easy to see where the peaks are occurring, especially if you zoom into a section of the **Timeline** more closely, as in Figure 4.51.

Notice also that if there are extended portions of peak audio, FCP will place extended markers in the **Timeline**. It may be an idea to bring down the overall levels on some of these clips to make the audio levels acceptable. Lower the levels with the tools we've seen, and run the analysis again.

4.49 Audio Mixer Keyframe Button

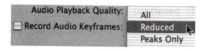

4.50 Audio Keyframe Preferences

⭐ Tip _____

Scrolling Sliders: FCP works with a scroll wheel. Wherever you place the cursor—in the Timeline, Browser, Viewer—the scroll wheel will function. One great thing about this is that the scroll wheel can be used to control the audio mixer sliders. Just place the cursor over a slider and twirl up or down with your scroll wheel to move the slider.

4.51 Audio Marks in the Timeline

You can clear audio peak markers either with the standard marker clearing tools (**Control- `** [grave accent]) or individual markers. To specifically delete audio peak markers, from the **Mark** menu choose **Audio Peaks>Clear**.

Voice Over

FCP has a **Voice Over** tool that allows you to record audio tracks directly to your hard drive while playing back your **Timeline**. Voice Over is most valuable for making *scratch tracks,* test narrations used to try out pacing and content with picture. It could be used for final recording, though you'd probably want to isolate the computer and other extraneous sounds from the recording artist. Many people actually prefer to record narrations before final editing, so that the picture and sound can be controlled more tightly. Others feel that recording to the picture allows for a more spontaneous delivery from the narrator. However you use it, **Voice Over** can be an important tool.

Voice Over is part of the **Tool Bench**. You can call it from the **Tools** menu, which brings up the window in Figure 4.52.

First you'll have to configure your recording setup for **Source, Input,** and **Sampling Rate**.

Source defines where the sound is coming from: the computer mic input, a USB device, a camcorder, or an installed digitizing card.

Input controls the type of signal being received, whether it's line level, balanced audio in, digital audio, or whatever your source device is capable of handling.

4.52 Voice Over Tool

Offset adjusts for the delay taken by the analog to digital conversion. USB devices typically take one frame. DV cameras can be three frames or more.

Let's look at some of the controls in this panel:

- The large red button, the middle of the three in the top portion of the window, is the **Record** button. It will also stop the recording, as will the **Escape** key.

- The button to its left is the **Preview/Review** button and will play the selected area of your sequence.

- The button to the right is the **Discard** button. Pressing it will delete the just-recorded or aborted file from your hard drive.

- The **Gain** slider, next to the **Input** popup, allows you to control the recording level based on the horizontal LCD display meter. This is fine for scratch tracks, but for finished work, it would probably be better to have a hardware mixer before the input for good mic level control.

- The **Headphones** volume does just what it says. If there is nothing jacked into the headphone output of your computer, the sound will come out of the computer speaker itself. To avoid recording it or the **Sound Cues**, pull the **Volume** slider down to the minimum level.

Note

More RAM for VO: Because Voice Over works in RAM (storing the sound before recording it to disk), you may need to put more RAM into your computer over and above the minimum requirements asked for by FCP because the audio is buffered in RAM as it's recorded. 48kHz audio consumes 6MB per minute. So a half-hour track would take 180MB. After the recording is finished, the audio is dumped from RAM to disk and stored in your *Capture Scratch* folder with the project name.

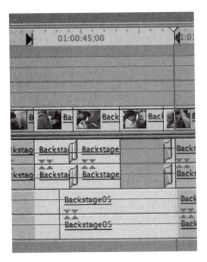

4.53 Timeline Marked for Voice Over

FCP gives the recording artist elaborate sound cues, which are turned on with the little checkbox. Together with the aural cues in the headphones, there is visual cuing as well, which appears in the window to the right of the **Record** button. As the recording starts, a countdown begins, with cue tones as the display, that starts pale yellow becomes darker and more orange until the recording begins. Then the display changes to red. There is a cue tone at 15 seconds from the end of the recording as well as beeps counting down the last five seconds to the end of the recording. Recording actually begins during countdown and continues two seconds after the end of the recording during finishing. Though this doesn't appear in the **Timeline** after the recording, you can just drag out the front and end of the clip if the voice started early or overran the end.

I think the best way to work with **Voice Over** in the **Timeline** is to define an In and Out point as in Figure 4.53. If no points are defined, recording will begin at the point at which the playhead is parked and go until the end of the sequence, or until you run out of available memory, whichever comes first. You can also define an In point and go from there, or define an Out and go from the playhead until the Out is reached. Because the **Timeline** doesn't scroll as the sequence plays, it might be helpful to reduce the sequence to fit the **Timeline** window. **Shift-Z** will do this with a keystroke.

Recording is always done to a destination track that has free space. If there is no free space within the defined area of the recording, **Voice Over** will *always* create a new track. So if you record multiple takes, they will record onto the next lower track or onto a new track. The **Audio File** window, just above the meter, will give you the track information. If there is no free space, a new track will be created. You can name the recording in the **Audio File** window, and each take will be numbered incrementally.

After a discarded take, **Voice Over** will record to the previously assigned track with the previously assigned name. After a few takes, you may want to discard a previous take and reassign the targeted track so that **Voice Over** will work with the empty tracks you vacated.

If you're going to be doing multiple takes, make sure you use the **Mute** button to switch off tracks with previous takes so that they do not play back during recording. Once several takes are recorded, you may want to play back the various takes to see which is the best. Just use the **Solo** button to hear individual tracks to assess performance. You can also solo individual items, which may be as simple. Select the VO track you want to listen to, and choose **Sequence>Solo Item**(s) or use the keyboard shortcut **Control-S**. For some reason, this function has never been made available in the shortcut menus.

After a recording session with **Voice Over,** it's a good idea to go into your hard drive and root out old unnecessary tracks that may be filling up your drive. It's probably simplest to do this from the application. Those takes you recorded that you no longer want can be deleted from your sequence, but they aren't automatically deleted from your hard drive. You can't make something offline from inside a sequence, but you can drag the unneeded takes into a bin in your **Browser** and from there make them offline, deleting them from the drive. Also remember, the recordings are only a part of your sequence and will not appear in your **Browser** at all, unless you put them there.

Note

Make Notes: Another handy use for the **Voice Over** tool is to make notes while you're watching the video. Use headphones to hear your track. Clip on a lavaliere mic as close to your mouth as you can get it, and set off to play your sequence. This is kind of like recording dictation, except that it records right in your Timeline in line with what you're commenting. Your comment, "That shot's too dark" appears right underneath the shot that's too dark. Another use for Voice Over is to record rough translations in foreign locations. It's often cheaper, and easier to get a translation done right on the spot, recording it to your PowerBook with its built-in microphone. If it's good enough you can use your location recording, or get it re-recorded later. But having the foreign language content translated on the spot can be a great time saver when you get into the cutting room.

Summary

In this lesson we looked at working with sound in Final Cut. Performing split edits, overlapping sound, cutting with sound, overlapping and cross fading tracks, as well as FCP's **Audio Mixer,** its **Audio Peaks feature,** and its **Voice Over** tool. Sound is often overlooked, seeming insignificant or of minor importance, but it is crucial to making a sequence appear professionally edited.

When you want to smooth out cuts or to change between scenes, you might want to use transitions. That's what we're going to look at in the next lesson: how they work, and how to use them.

Double System Sound

When you shoot film, the sound is recorded on a separate audio recorder, what's called *double system sound*. More and more people working in video seem to be returning to double system sound, often using a DAT recorder to get better quality recordings than is possible recording directly to the camera. Handling this material has often been a problem for editors working in video. FCP's **Merge** feature, which we saw earlier, makes this process simpler than ever.

1. First capture your video and your separate sound track. If your video and audio have locked timecode tracks, FCP makes this merge a quick menu trip away.

2. Select the two pieces of material, video and audio, that you want to merge, and from the **Modify** menu choose **Merge Clips**. This will bring up the dialog box in Figure 4.54.

3. Select the **Timecode** button and click **OK**.

4.54 Merge Clips Dialog

If your video and audio don't have shared timecode, it's still simple to do.

1. Open the video into the **Viewer** and find a common sync point that you can see and which is also audible. A clapperboard is, of course, the best way to do this, but a simple hand clap will suffice.

2. Mark the clap strike as your In point.

3. Open the audio file into the **Viewer** and find the audible clap strike there and mark that as your In point.

4. Now when you run **Merge Clips**, select **in points** in the **Merge** dialog box. Obviously if the clapperboards are end sticks marking the tail of the shot, you mark Outs on your media and **out points** in the **Merge** dialog. When you merge the clips, a new clip is created in your **Browser**. The new clip takes its name from the video clip and adds *Merged* to the name.

Audio and video do not have to have the same duration or have the same start or end times. The application will create a merged clip long enough to cover the whole duration of the media, beginning with the one that starts first, video and audio, and ending with whichever ends last.

Lesson 5

Adding Transitions

Transitions can add life to a sequence, ease a difficult edit into something smoother, or give you a way to mark a change of time or place. The traditional grammar of film that audiences still accept is that dissolves denote small changes, while a fade to black followed by a fade from black mark a greater passage of time. With the introduction of digital effects, any imaginable movement or contortion of the images to replace one with another quickly became possible—and were quickly applied everywhere, seemingly randomly, to every possible edit. They can be hideously inappropriate, garish, and ugly. But to each his own taste. Transitions can be used effectively, or they can look terribly hackneyed. Final Cut Pro gives you the option to do either or anything in between.

Loading the Lesson

Let's begin by loading the material you will need for this lesson on the hard drive of your computer.

1. If you don't already have it on your media drive, drag the *Lesson 3 Media* folder from the DVD to it. We'll use this media again to demonstrate how transitions work.

123

2. You should also drag the folder called *Transitions* from the DVD onto your media drive. This contains samples of each of the 60 transitions available in FCP.

3. Make sure you have the *Projects* folder on your system drive.

4. Eject the DVD and look inside the *Projects* folder on your hard drive, where you'll find a folder called *Lesson 5*.

5. Inside that folder, double-click the project file *Lesson 5* to launch FCP.

6. Once again, go through the reconnect process as in Lesson 3 on page 66.

Inside your copy of the project *Lesson 5* you'll find in the **Browser**:

- An empty sequence called *Sequence 1*
- A still image called *Gradient.pct*, which we'll use later
- The bin called *Clips*
- The bin called *Transitions*

We'll be working with the food clips again to see how transitions work and how to control them.

5.1   Effects Window

5.2   Video Transitions Window

Applying Transitions

Next let's look at the transitions themselves. In the **Browser**, usually behind the project window, is a tab called **Effects**. If you open it, you see a window with a group of folders—sorry, bins—as in Figure 5.1. You'll notice more than transitions in this window. For the moment, we're going to concentrate on the *Video Transitions* bin.

The **Effects** window does not maintain strict interface standards: for some reason, the **Name** column does not force alphanumeric ordering. The order is created internally in FCP, and the first bin is *Favorites*. You can park your special transitions and effects here. It's probably empty now.

Double-click on **Video Transitions** to open the bin. It should look like Figure 5.2. The **Video Transitions** window shows yet more bins, and these bins contain a total of 60 video transitions. I'd be very surprised if any one has actually ever used them all in earnest on real projects, not just playing with them to try them out.

The *Transitions* bin in your **Browser** contains previews of each of the transitions available in FCP. We're going to try some of them out in this lesson, but first let's see how the *Favorites* bin works.

Favorite Transitions

Click on the disclosure triangle to twirl open **Dissolve**, which holds seven different types of dissolves. Notice that **Cross Dissolve**, which is the most commonly used transition in video or film, is probably in bold. Whenever a transition's name appears in bold in either the *Video Transitions* folder or in the **Effects>Video Transitions** menu, that indicates that the transition can be played back in real time. These transitions only appear like this if your system is capable of real-time playback.

How many transitions appear as real time will also depend on your **RT** settings, which we saw in **Playback Control** in Lesson 1 on page 9. At **Safe RT** with the quality set to **High**, you'll get fewer transitions than with **Unlimited RT** set to **Low**.

Grab the **Cross Dissolve** and drag and drop the transition over to the *Favorites* bin. Twirl open the *Favorites* bin. You may notice that the transition in the *Favorites* bin is a duplicate. The usual behavior when moving items from one bin to another is that the item is relocated. But when moving an element to *Favorites*, a copy is created. You can put any transitions, video or audio; any effect; or even a generator into *Favorites*. Though multiple types of items can be placed into this bin, only the appropriate items will appear in the **Effects** menu below **Video Transitions** in *Favorites*, as in Figure 5.3. You can rename the transition or effect anything you want, so perhaps you'd like to keep handy an eight-frame dissolve. Just copy **Cross Dissolve** into *Favorites*. Change its name to something like *8Frames*, and then change its duration to your favorite length.

Notice in Figure 5.3 that below the *Favorites* menu item that's selected is the default effect, in this case, **Cross Dissolve**. It's simple to set the default transition. You can either:

- Set it with the menus by selecting the transition in the *Video Transitions* bin and choosing **Set Default** from the **Effects** menu, or

- **Control**-click on the transition in the *Video Transition* bin, and from the shortcut menu choose **Set Default Transition** as in Figure 5.4.

5.3 Video Transitions Favorites Menu (above)

5.4 Set Default Transition (right)

You can also create a favorite transition from one applied in the Timeline. This allows you set up a complex transition such as a page peel or a gradient wipe, which we'll see a bit later, and then save it into your *Favorites* bin.

1. To do this, create the transition and set it up to taste in the **Viewer**, which we'll look at a shortly.

2. With the **Viewer** window active, choose from the **Effects** menu **Make Favorite Effect**, or use the keyboard shortcut **Option-F**. The effect will appear in the *Favorites* bin just as you set it up.

After the default transition is set, it will appear underlined in the bin.

> ✒ *Tip*_____
>
> **Favorites:** Your *Favorites* are saved as part of your *Preferences*. If you trash your *Preferences* file, your *Favorites* go with it. There is a simple solution to this. Drag the *Favorites* bin from the **Effects** panel and place it in your **Browser**. This is a copy of the *Favorites* bin in **Effects**, and it will remain with the project, even if the prefs are trashed. I keep a *Favorites* project containing a **Browser** with a constantly updated *Favorites* bin as well as a sequence to which I add color mattes or slugs to which whole effects or groups of effects applied. I save the project regularly as part of my backup routine to external drives and DVD disks. You can also back up your preferences with FCP Rescue 5, which is in the *Extras* folder of the DVD.

The default duration for all transitions is one second. You can set any duration you want in the **Transitions** bin, and that will be the default duration for that transition.

So what's all this about default transitions? In Lesson 3 we skipped two items in the **Canvas Edit Overlay**:

- **Insert with Transition**
- **Overwrite with Transition**

The default transition will appear in your sequence when you select **Insert with Transition (Shift-F9)** or **Overwrite with Transition (Shift-F10)**, or use the keyboard or shortcut menu to enter a transition.

5.5   Transitition Error

Checking the Media

1. Let's begin by opening up *Sequence 1*.

2. Next select the two clips from the *Clips* bin, *Food2* and *Food4*, and drag them directly to the sequence.

Remember these are all subclips, and so each shot you just placed in the timeline contains the full extent of the media for that clip on the hard drive. Or at least Final Cut Pro thinks so.

Let's try putting a transition onto the sequence we've laid out, the two *Food* shots.

3. Grab the **Cross Dissolve** transition from the *Dissolve* bin and drag it onto the edit point between *Food2* and *Food4*.

You see that this isn't possible because you get the transition drag icon with a small **X** as in Figure 5.5. Why is this happening? The answer is simple. There isn't enough media in either clip to perform the transition. The shots must overlap; frames from both shots must appear on the screen simultaneously. For a one-second transition, both shots have to have one second of media that overlaps with the other shot.

1. Double-click *Food2* in the **Timeline** to open it into the **Viewer**.

2. Go to the end of the shot. Use **Shift-O** to take you to the Out point.

If **Overlays** are switched on in the **View** popup (Figure 5.6) as they normally are, you'll see the telltale film sprocket hole indicator on the right edge of the frame (Figure 5.7). This overlay tells you that you're right at the end of the available media for the shot. There needs to be extra media available to create the overlap for the transition, as shown in Figure 5.8.

The pale shot on the left has to overlap the dark shot on the right by half the length of the transition, and vice versa. If that media does not exist, you can't do the transition. FCP usually assumes

5.6   View Popup

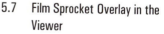

5.7   Film Sprocket Overlay in the Viewer

5.8 Overlapping Video

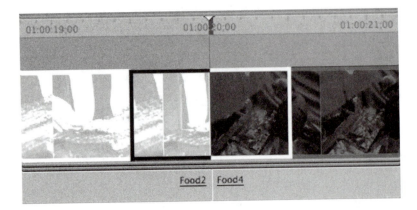

as a default that the transition takes place centered around the marked edit point, not that it ends at the edit point. Therefore, to execute the default one-second transition, you need at least half a second, 15 frames, of available media after the Out point on the outgoing shot, and 15 frames in front of the In point of the incoming shot. In this case there is nothing, hence the X. Unless you think of it ahead of time, which many times you don't, you'll have to deal with it when you're fine tuning your edit. Often you'd rather not deal with transitions while you're laying out your sequence, leaving them until you've laid out the shot order.

Note_____
Positioning the Transition: The only time FCP does not presume to center the transition on the edit point is when there is overlapping media available on the incoming side of the transition and not on the outgoing shot. Then, if there is extra material on the incoming shot, FCP will end the transition at the edit point. However, if there is media available on the outgoing shot, but none on the incoming shot, FCP will not create a transition properly. If there isn't enough media to create a transition of the duration requested, it will make one for as much media as there is available, centering it on the edit point.
_____

If you know you have extra media in the original clip, you can always go back to extend the media. If this option is available, it's easy to do in FCP. Select **Remove Subclip Limits** from the **Modify** menu.

However, in this case, extending the media will extend it into another shot, producing a flash frame during the transition, something to be avoided. To be able to put in transitions, we'll have to trim the Out point on *Food2* and the In point of *Food4*. Let's do that in the **Timeline**.

1. Select the **Ripple tool** from the **Tools** palette, or use the keyboard shortcut **RR.**

2. With the **Ripple** tool click just to the left of the edit point between *Food2* and *Food4* as in Figure 5.9.

3. With **Ripple** active, type in **–15** for a 15-frame ripple. Notice the display that appears in the middle of the **Timeline** window (Figure 5.10). Press **Enter.**

This is the navigation shortcut for going back half a second. Because we're using the **Ripple** tool, we're rippling back half a second.

4. Click on the right side of the edit point at the start of *Food4*.

5. This time type in **+15** and press **Enter** to ripple that side of the edit point by 15 frames.

We've now rippled *Food4's* In point by half a second, half a second off the end of the first shot, half a second off the beginning of the second.

6. Once you've rippled the two edits, go the edit point in the sequence between *Food2* and *Food4*.

7. From the menus, select **Effects>Video Transitions>Dissolve>Cross Dissolve.**

This adds a cross dissolve transition to the edit point. You can also go to the *Video Transitions* bin, either from the *Dissolves* bin or from *Favorites*, and drag and drop the transition onto the edit point. The transition does not need to be dragged only to the center line. It can also be dragged to the outgoing clip so that the transition ends at the edit point, or to the incoming clip so the transition begins at the start of the clip. This can only be done, of course, if there is sufficient material for this type of transition.

If you double-click on the transition itself in the **Timeline**, it will open into the **Viewer.** Here you can see how the video overlaps and why extra material—handles—are needed on either end of the transition to create the effect (Figure 5.11).

Once it's in the **Timeline**, the transition displays in one of three ways, depending on how it was placed. Figure 5.12 shows the center position; the other two appear as in Figure 5.13, an end-on-edit transition, and Figure 5.14, a start-on-edit transition.

Notice the sloping line indicators showing the type of alignment in each case, and also note that the two latter transitions can only be half-second dissolves. When the sequence was rippled by 15 frames on each side of the edit point, only enough media was

5.9 Ripple Tool in the Timeline

5.10 Ripple Value in the Timeline

Tip

Quick Transition: The quickest way to add a transition to an edit is to go to the edit point, park the playhead over it, and press **Command-T.** This will add the default transition with the default duration.

5.11 Clips Overlapping in the Transition Edit Window

5.12 Center on Edit Transition

5.13 End on Edit Transition

5.14 Start on Edit Transition

made available for a center-aligned transition. If the transition is to end on the edit point, the incoming shot has to be extended a whole second underneath the outgoing shot to accommodate it. Similarly, if you wanted to start the transition on the edit point, the outgoing shot has to extend one second into the incoming shot, one second beyond the start of the edit point. If we made these changes, then we could also easily change the type of transition alignment with a shortcut menu on the transition in the **Timeline** (Figure 5.15).

Using the Canvas Edit Overlay

Let's back up a bit to see another way to do this.

1. Delete everything in the **Timeline**.

2. Open up *Food2* from the **Browser** into the **Viewer**.

5.15 Transition Shortcut Menu

5.16 Video Transition with Audio Cross Fade

5.17 Transition Shortcut Menu

Because this will be the first shot in the timeline, I won't need to shorten the front of the clip.

3. Press the **End** key to take you to the end of the shot.

4. Type *–1.* (minus one period) and press **Enter**. This will move the playhead back one second.

5. Press **O** to enter the Out point and drag to the **CEO Over-write** box, or press **F10** to overwrite it into the **Timeline**.

6. Open *Food4* in the **Viewer** from the **Browser**. This clip we will shorten front and end.

7. Go to the beginning of the clip and type *+1.* and enter an In point.

8. Then go to the end of the clip and enter an Out point one second before the end (type *–1.* and press **O**).

9. Drag *Food4* from the **Viewer** to **Overwrite with Transition**—not to **Overwrite**. Or enter **Shift-F10**.

The clip immediately drops into the **Timeline** after the first clip. The default transition has been added at the beginning of the clip, as well as a default audio cross fade (Figure 5.16). Adding the audio cross fade is a bonus that often enhances the edit and helps to smooth the transition.

Shortcut Menu Transition

A third method can be used to add the default transition.

1. **Control**-click (or right-click with a two-button mouse) on an edit point as in Figure 5.17.

2. Select **Add Transition**.

This procedure will evoke the defaults for transition type and duration, if sufficient media is available. If not, FCP will make a transition of whatever length is available. If no media is available, no transition will be created. If media is available only on one shot, the transition will be created offset on one side or the other. The shortcut menu transition will also add the audio cross fade.

Rendering

After you've entered a transition, you'll see that the narrow bar at the top of the **Timeline** has changed color from the normal mid-gray. It will have changed to red, green, yellow, or orange, depending on the type of transition you applied, your system capabilities, and your **RT** settings. If you are working with a system with no real-time capabilities, then a bright red line will appear over the transition, indicating that a portion of the sequence needs to be rendered. Newer systems, especially if you're switched to **Dynamic** settings in **RT** controls, which you should use, will probably give you real-time playback for many transitions.

Rendering means that the application has to create media for a portion of your timeline where none exists. Most of the two shots in your sequence are on your hard drive, but not for the 30 frames that make up this one-second cross dissolve, during which one shot is changing into the other. The material of one shot mixed together with another is not on your hard drive. All you've done is give the computer instructions to create that media.

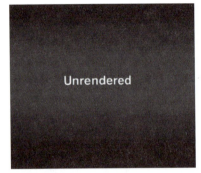

5.18 Unrendered Warning in the Canvas

If you try to play across that part of the timeline with a non–real-time system, the **Canvas** will display the message in Figure 5.18. If you do have real-time capabilities, Final Cut can play through the timeline without prior rendering. It processes the transition on the fly in real time as it plays. If your system is capable of real-time transitions, this bar will appear green. Real-time transitions will be highlighted in bold in your bins and in the menu.

If you have your **RT** settings, which we saw in Lesson 1 on page 9, on **Unlimited RT**, you may get a yellow or an orange bar. The yellow bar indicates that playback is a proxy only; that is, if you've created a complex setting for your transition, only the default will be visible in real time. Orange indicates that you will likely get dropped frames when playing through this area. If you do playback through you will normally get the dropped frame warning message in Figure 5.19. If you switch this warning off in the lower right corner, you can then work in **Unlimited RT** without hindrance, though with the occasional frame drop.

To turn on the dropped frame warning, you'll have to go back to your **User Preferences** and switch it back on in the **General** panel. Remember that even though you use **Dynamic RT** and have a great deal of real-time playback, most of your effects, including

5.19 Unlimited RT Dropped Frame Warning

5.20 Sequence > Render Selection

transitions, will have to be rendered before you can output your material.

Render Commands

FCP's render controls are extremely flexible, but they can also be quite complex and bewildering for many users. What gets rendered when is controlled by a complex combination of settings in the **Sequence** menu under **Render Selection**, **Render All**, and **Render Only**.

The **Render Selection** menu (Figure 5.20) controls rendering of a selection, either a clip, clips, or a segment of the **Timeline** marked with In and Out points. Normally only the red **Needs Render** bar is checked for both video and audio. If you want to force a render on any of the other available items, select it. It will remain checked in the menu. Whenever you give the **Render Selection** command (Table 5.1), those items that are checked will be rendered. Remember, though, that if you select a checked item, you will be unchecking it, effectively switching off that render command.

One of FCP's render settings is the ability to render audio at item level. This allows you to render a piece of audio such as an MP3 file or a piece of 44.1kHz CD music into the correct sampling rate as a separate item. Wherever you place a piece of audio into a sequence that doesn't match the sequence settings, it will appear with a green line through the top of the track (Figure 5.21) and the red render bar in the **Timeline**. If you look closely, you'll see that the render bar is in two halves, like the **Timeline** itself. The video render indicator is above and the audio render indicator below (Figure 5.22).

5.21 Unrendered Audio in the Timeline

5.22 Audio Render Indicator

5.23   Sequence > Render All

5.24   Sequence > Render Only

Table 5.1   Table Render Commands

Render All	Option-R
Render Selection	Command-R
Render Audio Selection	Control-Option-R
Render Proxy	Command-Option-P
Render Preview	Control-R
Mixdown Audio	Command-Option-R

You can select the audio item from any of the menus render it at **Item** level. After that audio in your **Timeline** has been rendered to the correct settings, it will have a blue indicator bar showing that it's been rendered as an item and will not need to be re-rendered. The item can then be moved to any part of the sequence without needing re-rendering.

The **Render All** menu (Figure 5.23) gives you same list except many more items are checked by default. The **Render Only** menu (Figure 5.24) is similar. It allows you to render selected items without changing the settings in **Render** and **Render All**. Note the inclusion in the **Render Only** menu of **Mixdown** for audio. This allows you to render out a mixed audio file of all your tracks, allowing easier playback. This is particularly important when exporting or outputting to tape.

Render Previewing

If you want to look at your material without rendering it, in real-time, you have a couple of different options. One is **QuickView**, in the **Tools** menu. The **QuickView** window (Figure 5.25) allows you to play through a section of video by building a cache file in RAM. The more RAM you have available, the more the application will able to store.

There's only one button on the window, a **Play** button. Click to play; click to stop. Of course, you can also use the spacebar. No **J**, **K**, and **L** keys, however. There is only one direction and one speed: forward and looping. The **QuickView** window is like the Energizer bunny: it just keeps playing and playing, trying to cache as much as it can with any available RAM, until you press the spacebar to stop it. With the window set to **Auto** (in the **View** popup menu at the upper right), it will keep doing RAM previews of whatever is in the active window. Switch to the **Timeline**, and it will start previewing around the position of the playhead. Switch to the **Viewer**, and it will start playing that.

5.25 QuickView Window

The little popup also allows you to designate a screen to preview: **Canvas**, **Viewer**, or **None**. **None** simply lets you switch it off so it doesn't update, without closing the window.

The **Resolution** popup in the upper left does just that: sets the resolution of playback to **Full**, **Half**, or **Quarter**. The lower the resolution, the more you'll be able to preview, but the poorer the quality. The default duration for **QuickView** is two seconds, which is ideal for checking one-second transitions. To increase the amount of time previewed, use the **Range** slider at the bottom of the window. It goes up to 10 seconds. If you do increase the range to its maximum and you don't have enough RAM to hold 10 seconds of video as well as do the processing, **QuickView** will never be able to get the preview up to speed. It will always be dumping cached frames to pick up new ones. So either reduce the range or reduce the resolution.

Another way that I like to play through a section that needs rendering is to use the keyboard shortcut **Option-P** or **Option-**. This is a good way to see if the transition will play smoothly, if there are any other unpleasant hiccups in the effect. The faster your system, the faster it will play through the transition. What's nice about this is that FCP caches the playback, so that the first time you play back using the shortcut, it might take quite a while, but the next playback using **Option-** will be considerably faster, even in real time on the slowest systems.

5.26   Render Control

Note

Exporting: Changing the Record to Tape settings in the RT popup will not affect export settings. If you export a sequence, it will export your material as it's currently rendered, regardless of the settings in Render Control. So if some of your material has been rendered in low resolution, when you export there will be no warning that your material needs to be re-rendered at high resolution. There is also no way to force the application to do that.

Render Control

As real-time playback is becoming more and more the norm in FCP, render control, which sets the quality level of your renders and was an important feature in earlier versions of the application, has been greatly simplified. Normally FCP renders at full resolution, but it's still possible to adjust your render settings to render at reduced quality for greater speed.

Render settings are now set in the **Render Control** panel (Figure 5.26) at the back of the **Sequence Settings**, which can be called up from the **Sequence** menu or with the keyboard shortcut **Command-zero**. Here you can set what you want to render, as well as control your render quality with the **Frame Rate** and **Resolution** popups. Setting these two popups to lower numbers will greatly speed up your rendering process. You can change your render settings at will, which allows you to have material in various render resolutions throughout your sequence simultaneously.

Render Manager

The **Render Manager** is in the menus under **Tools>Render Manager**. This feature lets you selectively delete unwanted or old render files from your hard drive. What's nice about the **Render Manager** is that you can delete files not only from the project you're working on at the moment, but also from any other projects that are on your Scratch Disks. (Figure 5.27).

It's simple to delete files. Check in the **Remove** column the items you wanted deleted and press **OK** or the **Enter** key. It's good practice to go through the **Render Manager** periodically to weed out old render files. You might find some lingering items you'd long forgotten. It's probably a good idea to check through the **Render Manager** about every month or so.

Render Manager				
Name ▼	Type	Size	Remove	Last Modified
▼ ☐ Additional Render Files	Bin	918.3 MB		
▶ ☐ Animated Cutout	Bin	40.7 MB		
▼ ☐ FCP	Bin	577.2 MB	✓	
▶ ☐ Animated Comp	Bin	14.3 MB	✓	
▶ ☐ Drop Shadow	Bin	14.3 MB	✓	
▶ ☐ Sequence 1	Bin	265.6 MB	✓	
▶ ☐ Sequence 11	Bin	15.0 MB	✓	
▶ ☐ Sequence 11 1	Bin	207.1 MB	✓	
▶ ☐ threeLayers.p	Bin	34.3 MB	✓	
▶ ☐ Title 3D pan	Bin	26.4 MB	✓	
▶ ☐ FCP3	Bin	30.8 MB		
▶ ☐ Lesson 1 copy	Bin	146.7 MB		
▶ ☐ Lesson 2	Bin	3.4 MB		
▶ ☐ Lesson 5	Bin	15.1 MB		
▶ ☐ Sample Project	Bin	45.1 MB		
▶ ☐ Tips Project	Bin	59.3 MB		
▶ ☐ Lesson 5	Bin	3.4 MB		
▶ ☐ Lesson 5a	Bin	3.4 MB		
☐ Render Files in Undo Queue	Render Files	23.3 MB		Unknown

Render Files Selected: 577.2 MB

Check in the Remove column to delete unwanted render files or free up disk space.

Cancel

5.27 Render Manager Window

Controlling Transitions

Once you've played back your transition a few times in **Quick-View,** you may discover that it doesn't look quite the way you'd want it to. You may want to shorten or lengthen it or shift the actual edit point. Assuming you have material available for this, it is easiest to do in the **Timeline** itself. To change the duration of the transition, grab one end of it and pull, as in Figure 5.28. It's a good idea to switch **Snapping** off before you do this, because it's easy to snap the transition down to nothing. As you pull the transition, a little window displays the amount of change as well as the new duration of the transition. If you have an audio cross fade as well as a transition, that will also change with your action. While you're dragging the transition end, you'll get the two-up display in the **Canvas** that shows you the frames at the

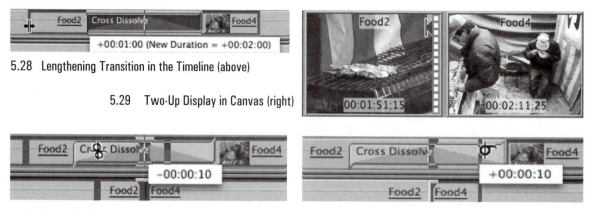

5.28 Lengthening Transition in the Timeline (above)

5.29 Two-Up Display in Canvas (right)

5.30 Rolling the Transition Edit Point

5.31 Rippling the Transition Edit Point

ends of the transition (Figure 5.29). Notice the tell-tale film sprocket holes on the right edge of the frame. While extending the transition, I reached the limits of media available to one shot.

You can also change the edit point in the center of the transition. Move the **Selector** to the center of the edit, and it will immediately change to the **Roll** tool, allowing you to move the edit point and the transition along the timeline, left and right as desired (Figure 5.30). You can also ripple either shot, but to do that, you have to call up the **Ripple** tool (**RR**) and then pull either shot left or right, shortening or lengthening the sequence while not affecting the transition (Figure 5.31). Again, the two-up display in the **Canvas** will show you the frames you're working on.

Transition in the Viewer

Final Cut gives you another way to control the transition and fine tune it. This is done in the **Viewer** (Figure 5.32).

Double-click on the transition itself in the **Timeline** window to bring up the window, which opens in place of the **Viewer**. The **Viewer** displays the transition as a separate track between the two video tracks on which the clips sit.

Here you can control the transition. At the top is a small group of buttons (Figure 5.33) that let you position where the transition will occur. The transition will be placed in the default centered position between the two clips, shown by the middle button in Figure 5.33. Using the left button moves the transition so that it begins at the edit point. The right button in moves the transition so that it ends at the edit point.

5.32 Transition in the Viewer

5.33 Transition Alignment Buttons

The primary purpose of the **Viewer** for transitions is to access the controls some transitions offer you. Here you can also fine tune the effect, to shorten or lengthen it as needed. As in the **Timeline**, you can do this by dragging either end of the transition. The **Canvas** displays the end and start frames for the two shots.

By grabbing the center of the transition, you evoke the **Roll** tool, which allows you to drag the transition forward and backward along the clips, provided there is available media.

You can also ripple edit either the end of either outgoing or incoming clip by pulling it. You don't have to call up the **Ripple** tool. Moving the cursor into position will change it to the appropriate tool. Different shades of blue indicate the limits of the media. As with all ripple edits, you are changing the duration of the tracks involved and may be pulling the alignment of clips on different tracks out of kilter.

Notice in the **Viewer** the two sliders, one for **Start** and the other for **End**, each with adjacent percentage boxes. The transition starts at 0% completed and ends at 100% completion. You can adjust these sliders so that the **Cross Dissolve**, for instance, will pop in at more than zero to start or suddenly finish before the transition reaches completion. In **Cross Dissolve** this produces a rather ugly effect. The small arrow button to the right of the **End** slider will swap the effect for you. Below that is a small circle with a red cross in it, the **Parameters Reset** button. Neither of

Tip

Alignment Shortcuts: You can switch between the three transition alignment types with keyboard shortcuts. **Option-1** sets to begin at the edit point, **Option-2** to center on the edit point, and **Option-3** to end on the edit point. These are the numbers on the keyboard, not the keypad numerics. Using the **Option** key with the keypad controls the **Autoselect** function for the audio tracks.

Transitions between Sequences

Because FCP allows you to place sequences within sequences, it sometimes becomes necessary to create transitions between them. This presents some problems. FCP treats each sequence as a complete piece of media. So as we've seen, if you have used the media to its limits, you can't create a transition.

If you want to create a transition between sequences, you have to either ripple the sequences in the **Timeline** or open the edit point into the **Trim Edit** window and ripple the outgoing sequence and the incoming sequence to allow room for the transition.

5.34 Sequences Overlapping for Transition

Another way (for many transitions, except those that don't require both clips to move) is to place the second sequence on **V2**, overlapping the first sequence, and place a start on edit transition at the head of the sequence on **V2** as in Figure 5.34. This will bring it in over the outgoing sequence without having to fuss with trimming.

these has value in **Cross Dissolve** but will be important later for more complex transitions, as we shall see in a moment. Also note that the **Reset** button does not reset the sliders nor the arrow, only the other parameters.

✎ *Note*
Navigating the Transition Viewer:
The **Grab Handle** in the upper right corner lets you pull a transition from the **Viewer** onto an edit point in the Timeline. This is useful if you've opened the editor directly from the *Video Transitions* bin. This is the only way you can grab it to drag the transition to the **Timeline**.

Using Transitions

Now that we know how to add and trim transitions, let's look at some of the transitions themselves. To change the transition from **Cross Dissolve**:

- Drag the new transition from *Video Transitions* bin in the **Effects** window and drop it on the existing transition in the **Timeline,** *or*
- Select the transition in the **Timeline** and then select a new choice from the **Effects>Video Transitions** menu.

I'm not going to go through each of the transitions, though I would like to highlight a few because they are representative and show you how the controls work in some of the other changeable transitions. To see what the transitions themselves look like, take a look at the *Transitions* bin in the **Browser.** This contains short clips that show how each of the transitions behave, with a couple of exceptions, all at their default settings. Many of the transitions have lots of variables, such as colored borders and the direction in which a motion transition occurs. Here are grouped samplings of

5.35 Cube Spin (above)

5.36 Cube Spin Controls (right)

the FCP's 60 available transitions. Most of the transitions under one heading, with the exception of the **QuickTime** group, will have similar controls and features.

Cube Spin

Cube Spin is a typical 3D simulation transition. It will roll your clips around as though they were stuck to either the outside or the inside of a cube (Figure 5.35).

The controls for the transition are fairly simple: a couple of pop-ups, sliders, and a color picker (Figure 5.36).

Spin Direction lets you change between right, left, up, or down.

View can be either the default **Outside,** where you're looking at a cube turning in front of you, or **Inside,** with you inside the cube watching it turn around you.

The **Border** slider controls the width of the border, and **Color** lets you pick a color for the border either from the swatch, an eye-dropper, or opening the disclosure triangle for **Hue, Saturation,** and **Brightness (HSB)** controls.

The little arrow on the right edge of the controls will switch the direction of the motion from the currently set to the opposite. If it's set to right, it'll make it go left, for example, so it's not much use.

5.37 Dip to Color Controls

Dip to Color Dissolve

The default setting of the **Dip to Color Dissolve** using black as the color is the same as FCP's **Fade In Fade Out Dissolve**, but a couple of controls (Figure 5.37) make this unique.

One is **Threshold**, which determines when the fade will occur in the transition. The earlier the **Threshold**, the quicker the fade out will be, and the slower the fade in. The higher the **Threshold**, the slower the dip to color, but the faster the transition comes out of the color. Basically this allows you to create an asymmetrical fade out and fade in, which is often very useful.

Soft controls how long the color is held on the screen. Set at the default 100, the color (or the center of the fade) is no more than a couple of frames on either side of the edit point. By moving the slider into lower numbers, you can control how long the color remains on the screen. With the slider at zero, the color will pop on the screen and last the full length of the transition before popping off again. Combined with **Threshold**, you have full control to create an asymmetrical fade out and to specify how long the fade lasts on the screen before it comes back up again.

Another popular—perhaps overly popular—use of this effect is to specify a very pale color instead of black and then to make the transition very short to produce a flash effect. It's commonly used for bridging two sections of an interview that would otherwise be a jump cut. There are other ways to do this, such as using a bright color for a **Luma Map** transition, which works well too.

Star Iris

Star Iris does exactly what its name says. It uses a star shape to wipe the image on or off the screen (Figure 5.38). The difference between an iris transition and a wipe transition is that an iris can have a variable center point. You can iris out from a person's head, for instance, while a wipe is always fixed around the center of the image.

Food2				
Start:	0 %	End:	100 %	
Points		5	
Sharp		100	
Center	+	0 ,	0
Border		6	
Color			
Feather Edges			

5.38   Star Iris and Controls

The **Star Iris** controls include a **Points** slider, which varies the numbers of points in the star. The default is 5.

Sharp controls how pointy the star is. When set at the normal 100, the star is very angular. Bringing the value down toward zero, you can create an almost circular shape.

You can add a **Border** here, like in **Cube Spin**, or you can use **Feather Edges** of the iris. In this case, the **Border** slider controls the softness of the feathering.

Page Peel

Page Peel is often overused, but sometimes it really is the right effect, particularly for wedding videos (Figure 5.39). This transition has a number of controls that allow you to modify its look (Figure 5.40).

1. The **Direction** dial sets the angle at which the page turns back. The default is −30 and pulls the lower right corner toward the upper center of the image.

2. The **Radius** slider sets the arc of the page peel. A small number will make it peel very tightly, while a high number will make the turn of the page quite loose.

3. The **Highlight** slider puts a gleam of light on the back of the turning page. The farther to the left you move the slider, the more muted the shine becomes.

4. The **Peel** checkbox is defaulted on. With it unchecked, the page not only peels back, it also curls under as it goes. The smaller the **Radius** value, the tighter the curl becomes.

5.39 Page Peel

5.40 Page Peel Controls

Static Well: Unfortunately, the Well won't track an image or change if a video clip is used. The Well uses the In point of the video clip as its map. In the case of **Page Peel**, there is no movement on the backside of the page. Sorry.

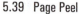

5.41 Generators Button

5. The tiny arrow checkbox in the upper right corner toggles between peeling the page off, the default, and peeling the page on, an unusual variation.

One of **Page Peel**'s interesting features is the **Well**, which lets you use another image as part of an effect. The **Well**, the indented filmstrip icon that controls the **Back** function, lets you map another image onto the back of the page peel. The default is to place the same image, flopped, on the back of the page, but you can use any image in your project.

To put a color on the back, as in Figure 5.39, use the **Generators** in the **Viewer** to create a color matte.

1. Open any clip into the **Viewer**. The **A** with the **filmstrip** icon in the lower left corner evokes the **Generators** (Figure 5.41).

2. Select **Matte>Color**.

3. On the **Control** tab (Figure 5.42), click on the color swatch, the small gray box to choice a color for your backing.

4. Drag the matte from the **Video** tab of the **Viewer** into the **Browser**.

5. Reopen the **Page Peel** transition from the **Timeline**, and pull the **Color Matte** from the **Browser** to drop it into the **Well**, making it part of the transition.

Push Slide

The **Push Slide** is often used when making still slide shows where one images pushes the other out of the frame and replaces it. The controls (Figure 5.43) are pretty straight forward, an **Angle** dial and controls for adding a **Border**.

5.42 Color Matte Controls Tab

Angle defaults to straight down, but you can set to any angle you want. At –90 the incoming image will slide in from the right and push the outgoing image off the left side of the screen.

The **Border** can be quite useful. It not only helps in separating the images more clearly, but it also covers the black band that appears on the edge of some digitized images. This is normally in the blanking area under the television mask and not seen by the viewer. However, if the image is moved, as it is here and in other digital video effects, the black edge becomes visible. The **Border** will help to disguise that, or at least make it a feature.

Gradient Wipe

The **Gradient Wipe** is a deceptively simple-looking filter with very few controls. Its real power lies in the **Gradient Well**

Note
Color Picker: The Color Picker offers a number of different color samplers. The RGB picker uses the Photoshop standard of 0–255 colors and is the best to work with for video. To keep colors NTSC safe, don't let the slider for any color exceed 235. This may produce color on the computer screen that looks muddy, but in video they'll be vivid without being oversaturated.

5.43 Push Slide Controls

5.44 Gradient Wipe Controls (above)

5.45   Gradient Wipe (right)

(Figure 5.44). In its default condition, it's nothing more than a simple wipe from left to right.

In the **Browser** is an image called *Gradient.pct*. If you open it up and take a look at it in the **Viewer,** you'll see that it's a complex, grayscale checkerboard pattern. This is the basis of patterning in a gradient wipe. The image will be wiped on or off, based on the grayscale values of pattern image. The darkest parts of the pattern image will be where the incoming image will appear first, and the lightest parts will be where the image will appear last. In the gradient pattern we have, some of the outside boxes will appear first, as in Figure 5.45. The lower left to upper right diagonal of the image will still be from the outgoing shot. There is no end to the variety of patterns you can get to manipulate this control. If you don't like a pattern, replace it with another. To really see the power of transition effects, you should look at what Michael Feerer has created with his Video Spices. Check them out at www.pixelan.com. They add an important tool to Final Cut's transitions. His patterns can be used not only inside his own transitions, but inside **Gradient Wipe** as well.

Everybody has their favorites. **Gradient Wipe** is probably mine, after a simple cross dissolve. Klaus Eiperle has created an even more powerful version of **Gradient Wipe,** called **Softwipe,** which is well worth having. Find out about it at http://cgm-online.com. I like it because it is infinitely variable, and you can always find some way to make it look just a little different and just right for the effect. A trick I've used in the past is to use a grayscale frame of either the outgoing shot or the incoming shot as the image for the **Well.** It makes the transition like a slightly sharp-edged dissolve because the elements of the shot itself are affecting how the transition happens.

Conclusion

That's it for transitions. Everybody has their favorites, and there are probably many that you'll never use. Many should probably never be used. Next we'll look at the text and titling tools within Final Cut Pro itself.

Lesson 6

Adding Titles

Every program is enhanced with graphics, whether they are a simple opening title and closing credits or elaborate motion graphics sequences illuminating some obscure point that can best be expressed in animation. This could be a map with a path snaking across it or a full-scale 3D animation explaining the details of how an airplane is built. Obviously, the latter is beyond the scope of both this book and of Final Cut Pro alone. But many simpler graphics can be easily created within FCP. Each version of Final Cut has brought new titling options, and FCP5 is no different, providing an enhanced version of Boris Calligraphy. Of course, there is also LiveType 2 as a separate stand-alone application. LiveType warrants a book all of its own, which can't be included in this work. It is certainly a powerful special effects and motion graphics tool, a worthwhile investment of the time to learn its capabilities.

In this lesson, we will look at typical titling problems and how to deal with them. As always, we begin by loading the project.

Loading the Lesson

This should be familiar to you by now. Let's begin by loading the material you need onto your media drive.

1. First, drag over the *Lesson 6 Media* folder from the DVD onto the media drive of your computer. We'll be using some of this material as background media of our titles.

2. Make sure you have the *Projects* folder on your hard drive.

3. Make sure the DVD is ejected from your computer, and double-click the *Lesson 6* project file to launch the application.

4. Reconnect the media files as you have done in previous lessons.

Setting up the Project

Inside the project in the **Browser** you'll find a number of sequences that we shall explore in the course of this lesson. One of the sequences, *Sequence 1*, is empty, ready for you to use. There is also a master clip called *Kabuki* in the *Clips* bin.

1. Begin by opening *Sequence 1*.

2. Drag a clip—let's say, *Kabuki3*—from the *Clips* bin and drop it on **Overwrite** in the **CEO** (**Canvas Edit Overlay**).

Text Generator

FCP still has its legacy titling tools included in the Generators. They are really obsolete and should only be used for the simplest titling functions. We'll look at just the basic titling tool before working with Calligraphy.

1. To get to the **Generators**, click the small **A** in the lower right corner of the **Viewer**.

2. Go into the popup menu, drop down to **Text**, slide across and pick **Text** again, as in Figure 6.1.

6.1   Text Generator

You'll notice that in the **Generators** there is a separate submenu for **Boris**. We'll look at the **Boris** tools a bit later in the lesson, but let's start by looking at the way FCP's basic **Text** tool works.

Text

This is for very basic text graphics indeed, simple on-screen words. By selecting **Text** from the **Generator** popup, a generic text generator loads into the **Viewer** (Figure 6.2).

Notice that this generator has:

- A default duration of 10 seconds.
- A default length of two minutes.

You can assign any duration for a text file, up to almost 12 hours, if you wanted. However, once the text file has been placed in a sequence, its duration can no longer be extended beyond the media length when it was originally created in the **Viewer**. So if you accept the default length and place the text file in a sequence, you can no longer make the duration go beyond two minutes. I don't know why it's limited this way. If you need to change to a long text file, you can drag it into the **Browser** and dial in a very long duration and then place it back in the sequence. You can always make it shorter, but not longer. It's a good way to create a video bug, that little graphic that's always in the bottom right of your TV screen—or your warning that a tape is only a check copy and not for distribution.

The first point to realize about this text generator is that at the moment it only exists in the **Viewer**. Usually the next step I take is to put it somewhere useful, either into the **Browser** or the **Timeline**. If you park the playhead anywhere over the shot in the **Timeline** and then drag the generic text generator from the **Viewer** to the **CEO** to **Superimpose**, the text will appear above the shot, with the same duration as the shot (Figure 6.3). It will create a new track above the set destination track.

You can also drag and drop the generator into the **Timeline** onto an empty track or the space above the tracks. If your system has real-time capabilities, the title will playback without rendering.

Whether you drag the generic text generator to the **Timeline** or the **Browser**, remember that you are creating a copy of that generator. Be careful not to do anything to the generator in the **Viewer**. I've seen countless people do this. They lay the generator in the **Timeline**, work in the **Viewer**, and then wonder why the text in the sequence still says "Sample Text."

After you have moved the text into the **Timeline**, double-click on the **Text Generator** in the **Timeline** window to open it back into the **Viewer**. The **Viewer** screen will look exactly the same, of course, except now you'll be working on the generator in the **Timeline**, which is what you want. The label area at the top of the **Viewer** will tell you where the text came from. Figure 6.4 shows

6.2   Generic Sample Text in Viewer

⭐Tip

Launching Text Generator: The default, basic text generator can be opened into the **Viewer** with the keyboard shortcut **Control-X**. It's handy if you need to create a lot of basic titles quickly.

6.3   Supered Text in the Timeline

6.4   Viewer: Text

Viewer: Text from Sequence 1

6.6   Plain Scrubber Bar on Clip Opened from Browser

6.7   Dotted Scrubber Bar on Clip Opened from Timeline

6.8   Text Control Window

the label for text generated in the **Viewer**. Figure 6.5 shows the label for text that's been opened from a sequence.

The other telltale sign that indicates whether a title or a clip has been opened from the **Browser** (or generated in the **Viewer**) rather than one that has been opened from a sequence is in the scrubber bar at the bottom of the **Viewer**. In Figure 6.6 the text has been generated in the **Viewer**. The scrubber bar is plain. In Figure 6.7 the text has been opened from the **Timeline**. The scrubber bar shows a double row of dots, like film sprocket holes.

⇒ Tip

Viewing Nothing: If you place text in the **Timeline** over nothing, the blackness you see in the **Canvas** behind the clip is the emptiness of space. You can make it any color, or even a checkerboard, under the **View** menu, but this is only for viewing purposes. If you want an actual color layer, use the **Generators** to make a color matte. Make it any color you want and place it on the layer below all other material.

Now we're ready to start making that graphic.

1.   After you've opened the generator from the **Timeline** into the **Viewer**, click on the **Controls** tab at the top. You might also want to stretch down the **Viewer** to see all the controls (Figure 6.8).

These are the default settings. At the top is the text input window in which you type whatever you want to appear on the screen.

2.   Click on **SAMPLE TEXT** and type in *Kabuki*, then do a return, and type *Performance*.

3.   Click out of the window, or tab to the **Size** box. The default is 36 point, which is small even for these clips.

4.   Type in a size of **72** and press **Enter**, which loads the size setting.

Above the **Size** slider is the **Font** popup, in which you can pick whatever TrueType fonts you have loaded in your system. If some fonts on your computer are not showing up, then they are probably PostScript fonts. Unfortunately FCP's **Text** tool does not work with PostScript, only TrueType. Boris Calligraphy—that is, **Title 3D**, **Title Crawl**, and **Text Scrambler**—will work with both TrueType and PostScript.

The **Style** popup lets you set text styles such as bold and italic.

Below **Style** is the **Alignment** popup. Alignment is usually called *justification*.

A word of caution: though the default setting is **Center**, the words in the text window are left justified. Ignore that. The popup rules; the text window just doesn't display intelligently.

The left and right alignment is not to the screen but to the origin point, the way it works in Illustrator and Photoshop. So if you want left alignment on the left side of the screen, you have to move the origin point about –300 or a little less to keep it in the **Safe Title Area**, depending on your format.

This only applies in the **Text** tool. Other tools such as **Scrolling Text** align to the screen as you might expect, with left as the left edge of the **STA**, and right as the right edge of **STA**.

Note
No Word Wrapping: FCP's titler is limited in many ways, and word wrapping is one of them. You have to put in the line breaks where appropriate, or your text is liable to run off the screen.

Fonts and Size

Not all fonts are equally good for video. You can't just pick something you fancy and hope it will work for you. One of the main problems with video is its interlacing. Because video is made up of thin lines of information—the odd lines making up one field and the even lines the other field—each line is essentially switching on and off 30 times a second. If you happen to place a thin horizontal line on your video that falls on one of those lines (but not the adjacent

6.9   Serif Fonts

line), that thin, horizontal line will be switching on and off at a very rapid rate, appearing to flicker. The problem with text is that a lot of fonts have thin horizontal lines called serifs, the little footer that some letters sit on (Figure 6.9).

Unless you're going to make text of a fairly large size, it's generally best to avoid serif fonts. You're better off using a sans-serif font for most video work. You should probably avoid small fonts as well. Video resolution is not very high, the print equivalent of 72dpi. You can read this book in 10-point type comfortably, but a 10-point line of text on television would be an illegible smear. I generally never use font sizes below 24, and prefer to use something larger if possible.

Safe Title Area and Safe Action Area

6.10   **Safe Action and Safe Title Areas**

Televisions have a mask on the edge that cuts off some of the displayed picture area. What you see in the **Viewer** and the **Canvas** is not what you get—far from WYSIWYG—and can vary substantially from television to television. That is why the **Canvas** and **Viewer** are thoughtfully marked with a *Safe Action Area* and a still smaller area that is defined as the *Safe Title Area* (Figure 6.10)

These are turned on with the **Image** popup at the top of the **Viewer** and **Canvas**. Make sure that both **Show Overlay** and **Show Title Safe** are checked to see the **Safe Action and Safe Title Areas**. What's within the **SAA** will appear on every television set. Because television tubes used to be curved, and many still are, a smaller area was defined as the **Safe Title Area** in which text would appear without distortion if viewed at an angle. Titles should remain, if possible, within the **Safe Title Area**. This is not important for graphics destined only for web or computer display, but for anything that might be shown on a television within the course of its life, it would be best to maintain these boundaries. That said, more and more often you're seeing titles that are well outside the **STA** and lying partially outside the **SAA**.

✎ Note

Font Limitations: The Font popup and all the settings in the text block will change all the letters for *everything* in the text block. You cannot control individual letters, words, or lines of text. This applies to all of Final Cut Pro's text generators except for the Boris tools. The one unintentional benefit of FCP's limitations is that it may prevent users from going wild with fonts, sizes, and colors.

Font Color is self-explanatory. It includes a color picker and a color swatch as well as a twirly triangle that opens up the **HSB** sliders and **Value** boxes.

The small icon between the eyedropper and the color swatch changes the direction in which the color moves if it's animated.

Hundreds and hundreds of parameters can be animated in Final Cut. Wherever you see a small diamond button like those on the left edge of the text control window, the parameter can have a keyframe defined and therefore be animated, just as we keyframed audio by placing a little diamond-shaped dot on our audio tracks in the **Timeline**. Animation is a complex subject and beyond the scope of this book.

Set the Origin of the text with a **Crosshair** button or with *x,y* values. You can use the crosshairs by clicking on the button and then clicking wherever in the **Canvas** you want the center point for the origin of the text to be. With the crosshairs active, you can mouse down the **Canvas** and drag the text to whatever position you want. The value windows are more precise, of course. The first window is the horizontal, or *x* value; the second window is the vertical, or *y* value. The default is the center of the screen. This is centered on the baseline of the first line of text, in this case under the lower right edge of the *b* in *Kabuki*.

You can also position the text by moving it about the screen in the **Canvas**. If you change the **Image** popup at the top of the **Canvas** to **Image+Wireframe** (or use the **W** key to toggle through the wireframe functions), you can now grab the text block, or any other image for that matter, and move it about the screen and position it wherever you like. Make sure the text block in the **Timeline** is selected, and then a large cross will appear through the image with a blue border (Figure 6.11). This is the image with its wireframe outline. You can now move the text block about the screen. If you hold down the **Shift** key, you can constrain it to moving exactly vertically or horizontally.

Tracking is the spacing distance between letters. The higher the tracking value, the farther apart the letters will get. Small increases in tracking will have a large impact on letter separation, and animated subtlety makes a pleasing enhancement to a title. As you move tracking down below zero, the letters will scrunch together. If you go low enough into negative values, the letters will actually squeeze into nothing and disappear.

Leading (pronounced *ledding*, as in little bits of lead spacing used in hot metal typesetting) is the spacing between lines. The default is zero. A setting of –100 moves the text up so that it's all on one line. A value of 100 moves the text down a whole line.

Aspect adjusts the text's vertical shape. Low numbers stretch text, and higher numbers squeeze the text (Figure 6.12). Be careful

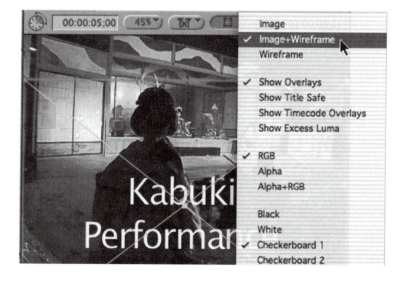

6.11   Image + Wireframe in the Canvas

6.12 Left: Aspect with a Value of 0.4
      Right: Aspect with a Value of 3

with the **Aspect** control. Very little movement from the default of 1 will cause ugly antialiasing (stair-stepped edges) to appear around the text.

Auto Kerning adjusts the letter spacing based on the letters' shape rather than absolute values and should be left on. Check the **Use Subpixel** box for better quality.

✎ Tip

Flickering Text: Interlace flickering caused by serifs and other fine lines can be alleviated somewhat by smearing the image across the interlace lines. It is easiest to do this with text created in Photoshop, where you can applying a one-pixel vertical motion blur. You don't have to soften the whole image like this. If there are particular portions that appear to flicker, you can select them with a marquee or lasso, slightly feathered, and then apply the vertical motion blur to just that portion of the image.

Or in FCP you can duplicate the **Text Generator** in the sequence and stack one on top of the other. Apply a slight **Blur** or **Antialias** filter to the bottom copy. Only the slightly blurred edge that sticks out from underneath the unblurred copy will be visible, smearing the edge. You can also darken the lower copy to give the text a slightly harder edge.

Drop Shadow

Drop shadows are important to give the text some depth and separation from the background image. It would be quite useful for our text where the white of the letters is over the bright highlights on the image below (Figure 6.13). You can add a drop shadow to your text in the **Motion** tab of the **Viewer**. The **Drop Shadow** control panel, when twirled open, shows all the expected features: **Offset, Angle** of offset, **Shadow Color, Softness,** and **Opacity** (Figure 6.14).

You have to activate the **Drop Shadow** with the checkbox in the upper left corner.

Offset controls how far from the image the shadow appears. What might be puzzling about the **Offset** slider is that it goes into negative numbers. You'd think this would just change the direction of the shadow. Doesn't the angle do that already? Yes, it

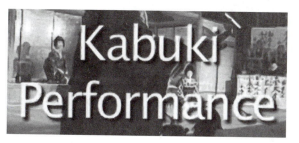

6.13 Drop Shadowed Text

▼ ☑ Drop Shadow			⊗	☑ ▾
Offset	←——[]——→	10	◁	◇ ▷
Angle	–(◉)–	135	◁	◇ ▷
Color	▶ ⊘ ↺ ▮		◁	◇ ▷
Softness	←[]———→	10	◁	◇ ▷
Opacity	←——[]——→	50	◁	◇ ▷

6.14 Drop Shadow Controls

does. But when you animate them they behave differently. When you animate **Offset**, the shadow slides underneath the image from one side to the other, while if you animate **Angle**, the shadow seems to circle the image.

The default **Offset** works well for stills, video clips, or other large images, but not so well for text. When using **Drop Shadow** with the basic **Text** tool, you'll want to bring the value down, probably into the 2–5 range.

The **Angle** dial will point your shadow in whatever direction you want. The default direction, falling off to the lower right, is the most commonly used drop shadow angle.

Softness lets you control the amount of blurring on the edges of the shadow. Though the slider goes up to 100, the shadow isn't as soft as it might be.

The **Opacity** slider defaults to 50%, which is probably too low for use with text. You might want to push up **Drop Shadow's Opacity** to 100 and use the **Softness** slider to take the edge off it.

Opacity

Opacity is the transparency of an image or text. There are two ways to control it:

- With the slider in the **Motion** tab of the **Viewer** (Figure 6.15)
- Directly in the **Timeline**

Adjusting opacity in the **Timeline** is exactly like adjusting audio levels.

▼ Opacity			⊗	☑ ▾
Opacity	←———[]——→	100	◁	◇ ▷

6.15 Opacity Slider

6.16 Opacity Level on Clip

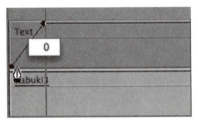

6.17 Fading In Opacity

1. Make sure **Clip Overlays** is turned on with the button in the lower left corner of the **Timeline,** or use the keyboard shortcut **Option-W.**

2. With the black **Opacity** level line visible in the **Timeline** (Figure 6.16), pull down on the line with the resizing cursor to make the image semitransparent.

Rather than pulling down the overall opacity of the image, let's undo that and animate the opacity to add a fade in and a fade out to our text.

3. Make sure that nothing is selected in the **Timeline** (**Command-Shift-A** to **Deselect All**) and that the playhead is at the very beginning.

4. Type in *+1.* and press **Enter** to move the playhead forward one second.

5. Take the **Pen** tool and click on the **Opacity** line at the playhead to add a keyframe.

6. Grab the line at the very beginning of the clip with the **Pen** and pull it all the way down, as in Figure 6.17.

7. To add the fade out at the end, go to the end of the clip. Use **Shift-O** to take you to the Out point, which is on the last frame of video.

8. Type in *–1.* and press **Enter** to move the playhead back one second.

9. With the **Pen** tool add a keyframe at the playhead.

10. Finally, grab the end of the **Opacity** line with the **Pen** tool and pull it down to complete your fade out, which should look like Figure 6.18.

Another way to add a fade in and fade out on text is to select the start or end of the clip and use **Command-T** to add the default cross dissolve. This will create either a start on edit or an end on edit to fade in or fade out the text as in Figure 6.19.

Reducing the opacity of a text block down to 90% will help to soften it and blend it better into the underlying image.

6.18 Opacity Fade In and Fade Out

6.19 Transition Fade In and Fade Out

Subtitles

Subtitling is a laborious, time-consuming business. The first problem is always the translation, especially making it match brisk dialog or narration. The best advice I can offer is to keep it simple and easy to read. The important thing is not to translate the text literally but to convey the sense. The text needs to follow the spoken words closely, which is why subtitles often need to be shortened and condensed.

Technically, the easiest way to generate subtitles in FCP is to make a couple of templates in your *Favorites* bin or in the **Browser** and keep bringing those into the sequence. Because the text is generally smaller than you would normally work with in video, you should always use a sans serif font. I prefer good old Helvetica. The size should be about 28. I prefer to use yellow with a saturation of about 85% for the text color, with a slight black drop shadow. Yellow shows against a white or pale shirt better than white with a drop shadow, I think. The text should sit on the edge of the Safe Title Area. Set the text at the bottom of the screen with the origin point of a 720 image with a *y* value of about 160. Try to keep to one line of text. Only go to a second line if you have to, but never go to three lines; it encroaches too much into the picture area. For two lines of text, set the *y* axis a little higher. A value of about 135 should do it.

Another trick is to use a black color matte behind the text. Keep it to just the size of the text and reduce the **Opacity** down to 10% or 20%, creating a translucent shadow area behind the text, making it more legible and reducing flickering in the text.

The **Superimpose** function can be useful in subtitling because it creates text clips that are exactly the length of a particular video clip.

Basic Animation

Though complex animation is beyond basic editing in Final Cut, understanding simple animation is important, and it's easy to do. Animation is based on the concept of keyframes. When you change the properties of an image—in text, for instance—you define how it looks. When you apply a keyframe, you define how it looks at a particular moment in time, at a specific frame of your video. If you then go to another point in time, some other frame of video—say, five seconds further into your video—and change

6.20   Text Tracking at –4   6.21   Tracking Keyframe Button   6.22   Text Tracking at 8

the values for the image, you will automatically create another keyframe that defines how it looks at that point in time. The computer will then figure out—it will *tween*—what each of the intervening frames of video has to look like over that five seconds. We've already done some animations, when we animated audio levels and when you animated the opacity of the text to fade it in and out. Let's do a simple motion animation.

1. With *Sequence 1* open, which should have *Kabuki3* and a *Text* clip on **V2**, make sure the playhead is at the beginning of the **Timeline**.

Let's animate the **Leading**.

2. If you have transitions applied to the beginning or end of the *Text* clip, or an opacity fade in or fade out, remove them.

3. Open the *Text* clip in **Viewer** and go to the **Controls** tab. Either grab the **Leading** slider and pull it down to **–40** or dial in **–40** in the value box. The lines of text should look scrunched together as in Figure 6.20.

4. Now click on the empty diamond keyframe button next to the **Leading** value (Figure 6.21). The little button will go green to indicate that you've added a keyframe.

5. Scroll down to the timeline to the last frame of the clip and change the **Leading** value to **13**. The **Canvas** will show the text spread out as in Figure 6.22.

6. Scrub the timeline to see the animation in the **Canvas**.

7. If you have a system with real-time capabilities, you're done. If not, you'll have to render out the animation to see it, or use **QuickView** from the **Tools** menu.

If you like, add the transitions back onto the *Text* clip to make a smooth effect. That's it. You've created your first Final Cut Pro motion graphics animation. The finished sequence is in the **Browser** called *Leading Animation*.

Boris Calligraphy

Apple has a number of other titling tools under the **Generators Text** menu, but they are really still there, I think, only to allow access to old projects you might have to open. For any new project, unless you need to use the simple text tool you should use Boris Calligraphy 2, which includes **Title 3D**, **Title Crawl**, **Text Scrambler**, and **Vector Shape**. These really supersede FCP's text tools in many ways, giving the user great control and flexibility with titling. It is a feature-packed tool, an application within itself, now with four separate tools with complex animation capabilities that are beyond the scope of this book. I'm going to show you some of its principal tools, but for a thorough look at its capabilities, consult the excellent PDF in the *Boris Calligraphy Docs* folder inside the *Extras* folder on the Final Cut installation DVD. The Boris Calligraphy tools are installed by default when you install FCP.

Title 3D

Let's look at **Title 3D** first. You can call up it up from the **Generators**, from inside the **Boris** submenu (Figure 6.23). This will load **Title 3D** into the **Viewer**. Go to the **Controls** tab and click on the button **Title 3D Click for Options** (Figure 6.24). This will bring up the **Boris** text window (Figure 6.25), which is the first of five

🐾 ***Note***

Navigating with Keyframes: Be careful when using the **Down** arrow key to go to the end of a clip. When FCP takes you to the next edit, it takes you to first frame of the next clip. So to get to the last frame of the clip, you need to use the **Down** arrow and then the **Left** arrow to take you back one frame. Where you want to go is not the next edit, but rather to the Out point, the last frame of the clip.

Visibility

It's sometimes helpful to see a single track of video in a multiple-track stack of clips. This can be done two ways, either with the **Visibility** button at the end of the track or with *soloing*. The **Visibility** button will switch off the visibility for the entire track. **Option**-clicking on the **Visibility** button will make all others tracks invisible. This can be handy, but it also means that if you have anything rendered out, everything that you've rendered will be lost. In **User Preferences** there is a checkbox for a warning if visibility changes will delete rendered files.

An option that avoids switching off a whole track is to use soloing. Select the clip you want to see, even if it's on **V1** underneath layers of other video, and choose **Solo Item(s)** from the **Sequence** menu, or use the keyboard shortcut **Control-S**. This will toggle off the visibility of all but the selected items.

Be warned that the **Preferences** warning does not apply to soloing. It only applies to switching off visibility of whole tracks. Switching off visibility of items using soloing *will* remove your render files and will do so without warning, but it will only be for the area that's affected by the soloing; it will not be for the whole track.

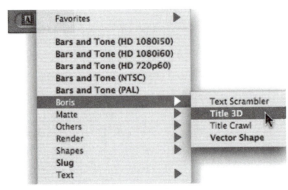

6.23 Generators > Boris > Title 3D

6.24   Title 3D Click for Options

tabbed windows that allow you access to **Title 3D**'s powerful and complex tools.

Unlike the FCP text box, this text window is truly WYSIWYG. Most importantly, each control can be applied to each letter or group of letters separately. So now, with little trouble, you can make a garish combination of colors and fonts, a regular ransom note.

Before you do anything in this window, you may want to click on the second tab and change the default **No Wrap** to **Wrap**

6.25   Title 3D Text Window

6.26 Text Wrap

(Figure 6.26). I don't know why it defaults to **No Wrap**. You can leave the wrap default at 512, which will fit inside a standard 720 video image's Safe Title Area.

The **Top-down Text** and **Right-to-left reading** checkboxes at the bottom of the window are great for vertical, Hebrew, or Arabic text.

After you've set text wrapping, go back to the text window to enter your text. The main window allows you to enter and select text, which you can then adjust with the controls at the bottom part of the window.

The text window works much like most text applications, such as Word. The ruler at the top of the text window allows you to set tabs for precise positioning of text elements (Figure 6.27). Use the **Tab** key to navigate from one tab indent to the next. After you've set a tab, you can double-click on it to toggle from left justified to right justified to center justified. This tool is especially useful when making long scrolls like movie credits that often use columns and indents for different sections.

The white area in the ruler is the active text part of the screen, within the Safe Title Area.

Let's look at some of the phenomenal text control in Calligraphy. In the bottom portion of the screen, the first popup obviously sets the font. The two buttons to the right will move you up and down through your font list. Below the **Font** popup is a **Point Size Value** box. The two buttons to the right of that will incrementally raise

6.27 Title 3D Text Window Ruler

and lower your point size. To the right of the font controls are six buttons that let you set:

- Normal
- Bold
- Italic
- Underline
- Superscript
- Subscript

Below that, three **Paragraph** buttons let you set justification:

- Left
- Center
- Right

The **Fixed Width** checkbox should be used only if you're doing text animation using randomization.

The **Tracking** slider adjusts the letter spacing globally while **Kerning** adjusts the spacing between individual pairs or groups of letters without affecting the overall spacing. It allows you to control individual letter spacing. It's important for many fonts, especially when you are writing words like *AVE*, where you need to slide the *A* and *V* closer together than fonts normally place them.

Leading controls the line gap between either all the lines in the window or between individual pairs of lines, a new feature in version 2.0 of Calligraphy.

The **Style** controls (Figure 6.28) allow you a truly astonishing degree of control over text and begin to show why this text tool is called **Title 3D**. Individual letters or groups of letters can be skewed left and right on the baseline with **Style Skew X**. They can be swung like doors with **Style Skew Y**. The value boxes in these controls let you set the degrees of skew (the lower box) and numbers of rotations (the upper box), which can be used in conjunction with the animation controls for keyframing.

Style Hue is an excellent feature that allows you to globally change the color values of text after you've created it. This means that if you've set the color values one way, you can easily change them globally with the **Style Hue** controls. Always start working with the **Style Hue** dial set to zero, and then when you need to change the values, try different color effects using the controls here.

✎ Tip

Scrubbable Values: Notice the underlined values in the **Title 3D** window. Wherever you see these underlined items, it means you can mouse down on the value and scrub it up or down, as needed. It works like a slider without taking up the space. Usually there is a slider as well for those who prefer that method of working. Or you can click in the value box and type in a number. The scrubbable numbers—in **Leading**, for instance—often go to values much higher than sliders do.

6.28   Style Controls (left)

6.29   Style Hue Adjusted (below)

In Figure 6.29 the text on the left held the original settings, and on the right the same text has been changed 180 degrees.

Style Baseline will allow you to raise and lower letters separately, while **Style Scale X** and **Style Scale Y** will let you scale individual characters on the *x* and/or *y* axis independently from each other.

The **Draft Typing** popup at the bottom lets you change to **All Styles** and **Basic Styles**. **Draft Typing** lets you set up your text without styles, which can slow down the image processing on your computer screen. So if you've set a style-heavy text and need to type more text, switch back to **Draft Typing** before you do it. **Basic Styles** limits in the text window and helps performance as well, while **All Styles** shows you the text in all its glory.

The **Percentage** popup lets you change the display size of the text window, a useful feature if you have a lot of text and want to move around in it quickly.

Boris FX Support will connect you to Boris's online web support system.

The **Reset Style** button will reset all the parameters for the words in the text window. It will not, however, reset fonts or font sizes, wrapping, tabs, justification, or margins.

The **Style Palette** is a great tool (Figure 6.30). The application comes with a bunch of style presets that will get to started, which you can easily modify to your needs. In addition, the applet allows you to create your own text style and to name and save it.

✍ *Tip*
Text Control Shortcuts: If any value box is active, you can make the values go up or down by holding down the **Option** key and tapping the **Up** and **Down** arrow keys to raise and lower the values. **Shift-Up** and **Down** will move in 10-unit increments. The **Tab** key will take you to the next value box, and **Shift-Tab** will take you to the previous value box.

This way you can efficiently replicate styles from file to file and even from project to project. Notice that there are separate tabs now for **Fonts, Color,** and **Gradient,** where you can save favorite fonts for easy access, favorite colors, and favorite gradients. **Color** and **Gradient** come with a number of presets catalogued in groups that you can select from a popup.

The **Import File** button allows you to bring into the **text** window a previously created plain text file or RTF (Rich Text Format) file. All the justification and styles applied there will be honored in **Title 3D.**

Cancel and **Apply** are self-explanatory.

This is only the first couple of tabs in **Title 3D.**

The third tabbed panel, **Text Color,** lets you set the text fill and opacity (Figure 6.31). The little checkbox in the upper left corner lets you turn off the fill, so that you have only the text outline.

The **Text Fill** popup lets you choose to fill the text with a color or with a gradient. If you choose **Color,** the **Style Color** swatch allows access to the system color picker that we saw earlier. If you choose **Gradient,** you will get access to an incredibly powerful gradient editor (Figure 6.32), which allows multiple color points as well as transparency. You can select different gradient styles from the **Type** popup. Notice the **Repeat Stops** slider that lets you

6.32   Gradient Editor

6.33   Text Edge (below)

create repeating gradients without having to set up multiple color stops. To add color points, click below the gradient bar display.

The fourth tabbed window lets you set the width and opacity for the **Text Edge**, and not just a single edge, but up to five separate edges for each letter (Figure 6.33). Each edge has to be turned on with the checkbox to activate it. Each of the five edges can be activated or switched off separately, which helps in trying out different looks. The edges can be **Plain, Bevel,** or **Glow,** and can be **Center, Inside,** or **Outside.** Notice the **Highlight** and **Shade** sliders to the right, which appear when the edge is set to **Bevel.** These allow you to create edges with subtle color shading and makes very nice images for display text. The variations possible with five edges are nearing infinite.

The fifth panel sets the five separate **Drop Shadows** (Figure 6.34). Like **Text Edges,** these have to be turned on with the checkbox to activate any drop shadows that you want to add. These can be either a standard **Drop;** a **Cast** shadow, which slopes away from the text; or a **Solid** shadow with sides. Drop and cast shadows don't have **Highlight** or **Shade** color, but they have a **Softness** control that appears when the shadow popup is changed. Each shadow also has controls for color, distance, opacity, and angle.

6.34 Drop Shadow

⚓ *Note*

Interlace Flickering: If you're doing text animation on interlaced video, check the 1:2:1 **Deflicker** box to reduce interlace flickering.

Unfortunately, while you're working in **Title 3D**, you cannot see the text composited on top of the image, but once you've created your text, drag it to the **Timeline** or **Superimpose** it over a clip that's already there.

If you need to change or adjust the text, double-click the **Title 3D** file in the **Timeline** to open it into the **Viewer**. Then click on the **Controls** tab to open all the controls for **Title 3D** (Figure 6.35). The new version of **Title 3D** has a huge number of controls. Figure 6.35 shows only part of them. We'll look at the **Type On** controls in a moment. Notice that all of the items that have the little diamond keyframe button on the right. Each of these parameters is keyframable, though there are some that you probably don't want to animate.

The **Geometry** section controls the text overall, changing:

- **Position**
- **Distance**
- **Scale**
- **Tumble**
- **Spin**
- **Rotate**

Use **Distance** and add a bit of **Scale** animation to make the text start from zero. This is the **Scale** value you want to adjust to get clean, large fonts, not the **Scale** in the **Motion** tab.

Tumble, Spin, and **Rotate** will turn the entire text block around on the *x, y,* and *z* axes, respectively.

The **Pivot** section controls the point around which the text tumbles, spins, and rotates. If the **Lock to Position** box is checked, the controls have no effect. With the box checked, the text will rotate around the selected pivot point, which can be set with numeric values or with the crosshairs button.

Neither **Tumble** nor **Spin** controls function with the **X/Y** controls, but their movement is affected when the **Z** slider is activated.

Transformation affects all the letters in the text block, but it affects them individually. In Figure 6.36 the image on the left has its **Geometry** tumbled –50° and spun 60° while the image on the right has its **Transformation** tumbled –50° and spun 60°. Notice that on the right each letter is tumbled, while on the left they are moving together. Also notice that on the right the **Tumble** factor appears quite limited when **Spin** is applied. You'll get more displacement of the text using **Letter Skew** rather than **Letter Tumble** if **Spin** is added.

6.36   Geometry vs. Transformation

Also notice that on the right the **Tumble** factor appears quite limited when **Spin** is applied. You'll get more displacement of the text using **Letter Skew** rather than **Letter Tumble** if **Spin** is added.

Type On

Type On is new to this version of Title 3D and allows you to create a typed-on effect with Title 3D's full text controls, making FCP's **Typewriter** finally obsolete. The **Type On** controls (Figure 6.37) are at the bottom of the **Title 3D** controls tab. To type text on the screen you need to animate the **Text Type On** value.

1. To start, open the sequence in the *Lesson 6* **Browser** called *Type On*.

It contains a piece of prepared text made in **Title 3D**.

2. Put the playhead at the beginning of the sequence (**Home**) and double-click on the text in the sequence to open it into the **Viewer**.

3. Go to the **Controls** tab and scroll down to the **Type On** area of the text.

6.35   Title 3D Controls

Video	Controls	Filters	Motion	
Name		Parameters		Nav
				⊗ ☑ ▾
		About...		
Text Entry and Style		**Title 3D** Click for options		
1:2:1 Deflicker		☐		
		_ Geometry _		
Position X/Y		⊕ 360 ,	240	◀◉▶
Distance		◀———⬦———▶	0	◀◉▶
Lock To Scale X		☑		
Scale X		◀—⬦———▶	100	◀◉▶
Scale Y		◀—⬦———▶	100	◀◉▶
Tumble		– ◉ –	0	◀◉▶
Spin		– ◉ –	0	◀◉▶
Rotate		– ◉ –	0	◀◉▶
		_ Pivot _		
Lock to Position		☑		
Pivot X/Y		⊕ 360 ,	240	◀◉▶
Pivot Z		◀———⬦———▶	0	◀◉▶
		_ Transformations _		
Opacity		◀———⬦▶	100	◀◉▶
Tracking		◀—⬦———▶	0	◀◉▶
Letter Skew X		– ◉ –	0	◀◉▶
Letter Skew Y		– ◉ –	0	◀◉▶
Lock Letter Scale		☐		
Letter Scale X		◀—⬦———▶	100	◀◉▶
Letter Scale Y		◀—⬦———▶	100	◀◉▶
Letter Tumble		– ◉ –	0	◀◉▶
Letter Spin		– ◉ –	0	◀◉▶
Letter Rotate		– ◉ –	0	◀◉▶
Leading		◀———⬦———▶	0	◀◉▶
Baseline		◀———⬦———▶	0	◀◉▶

6.37 Type On Controls

6.38 Keyframing Text Type On

4. The first value, **Text Type On,** is the one we'll animate. With the playhead at the beginning of the clip, click on the diamond button, which turns it green (Figure 6.38). You'll notice a little keyframe diamond appears in the keygraph to the right.

5. Drag the **Text Type On** slider all the way down to zero, or dial 0 into the value box. The text will disappear from the **Canvas.**

6. Go to the end of the clip. **Shift-O** right in the **Controls** window is the easiest way to do it.

7. Now drag the slider all the way up to 100, or type in the value.

8. You'll probably have to render this. With the text clip selected, press **Command-R** to render it.

9. Play it from the beginning and you'll see your text type onto the screen.

The rest of the controls in the **Type On** section are for complex animation features for make the text bounce, curve, and scale.

Title Crawl

Title Crawl is accessed from the bottom of the **Boris** submenu in the **Generators** popup and shares many of the same controls as **Title 3D.** The text window that's evoked when **Title Crawl** is called up functions identically in both these title tools. The real difference is seen in the **Controls** tab of the **Viewer** (Figure 6.39). There are somewhat fewer keyframable options here, no **Type On,** for instance.

The **Animation** popup lets you set:

- **None,** the default
- **Roll (Scroll)**
- **Crawl**

Mask Start and Mask End and Blend Start and Blend End allow you the softly fade scrolling text on and off the screen (Figure 6.40). You can set where the image starts to fade onto the screen and where it fades off the screen separately, as well as control the amount of fade, which is what Title Crawl calls *blend*.

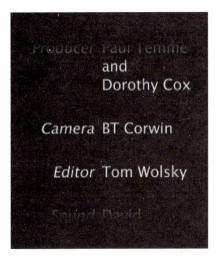

6.40   Blended Mask Start and End

The Reverse Direction checkbox does just that: makes a roll reverse from the default bottom-to-top direction to top-to-bottom, and reverses direction of the standard right-to-left crawl to left-to-right.

To do a crawl, make sure Word Wrap is switched off or use the Word Wrap Override popup in the controls, which toggles the condition currently set in the text panel.

The speed of the roll or crawl is determined by the amount of text in the text window and the duration of the text block in the timeline. The longer the block, the slower the motion. QuickView is especially useful here to determine whether the text speed is appropriate. A couple of seconds will be enough to give you an idea if the scroll is moving too fast or too slow.

6.39   Title Crawl Controls

	About...
Text Entry and Style	Text Scrambler Click for options
Continuously Rasterize	☐
	... Variations ...
User Text Variation	◁ ————— ▸ 0 ◁◉▹
Variation Mode	Random Text ⬍
Progress	◂ ————— ▸ 100 ◁◉▹
Progress Order	Left to Right ⬍
Scramble Characters	◁ ————— ▸ 0 ◁◉▹
Loop	◁ ————— ▸ 0 ◁◉▹
Random Seed	◂ ————— ▸ 50 ◁◉▹

6.41 Text Scrambler Controls (above)

6.42 Variation Mode
Popup (right))

Alphabetical Text
Random Text
Random User Text
Style Shift
Random Style
Style Shuffle
Style By Word
Style By Line
Style Shuffle By Word
Style Shuffle By Line

Text Scrambler

The **Text Scrambler** input panel is identical to **Title 3D** and shares all its features. The real controls for this text animation application are in the **Controls** panel on the **Viewer**. It has an enormously long list of controls divided into sections. The top section (Figure 6.41) gives control over how your text is scrambled, with the most important control being the **Variation Mode** popup that brings you the menu choices in Figure 6.42. Some of these scramble the letters themselves, while many of them scramble styles. You have to have multiple styles applied to the letters for the style variation functions to be active.

When **User Text Variation** is set to zero, as it is by default, the text will appear as you write it. When it's set to its maximum of 100, the text will be most varied. Like **Text Type On** function, you animate the **User Text Variation** value with keyframes to change from scrambled text to normal text.

Progress controls how far into the animation the scrambling continues. At 100 with a text variation of 100, the text will be fully scrambled.

Bitmap or Vector

How is this enormous flexibility of text possible? When you scale up text created with the FCP text tool, the image quickly becomes jagged around the edges, yet in Title 3D you can separately **scale, rotate, skew, pivot, and mangle** individual letters to very large sizes, and yet you'll see no apparent antialiasing or stair-stepping on the edges of the letters. This is possible because Calligraphy works with vector graphics, while FCP works with bitmapped graphics.

When a bitmapped graphic is created, the color and position of each pixel in the image is defined. If you then scale the image, you have to scale the pixels and try to create pixels where none previously existed. When a vector graphic is created, no pixels are actually defined; only the shape, based on lines and curves, is defined. So if you scale **the shape of the** vector graphic, you're redefining the **image, and** no actual pixels need to be created until the image is displayed on the screen.

The scaling for the vector graphics **in Boris Calligraphy should always** be done within **Title 3D** and should not be done using the **Scale** slider in the **Motion** tab.

_ Jitter _		
Jitter Seed	0	
Jitter Speed	100	
Jitter Position X	0	
Jitter Position Y	0	
Jitter Angle	0	
Jitter Scale X	0	
Jitter Scale Y	0	
Jitter Hue	0	
Jitter Opacity	0	
Restrictions	None	
Polarize	0	
Master Jitter Amount	100	

6.43 Jitter Controls

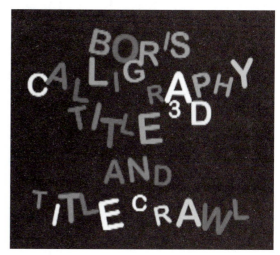

6.44 Jitter Effect

But with text variation at 100 and **Progress** set down to 50, half of the text will be normal, while the other half will be scrambled. The **Progress Order** popup lets you set whether the progress will be **Right to Left, Left to Right,** or **Random.**

Scramble Characters allows you to animate it the text variation further so the same letters do not consistently replace the letters in the text, while **Random Seed** can be used to even further randomize the text.

The middle section of the long **Text Scrambler** control panel handles letter and page transformations and also includes a section like **Title 3D** that allows for text to be typed on the screen as it's scrambled.

At the very bottom of the long control panel is a section that controls **Jitter** (Figure 6.43). Here you can animate text scale, position, angle, and hue. Make sure a color is set to the text; black or white won't work if you want to jitter the hue value. Using the **Jitter** function produces interesting animated text variations as in Figure 6.44.

Vector Shape

Vector Shape is a great addition to FCP because it allows for creative and animatable shapes. The only regret I have with the tool is that the fill color does not include a gradient. One that would

6.45 Shape Primitive Controls

do from color to transparency would be really useful. All the controls for **Vector Shape** are in a long list in the **Controls** panel. I've divided the list into three parts. The first (Figure 6.45) shows the first section that controls the primitive shape of the object, basically **Rectangle** or **Oval**. The sliders below that control the shape top, bottom, left and right, basically controlling its horizontal and vertical size.

The large middle section of controls (Figure 6.46) handles three separate sets of borders, similar to the edges in text. Notice the three borders default to **Center, Inside,** and **Outside**. As with text edges, to be visible the borders have to be activated with the checkbox just below the border name. The **Border Begin** and **Border End** functions allow you to animate the border so it appears to travel around the shape. With this tool, if you have an oval shape with no fill you can make a line appear to circle a word or an object on the screen, perhaps to highlight it.

The bottom section of the controls (Figure 6.47) include **Shape Fill**, which lets you set the color of the solid. There are also the typical Calligraphy animatable transformation controls for **Transformation**, which controls position, scale, skew, tumble, spin and rotation. At the bottom is a section for adding a shadow, either **Drop, Cast,** or **Solid**.

Nesting

The FCP titling workflow is based on the applications ability to built graphical elements in one sequence and nest them in another. In the **Browser** is a sequence called *Title and Background*, which is made up of a number of FCP titling tools. The first frame appears in Figure 6.48. If you open the sequence *Title*

	_ Border 1 _		
Border On	☐		
Position	Center		
Color	▶ 🖉 © ■		◁◈▷
Width	◀——⬥——▶ 10		◁◈▷
Opacity	◀————⬥ 100		◁◈▷
Border Begin	⬥——▶ 0		◁◈▷
Border End	◀————⬥ 100		◁◈▷
Border Offset	⊙ 0		◁◈▷
Softness	⬥————▶ 0		◁◈▷
Cap and Join	Flat/Round		
	_ Border 2 _		
Border On	☐		
Position	Inside		
Color	▶ 🖉 © ■		◁◈▷
Width	◀⬥———▶ 2		◁◈▷
Opacity	◀————⬥ 100		◁◈▷
Border Begin	⬥———▶ 0		◁◈▷
Border End	◀————⬥ 100		◁◈▷
Border Offset	⊙ 0		◁◈▷
Softness	⬥————▶ 0		◁◈▷
Cap and Join	Flat/Round		
	_ Border 3 _		
Border On	☐		
Position	Outside		
Color	▶ 🖉 © ■		◁◈▷
Width	◀⬥———▶ 2		◁◈▷
Opacity	◀————⬥ 100		◁◈▷
Softness	⬥————▶ 0		◁◈▷
Cap and Join	Flat/Round		

6.46 Border Controls

	_ Shape Fill _		
Fill On	☑		
Fill Opacity	◀————⬥ 100		◁◈▷
Fill Color	▶ 🖉 © ☐		◁◈▷
	_ Transformations _		
Opacity	◀————⬥ 100		◁◈▷
Position X/Y	⊕ 360 , 240		◁◈▷
Position Z	◀——⬥——▶ 0		◁◈▷
Master Scale	◀⬥———▶ 100		◁◈▷
Scale X	◀⬥———▶ 100		◁◈▷
Scale Y	◀⬥———▶ 100		◁◈▷
Tumble	⊙ 0		◁◈▷
Spin	⊙ 0		◁◈▷
Rotate	⊙ 0		◁◈▷
PreRotate Position X/Y	⊕ 360 , 240		◁◈▷
PreRotate Position Z	◀——⬥——▶ 0		◁◈▷
Lock Pivot to Position	☑		
Pivot X/Y	⊕ 360 , 240		◁◈▷
Pivot Z	◀——⬥——▶ 0		◁◈▷
	_ Shadows _		
Shadow Type	None		
Shadow Color	▶ 🖉 © ■		◁◈▷
Shadow Distance	◀⬥———▶ 5		◁◈▷
Shadow Opacity	◀———⬥—▶ 60		◁◈▷
Shadow Softness	⬥————▶ 0		◁◈▷
Shadow Angle	⊙ 45		◁◈▷
HighLight Color	▶ 🖉 © ☐		◁◈▷
Shade Color	▶ 🖉 © ■		◁◈▷

6.47 Fill, Transformation and Shadow Controls

6.48 Title and Background

and Background, you'll see that it is made up of two layers. On **V1** is the video clip *Kabuki1* twice, and on **V2** is a text block called *Title Composite* and another called *Title Composite Japan*. These are nests. Nesting is an important concept to understand in Final Cut. Because you can have sequences within sequences in FCP, you can also group layers together into nests to form a sequence of their own. Let's build these nests together.

Text

1. Start by duplicating *Title and Background* in the **Browser**. Select the sequence and use **Edit>Duplicate** (**Option-D**).

2. Open the duplicate *Title and Background copy* by double-clicking on it, or select it and press **Enter** or **Return**.

3. Use **Command-A** to select everything in the **Timeline** and then use **Delete** to empty the sequence.

4. Uncouple the audio patches on **A1/A2** and make sure **V1** is set as the destination track.

5. Next drag the clip *Kabuki1* from the *Clips* bin to **Overwrite** it at the beginning of the sequence on **V1**.

6. Move the playhead so that it is parked somewhere above the clip.

7. From the **Text Generator** popup in the **Viewer**, select **Boris>Title 3D**.

8. Before you set the text, drag from the **Viewer** to the **Canvas** to **Superimpose**. This will edit it into the timeline to **V2** above the video clip.

9. Double-click on the **Title 3D** block in the **Timeline** to bring it back into the **Viewer**.

10. Go to the **Controls** tab and click on the **Title 3D** button at the top of the **Controls**.

11. In the text box type in *DAMINE*, the name of the village where this video was shot.

12. You can, of course, use whatever text, color, or settings you want, but this is how I built this image. Make sure the text is selected first before you apply any changes.

Font	Arial Black
Point Size	96
Kerning	13
Justification	Center
Style	Bold

13. Because the letters looked too jammed together, I set the **Kerning** up to **13**.

14. In the second tab, text control was set to **Wrap**.

15. In the third tab for **Color** I used a **Gradient**, with these settings in the **Gradient Editor**.

First Control Stop	Muted red: Red 162, Green 63, Blue 76
Midpoint	0.25
Second Color Stop	Turquoise: Red 91, Green 218, Blue 211
Type	Contour
Fade	31

16. In the fourth tab for **Edges** I used two edges, the first the soft outer edge and the second the hard black edge. For the first edge I used:

Edge Style	Plain
Position	Outside
Color	White: 255, 255, 255
Edge Width	19
Edge Softness	3.34

17. For the second edge I used:

Edge Style	Plain
Position	Outside
Edge Color	Black: 0, 0, 0
Edge Width	4.15

18. Press the **Apply** button to fix the text and close the window.

One last thing: we need to reposition the text block lower in the frame. We could do this with **Image+Wireframe** in the **Canvas**, but it's better to do it using the **Title 3D Controls**.

19. Set **Position X/Y** values to **360** and **380** to lower the text in the frame.

That's it for the basic text block. Let's work on the background.

Background

1. Make sure the **Timeline** playhead is still over the clip (not at the end of the clip) and that **V1** is still the destination track.

2. In the **Viewer** from the **Generators**, select **Boris>Vector Shape**.

3. Drag the shape to **Superimpose**, which will edit it onto **V2** pushing the **Title 3D** text block up to **V3**.

Your **Canvas** should now look like Figure 6.49. This is going to be the background white glow.

6.49 Adding Vector Shape

4. Double-click on the **Vector Shape** in the **Timeline** to bring it into the **Viewer** and go to the **Controls** tab.

5. Obviously you can use whatever shape and colors you want, but to create my background shape I started with the default Rectangle **Primitive**. For the **Shape** values I used:

Shape Left	0
Shape Top	70
Shape Right	100
Shape Bottom	89
Corner Size	0

6. For the **Border** I used the default size, but changed **Position** to **Outside**, and using the system color picker (Figure 6.50) set the RGB values to 29, 158, 150.

7. For the **Shape Fill** color I turned the **Opacity** down to 75 and used RGB values of 179, 60, 75.

Your sequence should have three layers in it. We've now built a template to use for other titles, one we can use again and again without having to rebuild the graphics each time. Here's now to do that:

1. Select the **Vector Shape** and the **Title 3D** text in the **Timeline** by marquee dragging or **Shift**-clicking the objects. Do *not* select the video layer on **V1**.

2. From the **Sequence** menu, select **Nest Item(s)**, or use the keyboard shortcut **Option-C**.

3. This will bring up a dialog box that lets you name the new sequence you're creating (Figure 6.51).

4. Call it *Title Composite 2*, to distinguish it from the sequence in your **Browser** already called *Title Composite*.

This nest appears in the **Timeline** as a block called *Title Composite 2*. It will also appear in your **Browser** as a sequence. That block of text in your sequence can be moved around wherever you like and used again and again.

It's very simple to use this template to create new titles with the same layout and style.

1. Duplicate *Title Composite 2* in your **Browser**.

2. Change the name of the duplicate to *Title Composite Japan 2*. Double-click the duplicate sequence to open it into its own Timeline. Double-click on the **Title 3D** block to open it into the **Viewer**.

3. Go to the **Controls** tab, click on the **Title 3D** button, and in the text window, select the text and change *DAMINE* to *JAPAN*.

4. Because this will reset the **Kerning** value, you'll have to select the text and reset **Kerning** to 13 to match the original.

Nothing else changes, just the text block and all its settings. Easy, isn't it? Now you can place that new composite title in any sequence you want, just as it appears in *Title and Background* in the **Browser**.

6.50 RGB Color Picker

6.51 Nesting Dialog

Photoshop Titles

Adobe Photoshop should a part of every editor's toolset, perhaps not so much for titling any more, but for all the myriad other still image content that's so often required in editing.

What you should first know about working in Photoshop is that you should use only RGB color space—no CMYK, no grayscale, no indexed color. They don't translate well to video.

Note
Important Preset Update: Be aware that the DV and CCIR601 presets used by FCP5—720x540 and 720x547, respectively—are not the preset sizes that Adobe uses in Photoshop.

One problem with using Photoshop is the issue of square versus rectangular or non-square pixels. Because Photoshop is a computer program, until recently it worked in square pixels exclusively, while most video other than HD uses the CCIR601 or rectangular pixel. This presents a minor problem unless you are using a newer version of the Adobe product, Photoshop 7 or later, which allows you to preview images with rectangular pixels and has guides for both Title and Action Safe areas.

1. If you're working in the DV format using CCIR601 pixels at 720×480, create your PSD files at 720×540.
   If you're working in standard CCIR601 format, 720×486, then create your PSD files at 720×547.

2. After you've made your graphic, go to **Image Size** and, making sure **Constrain Proportions** is deselected and **Bicubic** is selected, change the height of the image to 480 or 486, as appropriate (480 for DV material, 486 for full-format digital video).

This squashes the image down, distorting it, changing it to a file that FCP recognizes as using CCIR601 rectangular pixels.

3. Save your file. I save out a separate PSD file that has been converted to CCIR601 format and keep the original so I can correct the typos I usually make.

When you bring a 720×480 PSD file into FCP, the editing software assumes it's been prepared to use in a DV sequence. When placed in a DV sequence, the image will work perfectly and be treated as a rectangular pixel image.

There are templates for the common formats in the *Extras* folder of the book's DVD. The images are black with white Safe Action and Safe Title Areas markers. Guides have also been set up for SAA and STA. Table 6.1 gives a list of these formats, their rectangular pixel size, and the square pixel equivalent that should be used in Photoshop with square pixels.

Table 6.1   Photoshop Specifications

Format	Rectangular pixel size	Square pixel size
NTSC CCIR601	720×486	720×547
DV NTSC	720×480	720×540
NTSC CCIR601 16:9 (Anamorphic)	720×486	853×486
DV NTSC 16:9 (Anamorphic)	720×480	853×480
PAL	720×576	768×576
PAL 16:9 (Anamorphic)	720×576	1,024×576

HD formats use square pixels, and graphics should be created in their normal sizes, either 1,920×1,080 or 1,280×720, depending on the format you're working in. HD formats are always widescreen formats.

You're not always making a graphic that needs to fit in the video format. Sometimes you're making a graphic that is much larger, one you want to move around on to make it seem as though you're panning across or zooming in or out. To do this, you need to make the image much greater than your video format, perhaps 2,000×2,000 pixels or more.

If you are working with a layered image in Photoshop, you should create it as before, using non-square pixels. You should squeeze the image down to rectangular pixels before you bring it into FCP. To do this, rather than using pixel values, use percentages and reduce the height of the image to 90%.

If you're using single-layer images without Photoshop transparency, create them in square pixels and don't do anything else. FCP understands these are square pixel images brought into a CCIR601 world and will handle them appropriately. If they are PSD-layered files with transparency, FCP treats them as separate sequences and does not adjust for CCIR601 pixels.

The easiest way to work with Photoshop files that you want to lay over video is to create your PSD files over transparency, PSD's checkerboard background. This transparency will be honored when you import the file into FCP. It's important to understand that PSD files come into Final Cut as separate sequences. This means that when you bring a PSD file with multiple layers, all its layers remain intact as separate layers in a FCP sequence. There each layer can be animated and affected separately, just as we recently saw with nested sequences.

The only time Photoshop files do not import as a sequence is when they are made up of a single background layer or are saved as flattened images or in some other file format, such as PICT.

Resolution

For people who come from a print background, it's important to note that video doesn't have a changeable resolution. It's not like print where you can jam more and more pixels into an inch of space and make your print cleaner, clearer, and crisper. Pixels in video occupy a fixed space and have a fixed size, the equivalent of 72dpi in the print world, which happens to be the Macintosh screen resolution. Dots per inch are a printing concern. Forget about resolution. Think in terms of size: the more pixels, the bigger the picture. Do not think that you can make an image 720×480 at a high resolution like 300dpi or 600dpi and be able to move it around in FCP. Certainly you'll be able to scale it up, but it will look soft, and if you scale it far enough—to 300%, for instance—the image will start to show pixelization. FCP is good at hiding the defects by blurring and softening, but the results are not really as good as they should be. FCP is a video application and only deals with pixel numbers, not with dpi.

Scanners, on the other hand, are designed for the print world where dpi is an issue. Because scanners generate lots and lots of pixels, this is very handy for the person working in video. You can scan even a quite small image at, let's say, 300 or 600dpi, and your scanner will produce thousands of pixels, which will translate into video as a very large image. You now have an image that's much larger than your video format of 720×486 pixels. If your scanner can generate an image that's 2,880 pixels across, it's making an image four times bigger than your CCIR601 video frame. You can now move that very large graphic around on the screen and make it seem as though a camera is panning across the image. Or you can scale it back, and it will look as though the camera is zooming back from a point in the image. Reverse the process, and it looks as though the camera is zooming into the image.

Summary

In this lesson we've gone through FCP's title tools, Boris Calligraphy, and the task of bringing Photoshop title files into Final Cut.

In the next lesson we'll look at the different forms of editing—documentary, music, multicamera, action, and dialog—and how to work in them using Final Cut Pro 5.

Lesson 7

Editing Forms

The moment of the edit, where one shot changes into another, is dictated by rhythm—sometimes by an internal rhythm the visuals present, sometimes by a musical track, more often than not by the rhythm of language. All language, dialog or narration, has a rhythm, a cadence or pattern, dictated by the words and based on grammar. Grammar marks language with punctuation: commas are short pauses; semicolons are slightly longer pauses; periods are the end of an idea. The new sentence begins a new idea, a new thought, and it is natural that as the new thought begins, a new image is introduced to illustrate that idea. The shot comes, not on the end of the sentence, not in the pause, but on the beginning of the new thought. This is the natural place to cut, and it's this rhythm of language that drives the rhythm of film and video, particularly so in documentary production. Dialog presents different problems. Cutting on speech from one speaker to the next, though apparently mandatory in sitcoms, is usually monotonous to watch. Action and music may not have language to guide their rhythm. Music, of course, will have its own, while action has the internal rhythm of movement within the frame that will drive the pace of the cuts. In this lesson we'll look at cutting these various forms.

Editing Considerations

Each of the many common editing forms requires a different approach to the material. The forms I'd like to look are:

- Documentary
- Music
- Multicamera
- Action
- Dialog

Obviously these will all overlap to some extent or other. Each has its own variations, and techniques that apply to one will get used in others, but these four offer the principal challenges an editor might face.

Final Cut Pro has been aiming in the direction of narrative film h since its inception. You can see this by the terms used in the application, which are not video terms, but film terms. This version of FCP enhances the metaphor further, integrating Cinema Tools into the application, adding to the **Browser** displays for **Film Slate, Camera Roll, Lab Roll, TK Speed, Key and Ink Numbers,** and others. In FCP5 the **Timeline,** the **Viewer,** and the **Canvas** can all be set to display film **Feet+Frames,** and **View>Timecode Over-lays,** which in previous versions showed timecode displays in the **Viewer** and the **Canvas,** now also can show **Keycode** and **Ink Numbers** in the overlay. Though narrative film, the Hollywood and independent feature film, is the most visible film and video production, it makes up only a very small fraction of production in America and around the world. On any single weekend day in June, probably more wedding videos are produced in America than all the feature films made in Hollywood in a year, and some of those wedding videos are longer than feature films. Or maybe they just seem that way. Final Cut Pro is being used on a vast range of projects—by three-time Academy Award–winning editor Walter Murch on *Jarhead* for Sam Mendes all the way down through television networks like CNN, to commercials, corporate videos, wedding videographers, and even serious hobbyists—and in every format from film resolution and High Definition down to HDV and DV and even web video. The extensibility of Final Cut is a significant factor in its popularity.

One of the first points to consider in any production is the form in which it will be delivered. This should not be happening when you are in postproduction, but rather when you are writing, and congruent to that, when you are planning production, when you are shooting, and then finally when you are editing. If your end product is a film to be seen on a large screen, it's shot in a certain way and edited in a certain way. Shots can be held longer because there is so much to see and so much space for the eye to cover and travel around. The same movie seen on the small screen of a television set will appear to be cut too slowly, because you take in the whole image without your eye moving, so you take it in more quickly. Of course, you also see less detail.

If your project is intended for delivery on television, it should be shot for television's limitations of luma and chroma values. If it's shot for delivery on a computer screen, you aren't bound by those limits, but perhaps by greater limits dictated by compression. If you're going to squeeze your video down for web delivery, you need to shoot it with as few moves as possible, use few transitions (which don't compress well), and shoot plainer, less busy backgrounds. Delivery should be the first consideration in a production, not the last, and every step of the process, from scripting through final editing, should bear the delivery mechanism in mind.

Film and video production starts with an idea and expands outward. It grows fuller and more detailed, but everything refers back to the original idea. What determines how the production is edited is in that original idea. It goes from the script which governs:

- What and how the video is shot
- Where the emphasis is placed
- What is looked at in the scene and from what angle
- What elements are created for juxtaposition

The elements are the shots. Often a scene will be shot all the way through repeatedly from a number of different camera angles to give the editor the greatest variety of selection material. This is conventional in all types of production, even sometimes in documentaries. It's certainly common in commercials, in corporate videos, and of course in narrative film.

On the other hand, a director who knows in his mind how the shots will be cut together will probably be more effective than one who shoots lots of cover material without a clear idea of how it will come together. Without having an idea how the material will be put together, it's difficult for the director to judge the pacing within each shot. If the action is slow within the shot, then the shots will have to be cut together slowly. If the action is fast paced, it will force the editing to be fast. The key to good editing is in timing, and that timing starts in the camera. For instance, if camera moves are not well timed, it becomes difficult to pace the material well when it's being cut. Whether zooming or panning, the camera movement itself should last no more than a few seconds. In well-shot material there are no random movements. The camera movements are deliberate and precise; the pan goes from object A to object B and stops. There is a tendency for camera-people, particularly novices, to use moves to make static material more interesting. Pans and tilts and zooms appear to enliven what might otherwise be dull or static material.

Shots are generally on the screen no more than 5–10 seconds. For faster paced editing—in commercials, for instance—shots often last a second or even less. That isn't to say that the camera shoots shots that are that short, but the editor cuts them down to just the few frames that best serve the material.

Every editor comes out of a movie saying he could take 10 minutes out of it. Maybe the picture would be improved by the trims, but often enough it would be ruined. There is a danger in chipping away too much, in too finely honing a piece, eventually cutting into the core and damaging the material. As the editor you get used to seeing the pictures again and again. You see the content more quickly. You understand the flow of the shots more quickly, and then the danger is that you mistake your understanding and comprehension of the material for that of the audience, an audience who has never seen the film before. This happens less often when a director has a clear vision of the picture and has been able to convey that vision. The greater danger comes when the director's concept is unclear both to him and to you. Then the risk of overcutting increases. Directors confident in their ideas, who know clearly what they want, tend to shoot less, with little extra cover. Sometimes this will get them and you as the editor into trouble in the cutting room. But when it works, when the director's vision is clear and well executed, the outcome can be very, very good, but when it doesn't, the results tend to be very, very mediocre. Uncertain directors tend to overshoot, giving the editor a vast range of choices and angles, more than he probably wants, certainly more than he needs. This is where the greatest danger comes in overcutting, putting in too many angles to fit in every vision—a bit of this, a bit of that, and in the end, not much of anything.

I am often asked how long it takes to edit something. The only answer I can usually find is that it takes as much time as you have. The constraints of time can have two causes: deadline, as in broadcast airtime, or cost, because of limitations of budget, or a combination of the two. I have worked on news pieces that should have taken an hour to edit that have been cut for air in less than 10 minutes. And I have worked on pieces that could have been cut in an hour that took weeks. An edit can go on endlessly. It never really finishes; it stops. Painters often talk about painting in this way, that you just reach a point where the work stops and you say that is it. Eventually you reach a point at which all your additional effort isn't making it better, just making it different, rearranging the shots, making adjustments so subtle that they can be seen only on the 20th viewing. It's often better to stop earlier rather than later.

Editing is about three things: selection, arrangement, and timing. Selecting which shot to use, which order the shots should be in, and how long the shots should be. The classic example of shot arrangement is the three shots of the burning building:

A. The building on fire

B. The building exploding

C. Three men running away

In this order the audience sees it as three men escaping the exploding building. If you see A, then C, followed by B, you might think the men are trying to escape the fire and are caught by the explosion. If you see C, then B, then A, you will probably suspect the men caused the explosion that left the building burning.

Whether the editing takes place when the writer scripts one shot and then another, or the director stages a scene to be shot with a certain continuity, or in some moment of serendipity in the cutting room when one shot is placed next to another, that is where movies are made.

Editors like to think they can make or break a project. They most certainly can break one, and they can certainly rescue one, but for a project to be really good requires not only that it be edited well but that it be shot in such a way that it *can* be edited well. This doesn't only mean that it is beautifully photographed; the most beautiful shots that can't be edited together effectively are pointless. That long, slow lingering zoom out becomes an anchor that drags down the video. That perfectly smooth pan along the treeline down to the shore brings the video to grinding halt. Do you know what the viewer looks at when he or she watches this type of pan? They're staring at the leading edge of the screen, watching for what's coming around the corner. It isn't only slow movement that will destroy a sequence, but the very camera angles chosen to show the scene. Poorly placed cameras, poorly composed shots and ineffective staging will do more to kill a video beyond what even the finest editor can resurrect.

Loading the Lesson

Before we begin looking at the various editing forms, let's load the material you'll need for the lesson onto the media hard drive of your computer.

1. Drag the *Lesson 7 Media* folder from the DVD to your media drive.

2. If you don't already have it, bring the *Projects* folder from the DVD onto your system drive.

3. Eject the DVD, open the *Projects* folder on your system drive, and double-click the project file *Lesson 7* to launch the application.

4. Once again, choose the **Reconnect** option to relink the media files when the **Offline Files** dialog appears.

Setting up the Project

Inside the project, you'll find these sequences in the **Browser**:

- An empty sequence called *Sequence 1*
- A bin called *Multicam* which contains a four clips and an empty sequence.
- A bin called *Action Cut*, which contains a master clip, two subclips and a sequence, which we'll look at later.
- Another bin called *Heartwood*, which contains the another master clip as well as some subclips and a few sequences.

Documentary

Documentary is a loosely used term for factual film or video production. Generally these are productions that usually present facts and have a narration, either a disembodied voice or one made up from those appearing in the video. Documentaries are the type of shows you might see on the Discovery Channel or National Geographic. Documentary, news, reportage, informational, and even instructional are all variations of the same type of video. Even wedding videos are forms of documentary production in the purest sense: they document an event, but they often include other material that records the couple's background, as well as poetic mood pieces with suitable music.

Documentaries fall into two large groups:

- Programs that are tightly scripted to start, shot to a pre-written narration, and edited from that, with few changes along the way

- Programs that are wholly made up in the editing room, with a structure and a narration that is crafted to fit the material.

Most documentaries fall somewhere in between. Again, wedding videos provide a common example: the ceremony is the tightly scripted portion of the production, while the reception might be largely unscripted. In its unscripted form, the documentary is created by the producer, director, and cameraperson on location. Good, experienced camerapersons, whether they realize it or not, are actually scripting the story as they shoot it. Certainly every good news cameraperson is shooting with the correspondent's voice reading the lines in his head. Chances are that if it isn't shot for any particular purpose, it will probably not find any use at all. Once the material has been shot, it's the director's and editor's responsibility to bring from that material all that it has to offer.

Documentary can be a factual, accurate representation of events, or it can be an imaginative, poetical, loose interpretation of reality. Either way, documentary can start fully scripted, wholly unscripted, or something in between. One feature that all forms have in common is the tendency to shoot vastly more material than necessary, sometimes with shooting ratios as high as 25:1, even 100:1.

Many documentary scripts aren't written so much as found, or so says my friend, Academy-award winning editor Loren Miller. There's much truth to that. The mass of material in a documentary is often best sorted out on paper before the picture itself is attacked. The paper edit is crucial, and the paper edit is the mining for the script that's in the material, Michelangelo finding the

Music and Narration

A common dilemma that's often posed is whether it is better to cut to the rhythm of the music or to the rhythm of the narration in a sequence. Personally, I don't think you should be having to make a choice between the two. If you're having to make that choice, then there is probably something more fundamentally wrong with the sequence. There should either be music you're cutting to or there should be narration. I very much dislike productions that slather music under everything. You should bring the music up for a purpose, and while it's up full, you should be cutting to the music. Then when you bring in the narration, you should fade out the music under the narration, but just keeping it there as a bed, I think, is almost always wrong (unless it's integral to the scene that's being narrated).

If you're having to choose between cutting to one or the other, the music or the narration, then either the music doesn't belong there, it's the wrong music, or it's the wrong narration. Even in a sequence where music is a key element—a video about dance, for instance—you are cutting to the rhythm of the music while the music is up, and then to the narration when it's up, even if the music continues underneath. Often with this kind of production, it's better to make the narration quite sparse and punctuated more frequently than you normally would with sections of music. So you get a phrase or a sentence or two at most, then go back to the music and dance briefly, before returning to another short piece of narration. What should be avoided in almost every instance is the tendency to have a blanket of narration lying on top of a blanket of music.

statue that's in the stone. The paper edit can be done from transcripts, from log notes, on an Excel spreadsheet, or on 3×5 cards. The idea is always the same: move the information around, find the links, find what flows together, find the conflicts, the drama, and visual strength in the material and put it together into a coherent plan that can be taken into the cutting room.

The unscripted documentary benefits greatly from the advent of nonlinear editing systems, because not only does it give the editor very powerful search tools, but it also allows quickly trying many combinations of images. You can try different sequences and archive them, but avoid taking this to extremes. Don't start a new version of a sequence every few edits. You'll probably find yourself getting confused, or at least undecided about which to use. Better would be to keep substantially different versions of a sequence or a show. As a documentary develops an idea for a structure of the material may come up, seem like a good idea at the time, but then lead to a muddle later on, forcing you to backtrack to an earlier version that flowed better and worked better as a whole. Because the structure of a documentary can change often and radically before it's completed (probably more so than most narrative films), it's important to keep these major changes as separate sequences. On large projects it's better to archive them as entirely separate project files for simplicity's sake, which also helps to prevent single FCP project files from being bloated and bogging down the application.

In loosely scripted documentary material, after you work through various shot orders, the frames themselves can seem to impose a continuity by being adjacent to each other. Certain shots will seem to want to go together, as will others. Then groups of images coalesce into clusters, and the clusters form logical strings, until the whole is built out of the parts and a structure has imposed itself on the material.

Organizing your material is crucial to working efficiently in the documentary form. Well-organized bins with many notes throughout are more than beneficial: they're mandatory. We looked at organization earlier in Lesson 2 on page 31. You may want to review that.

Documentary generally uses a narration track to carry the information, whether it's a disembodied voice of God speaking truths or an ever-present narrator who wanders through the scene, or even if it's pieced together from interviews. The narration becomes the bed for the video.

What many editors like to do is build a bed of the primary audio track and its synchronous video. So if the video starts with a short piece of music, lay down the music on a lower audio track, leaving the primary tracks open for the video. Then the narration comes in. Lay down the narration on a separate track. Then when a piece of an interview comes in, lay in the sound bites in their entirety with the sync picture, jump cuts and all. The picture can always be covered later. Then perhaps more narration, and then another musical break. You can go on and on, building the entire sound track like this until it looks something like Figure 7.1. FCP's **Voice Over** feature comes in handy here, for recording the kind of scratch recording, a rough narration, to lay down as the basis for the bed.

At this stage, the laid-out video might have a distinctly blocky look to it, but as the material is worked, more and more overlapping of sound and picture will begin to appear.

Some people like to work in a very linear fashion, tightly editing the material as they go. It's quite natural to build a sequence this way, this is the natural way a story progresses, linearly. On the

7.1 Documentary Sound Bed

other hand, I think the benefit of laying out the bed is that you get to see what the whole structure is like, where emphasis needs to be placed, where more graphical explanation is needed perhaps, where there are parts that may need to be cut because they're taking too much time, or a minor point is being dwelt on too long. Without the whole, it's hard to get that sense of how the material is paced and stands up as a structure.

Once the bed is laid out, the sound track flowing smoothly, the content making sense, progressing sensibly from point to point to conclusion like a well-crafted essay, then the pictures are put in to fill the gaps in the track. Having laid down your bed, you're ready to put in the B Roll material. The pacing of the editing is now dictated by language, the rhythm and cadence of speech, which can vary greatly from speaker to speaker, from language to language. Usually I add the B Roll material to **V2** over interview portions if needed. This makes it easier to go back to the interview at a later stage without having to edit it back into the **Timeline**, which may, in its early stages while the first B Roll material is being added, look something like Figure 7.2.

The bed, of course, is just a starting block and is not inviable by any means. It's often ripped open to insert natural sound breaks. The multiple track tool to select everything after a certain point in the timeline is very useful for this. You can call it up from the

7.2 Documentary Bed with B Roll

Tools or with the **T** tool. By tapping **T** four times, you'll bring up the **Select All Tracks Forward** tool (Figure 7.3). Or if you press **T**, the single track tool, and then hold down the **Shift** key, you'll toggle to **Select All Tracks Forward**.

In practice, of course, an hour-long documentary is usually not laid out as a single bed, but rather broken into sequences that are edited separately and then brought together into a final sequence. Opens are often built separately, often by entirely separate companies specializing in motion graphics, 3D, and compositing with tools such as After Effects. Even while staying in-house, specialist sequences can be laid down separately.

What is a B Roll?

You may have noticed that one of the FCP default **Labels** is called **B Roll**. In the old days that were not so long ago, a television anchorman or reporter would lay down a commentary track or do an entire on-camera narration, originally as film and later as videotape. Called the A Roll, it would be loaded on a machine, either telecine or VTR. Then shots illustrating the narration would be cut together and loaded on a second machine. This would be the B Roll. Both would be fed into a control room and gang-synced together so that the director could either cut back and forth or use effects to switch between the two. B Roll became the generic term for any cover video, regardless of how it was assembled into the production. B Roll is material that shows what someone is talking about, the shots of the car accident as the police officer describes it, or they can be contrapuntal shots, pictures of wealthy homes while the narration describes poverty in the country. All of these shots serve to illustrate, refine, or comment on the narration, interview, or other voice over.

B Roll can also be cutaways. Any editor will tell you that cutaways are the most useful shots. You can never have too many, and you never seem to have enough. No editor will ever complain that you have shot too many cutaways. A cutaway shot shows a subsidiary action or reaction that you can use to bridge an edit. It's usually used to contract time, as we'll see a bit later. It's the shot of the onlookers watching. It's that overly used shot of a person's hands. The shot of the interviewer nodding in response to an answer is called in England a *noddie*. The noddie allows you to bridge a portion of the interviewee's answer where the person has stumbled over the words or has digressed into something pointless. A wide shot that shows the whole scene can often be used as a cutaway. Make note of these useful shots as you log your material.

⭐ *Tip*

Misused Montage: Montage in its weakest form is used as a quick way to convey information. The travel sequence is the most clichéd: character leaves, plane takes off, plane lands, character walks out of terminal and gets in a cab, cab pulls up at curb, character walks into a building. This is superficial montage to convey minimal information.

Foreign Language Versions

French and Spanish are often spoken very quickly, yet seem to take many more words to say the same thing as English, so despite the rapid speech, the editing often seems contrapuntal because it is paced so slowly. Re-editing for different languages can be a frustrating experience. Extending material to fit a sentence or shot may not always be best. Because of the rapid speech, new material might have to be introduced. So more shots are used to match the cadence while maintaining the coverage of a single scene. If the material was originally shot for English, finding extra clips to fit foreign language versions can be an exercise in futility.

Editing documentaries is not often about continuity of action, but rather about continuity of ideas, putting together images that separately have one meaning, but together have a different meaning and present a new idea. This is the concept of *montage*. The term has come to be used in a few of different ways, but the original form established by Russian filmmakers in the 1920s was based on this idea.

In this powerful concept, you can put together two shots that have no direct relationship with each other and thereby create in the audience's mind a quite different idea, separate from the meaning of its parts. This juxtaposition of unrelated images to make the audience draw a continuity of ideas is often done with a sequence of usually quick, impressionistic shots, often with motion.

Montage can mean a collection of shots that serve to contract or expand time by being cut together. It can be used to create the sense of location or process—for instance, shots of various aspects of car production build up to create an impression of the process. A variety of shots of the Damine festival produce an effect that gives the flavor of the town and the event. The common trick to make montage effective is fast pacing, using speed to quickly build block on block, shot on shot, to construct the whole. Because of time limitations, montage is often used in commercials. It's a quick and concise way to convey a variety of impressions that make up a single whole.

The juxtaposition of shots with very different audio may preclude the use of natural sound because of the harshness of the edit. It often becomes necessary to use unnatural sound or music or to use a split edit to reinforce the point of the intellectual edit. By splitting the sound, the edit happens twice, multiplying its effect. When intercutting material to create tension, what's commonly done is not to cut the sound with the picture, but to keep a constant sound or music to which the editing and the action paces itself.

Another commonly used form of montage is a complex compositing effect to overlay multiple changing images on the screen. This type of montage was popularized by the great filmmaker, theoretician, and teacher Slavko Vorkapich and is now most commonly seen in program openings and main title sequences, where it incorporates graphical elements as well as photographic ones.

Music videos are often montages, metaphors repeated often enough to become clichés, such as the suitcase in the Country & Western video. One good thing about cliché is that the repetition can be honed ever finer. A shot of a guy flirting with a girl, shot of another girl's hand picking up the suitcase tells the whole tale of any number of C&W songs.

Montage isn't confined to documentary or music videos. It is occasionally seen in feature films such as the climatic baptism scene in *The Godfather*. Here, with Bach's music and the Roman Catholic liturgy as a background, Michael Corleone literally becomes a godfather while eliminating his principal enemies, the two ideas intercut and built up together into a classic piece of cinema editing.

Music

Music videos are the staple of MTV, VH1, and CMT. All popular music recording artists have videos made to accompany their music. It's an essential ingredient in artist and record promotion. The key point to remember about editing music videos is that it's about the music. Everything is dictated by the rhythm, the tone, and texture of the music—whether you're working on a project that will be created entirely from computer-generated animation or from a multicamera shoot of a performance—where the edit point comes on each shot is driven by the beat of the music.

Marking the Beat on the Track

Finding the beat is the first step you'll have to take. The simplest way is to mark it up. You probably have an excellent piece of music to try this out on; if not, there are a couple of pieces of music that come with FCP5's training tutorial material. They're on the *Apple Pro Training Tutorials* DVD inside the *Apple_Pro_Training Tutorials-NTSC* (or *PAL*) folder. Inside *Introducing_Final_Cut_Pro/Media* are two files called *30 Sec.aif* and *30 Second Shark Dive.aif*. Drag one or both of these files from the DVD onto the media drive of your system.

1. Open your project and import one of the music tracks from the media drive. It will appear in the **Browser** and have the speaker icon.

2. Once the file is imported, open it into the **Viewer** and play it.

7.4 Music Markers

3. Once you've got the rhythm, start again. As it plays, tap out the beat on the **M** key (or grave accent). You'll quickly fill it up with little green markers (Figure 7.4).

You'll probably notice how not all the markers line up exactly with the spikes in the beat. The visual display of the waveform is really helpful here.

4. Step through the markers (**Shift-down** arrow takes you to the next marker; **Shift-Up** arrow takes you to the previous marker), repositioning them as you go.

5. If the marker is late (after the beat), just add a new marker on the beat. Then go to the incorrectly positioned marker and delete it (**Command-`**).

6. If the marker is early (before the spike in the waveform), reposition the marker with **Shift-`**, which will pull the marker up to the playhead.

Once you get into the groove of it, you can quickly clean up your markers until they're exactly placed.

Now that you've marked up the music, you're ready to start laying in picture. First drag the track into the **Timeline** and then lock those music tracks with the handy little locks on left end of the **Timeline**. That music track shouldn't be going anywhere, and you don't want to accidentally overwrite it when you put in some video. You can also use the keyboard shortcut **F5** followed by the track number, so in this case you'd press **F5** followed by **1**, and then **F5** followed by **2** to lock **A1** and **A2**. You are now ready cut up your shots and edit them into the **Timeline** based on the markers attached to the music clip.

Marking the Beat on the Timeline

Another way to work with markers, rather than putting them on the clip itself, is to lay your music into your sequence first. Then rather than placing the markers on the audio track, you can tap out the markers in the **Timeline**. FCP has a way to work with markers that's handy for music videos: **Mark to Markers**.

1. Place your music track in the **Timeline**.

2. Lock the audio tracks so that nothing can move them or overwrite them.

3. Make sure nothing is selected in the **Timeline** (**Command-Shift-A**). With the playhead at the start of the sequence, begin playing the track, tapping **M** to the beat as the music plays. This will add markers to the **Timeline** itself. If the clip were selected, the markers would have been added to the sound track itself, not to the **Timeline Ruler**, which is what we want to do.

4. After you've placed the markers in the **Timeline**, move the playhead to a point anywhere between the first pair of markers, and select from the **Mark** menu **Mark to Markers**. Or press the keyboard shortcut **Control-A**.

Now all you have to do is find the shot to place between those markers and the In and Out points you've created.

5. Open a clip from the **Browser** into the **Viewer** by double-clicking on it.

6. Find where you want the clip to begin, and mark an In point.

7. Press **F10** to **Overwrite**. The shot will be cut into the **Timeline** in the marked position.

8. Move the playhead between the next pair of markers, and press **Control-A**.

By repeating the process a couple of times, your timeline will soon look like Figure 7.5. It's a very efficient way for quickly roughing out your shots for a music video.

If you to want to use any natural or sync sound with your music video, you could add a couple of tracks and move the music down, leaving the primary tracks, **A1** and **A2**, free for sync audio.

★**Tip**
Slugs: Some people like to lay a slug from the **Generators** into the video track and go along, with **Snapping** turned on, cutting the slug at each of the markers (Figure 7.6). Each of these slugs becomes the basis for a shot that's cut on the beat of the music. With **Replace** you can quickly drop shots onto each slug. Place the playhead over the slug you want to replace, and drag the clip to **Replace** in the CEO. You just have to make sure there is enough media for the length of the slug you're replacing.

It's no coincidence that many editors are musicians at heart and often play musical instruments. Editing is so much about rhythm and cadence, both of which are usually dictated by sound. Editing to music is editing to the beat or rhythm of the music. There is almost always something happening on the beat of the music: either the cut is on the beat, or an event in the shot is on the beat. When you cut on the beat, the edit appears on the moment of the beat, on the spike in the waveform. If you are cutting a drummer pounding the skins, if you cut on the beat, you are cutting on the moment he is striking the drum. The strike on the drumhead explodes the edit into the next shot. However, to see the drummer beat the drum, you really need to cut off the beat so that the edit occurs in the gaps between strikes. This way the action is placed on the moment of the beat, on the spike in the waveform.

For most music you can cut either on the beat or off the beat. I'd guess most music is cut on the beat, as in the tip about slugs. This works pretty well and will always produce acceptable results. Placing the cut on the beat works especially well for stills or other images without much action. However, if there is strong action in the shot, it's often better to cut off the beat.

Take the example of the drummer striking his drum. If you're cutting on the beat, you're cutting to or away from the drum on the

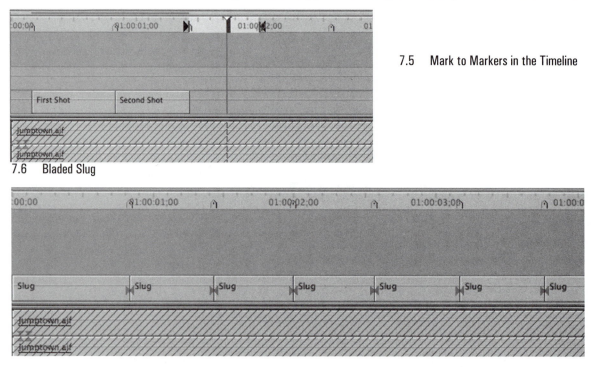

7.5 Mark to Markers in the Timeline

7.6 Bladed Slug

very frame on which it's struck. Here you might want to set up a rhythm that has you cutting off the beat and placing the action on the beat:

- The fist strikes the table.
- The door slams.
- The drum is pounded.
- The guitar chord is struck.
- The couple kisses.

All of these moments need to be seen. The impact event should happen on the beat; the edit, hidden between the beats. No video will have just one or the other, which would make it horribly monotonous, but a mixture of the two, changing back and forth through the rhythm of the music and of the images.

Multicamera Editing

Multicamera performance recordings, whether music, plays, narrative, speeches, or anything else, are edited somewhat differently from straight linear sequences. FCP5 has introduced some great new tools to facilitate this, letting you switch between cameras right in the **Viewer**, just as if you were directing a live television show.

The first step you have to take when working with multicamera material is to sync up the video from the various cameras. Ideally, the material is shot with cameras that can have their timecodes slaved to each other. One camera becomes the master camera, and all the other cameras run timecode that is jam-synced to the master, so that the timecode on each camera is identical. This means that at any single moment in a performance, the timecode on all the takes of the same event will be identical.

If this isn't possible, then you'll need to sync up the material. Hopefully there is a clapperboard or some other device, even a flashbulb going off, that can be used to sync the cameras together. If that's not available, then it's important that all the cameras record sound so you can use that to sync them up. Here's how you might do that.

1. Drag the shots into a sequence stacked one on top of the other, as in Figure 7.7.
2. Use the waveforms in the **Timeline** to line up the material as closely as you can get it.

Tip

Sequence Chorus: Music is about repetition: passages and choruses that often repeat. Using FCP you can create a sequence that repeats for each chorus. You may not want each chorus to be exactly the same, but have small variations, though the structure and rhythm and many of the shots may repeat. The simplest way to do this is to duplicate copies of the first chorus sequence, as many as you need, and make the variations in them. The various chorus sequences can then be dropped into the final sequence as needed.

7.7 Syncing Clips in the Timeline

3. Find a sync point, a sharp sound or a plosive *b* or *p* that's easy to see on the waveform of all shots.

4. Go in the **Viewer** and in the audio tab find the point precisely and add a marker to it.

5. Line up all the markers on the clips in the **Timeline**, and then use the **Blade** tool to cut off the beginning so that they all have an identical start point.

6. Drag the clips back from the sequence into the **Browser** and use these marked clips with defined In points as your clips for the next steps of your multicam edit.

Final Cut Pro lets you edit multicamera material using what it calls **Multiclips**. All your camera shots are placed into a single virtual clip that displays them together in the **Viewer**. You can embed up to 128 camera angles into a single multiclip, though only 16 can be viewed at a time. To edit our multicamera sequence, we're going to use a short section of material shot at the Coffee House during the Stanford Summer Jazz Workshop. The piece features Ambrose Akinmusire on trumpet; Patrick Wolff, tenor sax; Josh Thurston-Milgrow, bass; and Adam Coopersmith on drums.

Let's see how to do this with the source clips in the *Multicam* bin.

1. Select the *Cam1, 2, 3, 4* shots in the bin and chose **Modify>Make Multiclip**. Use the dialog box popup to set how the material is synced. In this case, select **Timecode** (Figure 7.8) and see how the clips line up. They don't all start and end at the same place.

After you've made your multiclip, it will appear in the **Browser** with an icon that's new to FCP (Figure 7.9). The number in brackets is the angle number. You can assign angle numbers when

Make Multiclip

In Points
Out Points
Timecode
Aux Timecode 1
Aux Timecode 2

Synchronize using:

Angle Name	Media Alignment	Sync Time
☑ [1] – Cam1		01:00:12;10
☑ [2] – Cam2		01:00:12;27
☑ [3] – Cam3		01:00:12;23
☑ [4] – Cam4		01:00:12;21

Cancel   OK

7.8 Multiclip Dialog (left)

7.9 Multiclip in the Browser (below)

▼ ☐ Multicam
  ▣ *Cam1 [1]–Multiclip 1*
  ▤ Cam1
  ▤ Cam2
  ▤ Cam3
  ▤ Cam4
  ▦ Multicam

you capture material in the **Clip Settings** tab of the **Log and Cap-ture** window, or FCP will assign angles based on reel number or clip name. Here it assigned *Cam1* as Angle 1.

2. From the Multicam bin, open the sequence called *Multicam*.

3. Double-click the multiclip from the **Browser** into the **Viewer**.

When you first open this multiclip into the **Viewer**, you'll notice that there is only video for *Cam1*.

4. Step through the video with the **Right** arrow until all cameras are visible in the **Viewer** and mark an In point (Figure 7.10).

7.10 Multiclip in the Viewer

7.11 Sync > Open

Notice the timecode in the corner of each camera and the **Viewer** display number. If you want to rearrange the way the clips are displayed in the **Viewer**, hold down the **Command** key and drag the clip to another position in the multiclip display. Note that although the numbers in the upper left corner of each camera remain in the same position, repositioning the shots in the **Viewer** does not change the clips' **Angle** number.

5. Edit the multiclip into the sequence.

You can use the keyboard shortcut to execute the edit, but you can't use the normal drag-to-**Edit-Overlay** function. To drag to the **Edit Overlay**, you have to hold down the **Option** key before you drag the clip. It's important that *Cam1* be the active clip when you perform the edit because that's the only camera that has audio.

6. When the clip is in the **Timeline**, double-click it to open it back into the **Viewer**. It's important that the clip from the **Timeline** is in the **Viewer**.

7. With the **Timeline** multiclip in the **Viewer**, set the **Sync** popup to **Open** (Figure 7.11).

8. In the same popup, set the selection to **Video**, not **Video + Audio**, because we want to cut only the picture and leave the *Cam1* sound as the track for our sequence.

Once you've got the **Viewer** set up, the right sources switched, the clips in the right place for you, and the **Sync** set to **Open**, you're ready to edit, which you do in the **Timeline**. Switch back to the **Timeline** and play the clip; as you play back the sequence in the **Timeline**, the **Viewer** will follow along. To cut from one camera

---

Audio Delay

Be careful where you monitor your work. Use either a video monitor with matching audio or the computer monitor with the computer audio. The latter shows you what your computer is doing, the former what's being fed out of your computer through some device that converts the digital signal to an analog display. The problem is that there is a delay in converting the signal. Do not mix the computer video with the external audio or vice versa. You really should either monitor your video and audio together on your computer, or better, monitor both video and audio together on your external monitors.

You can now offset the Canvas display so it matches your external audio speakers. This can be done using the **Frame Offset** function in **Playback Control** of **System Settings**, but it's really better not to use this at all and simply monitor video and audio together from a single source.

to another, click the clip you want in the **Viewer**, just as though you were directing a live program and calling the shots.

As you do, blue markers will be added to the **Timeline** (Figure 7.12). When you stop playback, the markers are immediately translated into edits (Figure 7.13).

This technique works fine if you want to great a virtual live switcher, but if you want to choose an angle at a specific point with accuracy, you can't simply click in the **Viewer**; this will only

7.12 Markers During Live Cutting

7.13 Edits after Live Cutting

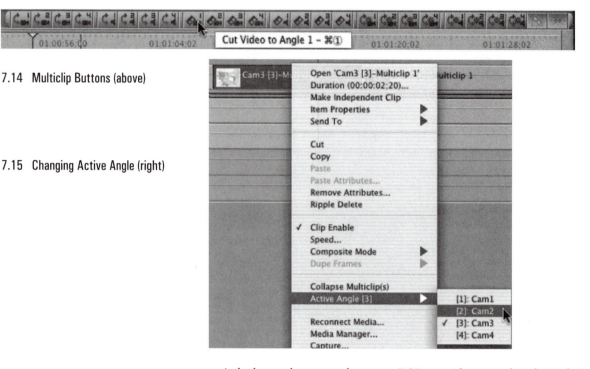

Cut Video to Angle 1 – ⌘①

7.14 Multiclip Buttons (above)

7.15 Changing Active Angle (right)

switch the angle, not make a cut. FCP provides some handy tools to help you, buttons and keyboard shortcuts. To get the multiclip buttons, go to **Tools>Button Bars>Multiclip**. This will load a set of buttons in the windows, including a string of them in the **Timeline** (Figure 7.14). The tooltip in the figure shows which buttons are used to make cuts. The first groups are used for switching, which just changes the active angle in the multiclip but doesn't actually make an edit; the middle group will cut video or audio. An even better way to cut is to use keyboard shortcuts, and FCP has a whole set of them for you. Go to **Tools>Keyboard Layout>Multi-camera Editing**. The **Command** and **Option** keys in conjunction with the keypad normally activate the **Autoselect** functions. Switching to the **Multicamera Editing** preset replaces these keyboard shortcuts with a new set that use **Command** and **Option** together with the keypad to edit your multiclip. **Command** and a number will cut to that camera angle, while **Option** and a number will switch to that angle.

After you've made your edit, you may decide to use a different shot, replace a shot with another one. It couldn't be simpler: Just **Control**-click on the clip you want to replace, and from the shortcut menu, choose **Active Angle**. Then in the submenu, pick a different angle (Figure 7.15).

After you've edited your material, you'll want to collapse the multiclip to replace all the virtual multiclip edits in the **Timeline** with the real clips from the **Browser**. The advantage of this step is that you no longer need the processor power to play back the virtual clip, and nothing will need to be rendered. To collapse a shot or shots, select it or all the shots in the **Timeline**, and either use **Modify>Collapse Multiclip(s)** or **Control**-click the clips to find the same option in the shortcut menu.

If you need to go back to the multiclip at any stage, select the clip or clips and choose **Uncollapse Multiclip(s)** from either menu.

Timecode Display

The **Viewer** will display timecode for the clips that make up the multiclip. If the clips don't have matched timecode, the easiest way to view and maintain sync across all the cameras is to use **Auxiliary Time-code**. Set Aux Timecode before you create the multiclip. Select the clip in the **Browser**—or with the clip in the **Viewer**—choose **Timecode** from the **Modify** menu. This will bring up the dialog box in Figure 7.16. In addition to setting the **Auxiliary Timecode**, you can also set an **Auxiliary Reel Number**, which might be useful to you. Notice in this box that you can change not only the **Auxiliary Timecode**, but also the **Source Timecode**. Use this with great care. This is one of the few functions within FCP that will actually affect the media on your hard drive. If you change the **Source Timecode** in this window, you will permanently change the timecode of your source media on your hard drive. To change from clip timecode to aux timecode, **Control**-click in the current time display and set it to the correct timecode display (Figure 7.17). You can help this further by changing the **Timeline** start time to match the timecode of the clips, so that everything, each clip and the **Timeline** itself, are all running to matching timecode references. You can change the **Timeline** start time in **Sequence Settings** (Command-Zero) under the **Timeline Options** tab by dialing a new **Starting Timecode** number.

7.16 Setting Aux Timecode (left)

7.17 Changing Aux Timecode Display in the Viewer (below)

After you've edited your material with the multiclip function, you can, of course, trim your edits. The **Roll** and **Slide** tools are very useful for this. Be careful, though, when using **Ripple** and **Slip** functions. They may leave your material out of sync with the audio.

Action

By action I don't mean only the movies of Governor Schwarzenegger or John Woo. The principals of action editing are not only for feature films. All forms of video might use elements and techniques of action, where what occurs in one shot continues smoothly into the next. While documentary is often based on noncontinuous shots and the juxtaposition of apparently unrelated images, action films are based, within each scene, almost exclusively on continuity, a smoothness that makes the film appear almost seamless. The director has to shoot the scene so that the elements match as precisely as possible, that movements repeat as exactly as possible, that the appearance of people and things (and the content of objects like beer glasses) change as little as possible from shot to shot. Editing action is often about finding that precise moment to match two events together as closely as possible.

The Line

The first lesson they teach budding directors in film schools is the Rule of the Line, sometimes called the 180° rule. It's a simple rule, and because it's simple, it always works. The rule is basically that through every scene the director stages, there runs a line, an axis, which his camera cannot cross. In the case of a couple speaking to each other—let's say the man on the left and the woman on the right—then the Line runs through their heads (Figure 7.18).

The director must keep his camera on the one side of his chosen line. He can move the camera anywhere he wants within that 180° arc. As long as he does, the man (A) will always remain on the left side of the screen and the woman (B) on the right. As long as the scene is shot from any position in that 180° arc, such as camera positions 1, 2, or 3, A will always be looking from the left side of the screen toward the right, and B will always be looking from the right side of the screen toward the left. As soon as the camera crosses the Line, such as in position 4, the relationship between the two will suddenly change. A will now be looking

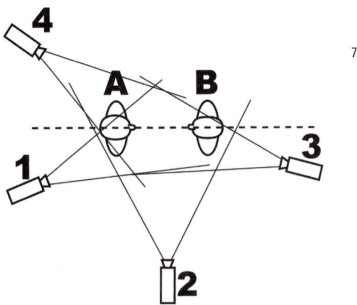

7.18 The Line

from right to left, B from left to right. The audience will become disoriented, thinking that one has turned his or her back on the other.

The convention is that the Line isn't crossed and that someone looking camera left is placed on the right of the screen, and vice versa. The viewer's eyes will sweep back and forth across the screen, like a voyeur eavesdropping on a conversation.

More and more, the directorial convention seems to be to place characters on the same side of the screen, so that someone looking camera left may be on the right side of the screen, but in the next shot the character facing them will be looking camera right, but will also be on the right side of the screen. The viewer's eyes now never have to move, but it creates an unpleasant framed shot for the character looking out of the frame rather than into the open frame. Placing the two characters on the same side of the screen evokes a sense of intimacy because the audience is (the director hopes) riveted, perhaps even mesmerized, by a point on the screen.

The principles of the Line are especially important to objects or people in motion. If a direction of movement is established, such as left to right across the screen, movement must continue in that direction, or the audience will think that the objects or people have turned around and are going back where they came from.

Tip

Two-Thirds: As a rule of thumb, cutting on action generally works best when the cut comes about two-thirds of the way through the movement, rather than right after the movement starts or at the mid-point. That way the movement really just finishes in the second shot.

To get over the problem of getting to the other side of the Line, directors use simple tricks like tracking around the subject, which visually defines for the audience that the line is being crossed. For objects in motion, the common trick is to place the camera directly on the line itself, so the car, for instance, is either going directly away from you or coming straight at you. After that shot, the director can then place the camera on either side of the line, because again the audience has received a visual clue that the line is being violated.

To achieve this continuity of action and avoid a lot of jump cuts, the director should vary the shot by changing the size/angle of the shot. A small change will create a jump cut. Shots should change a full size greater: close shot to medium shot to long shot, not close-up to close shot, nor medium shot to medium long shot. The angle change should be 40° or more to make it effective.

These are the most basic rules of action direction, but they do work and work effectively. And like most rules, not only are they often broken, but they're really made to be broken. If you do break them, though, you should know why, and break them on purpose to good effect.

These ground rules, of course, carry over to editing, so that the directions established on the stage or on location are maintained in the cutting room.

The basis of this type of editing is cutting on action. An action can be any movement:

- The moment when someone walks in the door
- When someone sits in the chair
- When the hero pulls the heroine into his arms

It's the moment the editor uses to draw the audience into the action or back them out of it. There are three possible places to cut an action:

- Just before the action takes place
- During the action
- After the action is completed

Each of these has a different contextual meaning for the audience. In the *Action Cut* bin in your **Browser** is a sequence called *Action Cut Sequence.* In this sequence, five separate edits are shown:

- In the first, the cut to the closer shot of the priest takes place before the priest rises. Placing the cut before the action occurs emphasizes the action.

- In the next edit, the cut occurs after the action is completed. This emphasizes not the action but the object or person you're cutting to. Cutting before the action begins or after the action is completed makes the edit more pointed, more apparent to the audience.

- The third edit shows the cut during the movement itself. Cutting during movement has the tendency to conceal the edit, probably the preferred edit in many circumstances.

- The fourth edit cuts away before the action takes place, but unlike the others, it moves from a close shot to wider shot.

- In the final edit, shot again changes from close to wide, but this time the edit takes place during the movement.

Sometimes it is important to mark the event before it occurs. Sometimes it is necessary not to disrupt the action but to let it complete before we move on. Sometimes it's best to make the action flow as smoothly as possible, to conceal the edit within the movement. In the first three edits in *Action Cut Sequence,* the edit goes from a medium shot to a closer shot. If the cut is going the other way, as in the fourth and fifth edits (close shot to wider shot), it generally works better to place the edit before the action takes place rather than during the action. None of these rules are by any means hard and fast. Every situation will vary; every cut will be different and require a different decision. These are the decisions you have to make, and you have to make them somewhere in one of those 29.97ths of a second.

Dialog

Dialog is the other key ingredient in feature and short-form narrative film and video. Action editing and dialog together form the main techniques used in narrative film. In dialog films, the order of shots often goes all the way back to the writer, whose choice of words, the sequence of imparting information within the dialog, will be the first steps in determining the order of shots. Eventually we arrive at the editor, who has a selection of material and an order of shots to some degree determined by the content, be it dialog, narration, or intellectual logic.

If your production is intended for theatrical release, be aware that the screen you're editing on is probably considerably smaller than the screen it will be projected on. It will take longer for the audience to read the image because there is so much of it and so much more detail. It's important to try to visualize your monitor as a theatre screen and not a television set. You need to be looking inside the picture that will be much larger than your audience, rather than simply at the image, which is what you do when you are watching TV, where you can see and absorb the whole image without your eye have to track or travel around the screen.

Modern editing is based on the idea of seamlessness; the narrative film especially stresses the hidden edit, both in action and in dialog. The editor in these types of film is often looking for the most natural place to cut. Editing is the decision of the moment, the one frame that precisely defines the moment of change from one image to another, the moment the great Walter Murch calls "the blink of an eye." This is the moment the viewer blinks, the moment he has enough of one image and is ready for the next. In a carefully edited sequence, that moment is predicated by the edits that came before it and by the sound that links them together.

Emotion is the key to storytelling. Fairy tales are driven by fear and elation. These are the key ingredients to the arc of Hans Christian Anderson's storytelling. For narrative fiction the elements of emotion are perhaps even more important than the story itself. Though some may say this is twice as important as the story, if the story is not there or not sustained, no level of emotional development will be believable or sustainable. The two are intrinsically entwined, and you shouldn't rely on simple numerical divisions, twice as important, or 54% more important. You have to weigh the emotional importance of a shot versus its narrative importance. If the narrative is lost, the emotion serves no purpose, but if the emotion is lost, the purpose of the narrative is lost. Mechanical devices such as the Line that allow the audience to suspend belief and help draw them into the reality of the story should not be dismissed as mere props. If the audience withdraws because it's abruptly jarred by poor direction and staging, the story and its emotional drive will suffer.

As so often in editing, sound is the principal driving force behind the timing of edits, probably none more so than in dialog sequences. This does not mean the edits come with the sound; they may in fact come against the sound, and most often do. You almost never slavishly cut with the person speaking; you often cut to a person after they begin speaking or perhaps more commonly before they begin to speak. It's often unnatural to cut on the gap; either you cut after the response begins, as though you're an observer reacting, or you cut while the first person is still speaking, anticipating the response.

Think of how you watch a conversation. You generally look at the speaker, perhaps occasionally glancing at the listener. When the listener interjects, you hear the voice and then turn to the source of the sound. The audio precedes the video; you hear the sound and then you see the source of the sound. Sometimes this is overt, such as the famous Hitchcock transition from seeing a woman's mouth opening to scream, hearing a train whistle, and then seeing the rushing train. More usually, the transition is considerably more subtle. In narrative film the editor often works on the assumption that the viewer grasps the situation and anticipates the response. One person speaks, and while they're talking, you cut to the other, to see the reaction and anticipate the response before it begins. The second person responds, and during the response, after the subject and verb establishes the sense, you cut back to the first person to await another response. Murch contends that you blink as you change your point of view, and this blink is the edit. You hear the door open; you turn to see who is entering the room. When we turn our heads, we often blink. When we're looking at the door to see who has entered, the door is already open. It is unnatural to see the door before it begins to open, though it's often used to create anticipation and suspense.

Sometimes you hold longer on the listener, especially when they're being told some piece of news that you already know. When your wife is telling a story that you've heard many times, usually you don't watch her retelling the tale; you watch her audience to see their reactions. This is especially true when someone is being told terrible news like a death in the family. If you know the news, you watch the reaction; but if you don't know the news, if it is being revealed to you for the first time, you usually watch the messenger, at least at first.

How long you hold an image on the screen is dictated by how long you want the viewer to look at it. Sometimes this is very brief. You look left and right to cross a street, and you see the two images of the street for only the briefest of moments, probably less a second each. Often you hold on an image much longer to give the viewer a chance to look around it, to study the image. The more complex the image the longer it needs to be on the screen. The word STOP in white letters in a black ground can on seen in a few frames; an Ansel Adams photograph of Yosemite's Half Dome needs to be lingered over.

Because editing dialog is such a unique, yet common, problem, let's look at a short, simple scene and see how to put it together. There is no right way to edit any scene of dialog; no two editors will pick exactly the same frames, or perhaps even the same takes, or the same pacing, to assemble a scene.

There is a conventional pattern to structure scenes, still followed so much of the time that the audience notices when it's not. The convention is to begin with a wide, establishing shot, then move from there to medium shots, move in to close-ups as the scene intensifies, and perhaps return to the wide shot after the climax of the scene.

Another convention is to follow your character:

1. We see the character.
2. We see what the character sees.
3. We see the character react.

The shot progression quickly goes from wide shot to a series of *singles*; these singles being simple close-ups and their respective *reverse angles*. It is important in this structure that the characters are consistently sized on screen. It would be unsettling for the audience if the sizes of the close-ups varied greatly while we're switching from one character's point of view to the other. It's important to establish the frame size for the scene so that the actors maintain their relative size in the frame.

In your **Browser** is a bin called *Heartwood*, which contains the clip *Heartwood*. This is a master clip made up from the slightly edited rushes of a movie called *Heartwood*, an independent production, directed by Lanny Cotler and produced by Steve Cotler, starring Hilary Swank, Eddie Mills, and the late Jason Robards. This is a short scene between Sylvia (Hilary Swank) and Frank (Eddie Mills) in which he's trying to persuade her to run away with him. The scene was shot, as is common in film production, with a single camera. Editing the scene shot with multiple cameras is somewhat easier, especially if you can use FCP5's new multicamera editing tools.

This scene opens as the couple comes out from an old trailer. The camera tracks slightly with them to their marks, and then becomes the master wide shot for the scene. The wide shot is followed by singles of Frank and Sylvia, close-ups of each of the actors' performances. There are a couple of flubs at the beginning, but the singles are only one take of many. By giving you only one real take, I've simplified your editing choices considerably. In reality, you could choose lines from a number of takes, as long as you maintained the integrity of the performance.

1. Look through the material. It's only about four and one-half minutes long.

In the *Heartwood* bin I have already made up the subclips for you—*Frank*, *Sylvia*, and *Master*, which is the wide, two-shot of the argument. You can use the empty *Sequence 1* in the **Browser** to do your edit.

In this scene, let's begin with the wide shot because that's the only cover until the actors reach their marks.

2. Drag the subclip *Master* directly into the **Timeline** or to the **Canvas** to **Overwrite** to edit it into the sequence. Leave it stretched out for the whole length of the scene.

3. Play the master shot until the first line of dialog, "Look, we can make it."

4. Mark an In point in the **Timeline**. This is where we're going to edit in the first close-up. The timing can be trimmed and adjusted later, but this is your staring point.

5. Switch off the audio for the master shot tracks **A1** and **A2**.

6. Create a new video track by **Control**-clicking in the head of track and choosing **Add Track** from the shortcut menu.

7. Set the new **V2** as the destination track, and set **A3** and **A4** as the destination audio tracks (Figure 7.19).

8. Open up Frank's and Sylvia's subclips into separate viewers. **Control**-click on each of the clips and select **Open in New Viewer.**

Though you can't gang-sync the two **Viewers** in FCP—both windows playing at the same time—it's nice to have them open at the same time (Figure 7.20).

7.19 Destination Tracks

7.20 Multiview Arrangement

9. Cut the dialog up in the subclips line by line starting with Frank, and Overwrite each piece of video and audio into the destination tracks, back and forth between the couple.

Sometimes it's easier to find the edit point in the **Audio** tab of the **Viewer**, such as when Frank says, "I'll do anything for you." (Figure 7.21).

After you've worked through the lines, you'll have the basic structure of the scene in close-ups, cut in its most boring, conventional manner. The audience sees who's speaking, each in turn. By covering up the master shot but leaving it on **V1**, you have it available when you want to cut back to it (Figure 7.22).

At any point when you want to pull back to the master shot—for instance, where Sylvia shoves Frank—just cut out the close-ups on **V2** to reveal the master clip. Unfortunately, Sylvia's shove doesn't come in the same place in the dialog in the master shot as it does in the close-ups. You might need to slide the master clip up the timeline a bit. Generally good, professional actors will keep the pacing of a scene and the timing of each take remarkably consistent so that shots can match easily. Because Frank's performance varies a bit, you'll probably need to cut off some of the close-up so the lines don't repeat in the wide shot, but if you pull up the master shot and overlap the audio on the close-up tracks, **A3/A4**, it'll match pretty closely. Delete what you don't need from the close-ups, and then cut back to them on **V2**. Use the **Track** tool (**T**) to select **V2** and **A3/A4** when you need to pull up the close-ups. You might want to return to the wide shot for the end after Sylvia turns away (Figure 7.23).

Despite the inconsistent dialog, the performances here are paced carefully. There is nothing worse than trying to cut together a scene in which the actors rush the performance for the takes on which they are off camera.

After you've cut through the dialog like this, you'll immediately see how arid it is, the beginning rushed as the lines trade back and forth quickly, the middle section slower where they're longer

7.22 Close-ups Laid in Timeline

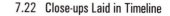

7.23 Final Cut

pieces of dialog. Where you adjust the shots is up to you and the director and the weight you want to give the scene. The basic question is usually, whose scene is it? Though *Heartwood* is really Frank's movie, a coming of age story complicated by timber and environmental issues, the scene is more Sylvia's, I think, and Hilary Swank gives a lovely performance. If you accept the premise that it is Sylvia's scene, you should cut it so it weighs more heavily in her favor; if it's Frank's scene, it'll weigh more on his performance and on his reaction to what she says.

I find it best to leave the sound mostly untouched, except to tweak it for any extraneous dialog. I work primarily by **Option**-clicking the video edits and using either the **Roll** tool in the **Timeline** or **E** to **Extend Edit** to alter the cut point while leaving the sound track as the bed.

At the end of the first close-up of Sylvia, I let her remain on screen over the beginning of Frank's line, "I'll do anything." Letting the dialog start first motivates the cut as though you are a bystander following it. You hear the voice, and then you turn to see Frank. Because Frank's line is short, I again waited for Sylvia's responding question "Anything?" before turning to her.

One problem is the type of lengthy speech like Sylvia's where you might want to drop in a cutaway of Frank to see his reaction to her words. I looked through Frank's takes in the **Viewer** and found a reaction I liked to use. The truth is the reaction I used doesn't come quite at the moment Sylvia says her dialog, but it seems to fit nicely as a reaction to her simile about her father. After deselecting the audio destination tracks (because we only want Frank's picture and not the sound that goes with it), I dragged it into the empty space above **V2** to create a new **V3**. The nice thing about stacking the cutaway vertically rather than editing into *Sylvia* is that it's much easier to move up or down the timeline or stretch it or shorten it as I like.

I also added a couple of other cutaways, one of Sylvia when Frank says, "This is what people do." Again, the moment Sylvia's shoulders sag didn't quite come on the line, but I think it works nicely here. I like using cutaways because it gives the audience a chance to see the other person's response without losing the intimacy of the scene by backing out to the wide shot.

In the *Heartwood* bin there is a sequence called *Heartwood Sequence*, which is my version of the scene. There are endless possible variations. In the film the scene was played largely in the master shot with one close-up of Sylvia and one of Frank. The movie edit is in *Movie Sequence*. It was probably right for the movie, but for this little exercise, I went for the intensity of the close-ups rather than standoffish look of the wider shot.

You might not have the opportunity to edit material shot by an excellent director and cameraperson, with an Academy Award winning actor and outstanding performances. If the direction, camerawork, and acting isn't there, it's much harder to edit the scenes. There is only so much you can do, and sometimes no amounting of stitching will be able to make a silk purse out of a sow's ear.

Summary

There are many film and video forms, and the lines between them are sometimes blurred, sometimes to the detriment of the content and of the medium. Sometimes though the blurring of documentary and narrative film, music, and dialog, which is basis of the American musical, can give a richness and texture to a film that would be missed if the story were told conventionally.

We've only looked at some of the most common editing forms, but there are others that have conventions of their own—corporate videos, informational, weddings, special interest videos, and on and on.

In the final lesson, we'll look at outputting your material from Final Cut Pro.

Lesson 8

Outputting from Final Cut Pro

This is the easiest part of working with Final Cut Pro, I think, the part where you output your material to tape or for export for the web, DVD, or myriad other uses.

The two basic ways of outputting are:

- Recording to tape, if you're going to traditional broadcast or analog tape delivery.
- Exporting, if you're going to another computer application or CD or DVD or web delivery, or

Because it's probably the most common requirement for Final Cut Pro users, let's look at outputting to tape first. We'll see exporting later on page 227.

There are basically three ways to get material from your computer to tape:

- **Record to Tape**
- **Print to Video**
- **Edit to Tape**

Record to Tape

You can get your edited material back out to tape in several different ways. The simplest way is to record to tape. Put the playhead at the beginning of the timeline, put your deck into record mode, and hit the spacebar. This is a fast, effective, and simple-to-use method.

Before you record to tape, you should always mixdown your audio. Use **Sequence>Render Only>Mixdown** or the keyboard shortcut **Command-Option-R**. Do this even if you only have a single stereo pair of audio. It's much easier for your computer and your drives to play back a mixdown file than it is to mix your audio on the fly. Also, the default audio quality playback is set to **Low**. If you just record to tape, you will get low-quality playback. However, whenever you mixdown your audio, it's always done to high quality, and that's what you'll get when you record to tape.

The **RT** button setting in the upper right corner of the **Timeline** lets you switch between **Use Playback Settings** or **Full Quality**. This actually has no effect on recording to tape manually. It only affects the other record functions that we'll see in a moment.

There is one other trap in recording to tape, either manually or with **Print to Video** or **Edit to Tape**. If you have set your **Render Controls** in **Sequence Settings** down to low values to speed up rendering, that's the playback quality you'll get. You cannot switch to high quality and automatically force a re-render. You have to switch to high quality and then reset each effect that was rendered at low resolution to force it to re-render at high quality. There is no force re-render function, unfortunately. This is also true of exporting to tape and is still a significant issue in Final Cut Pro.

Playing back from the **Timeline** has the advantage of speed and convenience. It is useful also for make quick test recording. In addition to the traps we've have already seen, some other disadvantages are that you don't get to put in bars and tone and neat countdowns, slates, black leaders, and trailers, unless you physically add them to your sequence. If you want these features, you can use **Print to Video** or **Edit to Tape**.

Print to Video

Print to Video and **Edit to Tape** are both found under the **File** menu. If you have a sequence selected in the **Browser** or an active **Timeline**, you can call up **Print to Video** from the menu or use **Control-M**. This brings up the dialog box in Figure 8.1.

In this dialog you can set any number of options for program starts and ends. You can add bars and tone and set the tone level, depending on the system you're using. A number of different digital audio standards are used, if you can call anything that has variables as being a standard. Different systems use –12, –14, –16, or –20dB as digital audio standards. Analog uses a variety of other standards around 0dB. Check with your final destination before selecting a tone level.

The **Slate** popup lets you use the:

- **Clip Name**
- **Text**, which you can add in the text window
- **File**, which is any still image, video, or audio file

Note

PtV Limits: You can loop FCP's **Print to Video** as many times as you want, but the duration of any **Print to Video** recording is limited. It can't be longer than 12 hours, which is probably more than enough for most people.

✎*Tip*
Academy Leaders: On your *FCP Install* DVD is an *Extras* folder that contains a folder called *Head Leaders for Cinema Tools.* Inside are pre-built, standard, motion picture Academy leaders in various formats. There's also an FCP project that will let you customize an Academy leader with your own logo or look.

So if you have an audio slate recorded, selecting the file and navigating to it with the little **Load** button will play the sound during your mastering session.

You can use FCP's built-in countdown, which has *Final Cut Pro* splashed across it. Or you can use a countdown of your own by selecting **File** in the **Countdown** popup.

Notice the **Automatically Start Recording** checkbox in the lower left of the **Print to Video** dialog window, which was introduced in FCP4.5. This works regardless of the automatic **Print to Video** option in **Device Control**.

One of the hardest tasks for a hard drive to do in digital video is finding and playing back multiple tracks of audio simultaneously. As in recording to tape, it is important to always mixdown your audio first. FCP will render out a single audio file that mixes down all your tracks. Your system will run more easily, and you're less likely to have dropped frames during that crucial playback to tape. I suggest mixing down every time you output to tape, whatever method you use.

When you start **Print to Video**, FCP will write a video and, if necessary, an audio file of any material that needs to be rendered. It should only need to go through this routine once, even if you need to do multiple **Print to Video** functions in succession.

Again, be aware of the render issues mentioned previously on page 222. Material rendered in low resolution will still be maintained in your final output unless you manually find it and force it to be re-rendered at full quality. If you have rendered with low resolution, mixed resolution, or think you may have done so, the only safe and sure method around this problem is to use **Render Manager** from the **Tools** menu and to delete the render files associated with that the sequence you want to export. Make sure your **Render Control** settings are at full quality and re-render everything.

After it's finished writing the video and audio files, FCP may prompt you to put your deck into record. Press **OK** for playback to start.

Edit to Tape

Print to Video is an excellent tool, but if you're working in DV with a camera or deck that allows assemble editing, which is pretty much all of them, or if you have a professional deck that allows insert editing to tape, then **Edit to Tape** is the tool for you. It's also called up from the **File** menu.

To do an **Edit to Tape**, the tape you're recording onto must have some video and timecode already recorded on it. You don't have to record on the entire tape, but I usually use **Black and Code**, at least the first minute before I begin using **Edit to Tape**.

Edit to Tape uses the same type of window as **Log and Capture**, only with an edit overlay (Figure 8.2). To perform an Assemble edit or Insert edit, you have to enter at least an In point. Dragging a sequence from the **Browser** into the **Edit to Tape** window will activate the **Edit Overlay**. It offers you the choices of **Assemble**, **Insert**, or **Preview**, assuming your deck is capable of those functions. Most DV camcorders and decks can do an Assemble edit. If so, you can select your edit mode here or with one of the buttons in the lower left corner, if the sequence is loaded into the **Viewer** first.

The controls will operate your deck with the usual buttons or the J, K, L keys. You can assign In and Out points on the deck for

8.3 Insert Selector Buttons in Edit to Tape Window

8.4 Buttons at the Top of the Edit to Tape Window

Assemble or Insert edits, either with the usual buttons as in the **Log and Capture** window or with the **I** and **O** keys.

On the lower right side of the **Edit to Tape** window are selector buttons that let you choose the tracks you want to enable for insert editing, any combination of video or two audio tracks (Figure 8.3). The little stopwatch button allows you to insert timecode onto a tape.

At the top of the **Edit to Tape** window, in addition to the duration on the left and the current time on the right, are two buttons (Figure 8.4). The one on the left is a popup that lets you select between **Mastering** and **Editing**.

At the back of the **Edit to Tape** window is the **Mastering Settings** panel. Here you have access to **Bars and Tone, Leaders and Trailers,** and **Looping,** just as you do in **Print to Video.** In the **Mastering Settings** panel, you can set whether you record whole or part of a sequence by selecting from a popup **Entire Media** or **In to Out.**

With the **Editing** option, you can do an Insert edit, assigning both In and Out points on the tape or In and Out points in your sequence in any combination to define a three-point edit. Insert editing is only available on decks that support it and is not a function that can be used with FireWire device control. In the **Editing** option, you don't have access to leaders and trailers and the other extras you get with **Mastering.**

The button on the right will black a tape for you. This lays down on your tape a video black signal with continuous timecode. You need this for an **Insert** edit, and you'd certainly want to black at least the first minute of a tape before you do an Assemble edit. Clicking the **Black and Code** button brings up a dialog where you can select any of your **Sequence Preset** types and use them as the type of Black and Code to be laid down. Or you can use the **Current Settings** or make up a new one with the **Custom** selection. After you click **OK,** you'll get a warning dialog before you can proceed. Clicking **OK** will take the tape in the record deck back to the head and begin the process of recording Black and Code to your tape. You can quit the Black and Code process at any time by hitting the **Escape** key.

When you're ready to begin the edit, drag the sequence into the **Edit Overlay,** and the process will start. As in **Print to Video,** FCP will first render out what's necessary before beginning the **Edit to**

Tape. As soon as that is completed, FCP will take control of your deck, queue it to the correct point, pre-roll it, and put it into Record mode as frame accurately as your system can manage.

During the recording you'll see on your computer monitor the video output, poorly displayed as during capture. If you have **Mirror on Desktop During Recording** switched off in your **External Video** preferences, instead of the picture you'll see a large black box the size of your output with the words "**Output of Video in Progress.**" The **Escape** key again will allow you to abort the edit at any time.

If you only want to insert a portion of the timeline into a portion of the tape, you'll have to do an Insert edit. If your deck is accurate enough, it's easy to do. What you'll really be doing is a linear, tape-to-tape, three-point edit, only in this case, one of the tape decks (the player deck) is your computer. Set the In and Out points on your record machine, and mark the In point in the timeline to create the three-point edit. Drag the sequence to **Insert** to execute the edit.

> **✎ Note**
> **Preedit Calibration:** Before doing either an Assemble and certainly an Insert edit, you should calibrate your deck in **Device Control** preferences, making adjustments in **Playback Offset**.

Export

You can access the different formats and ways of exporting from FCP from the **File** menu (Figure 8.5). From here you can export:

- As a **QuickTime Movie**
- **Using QuickTime Conversion**
- **For Soundtrack and For LiveType**
- As **Audio to AIFF(s)**

Other export options include:

- **Audio to OMF,** an Avid standard audio file format for digital audio applications such as Pro Tools.
- Batch List
- Various **Cinema Tools** options for film editing
- Edit Decision List (**EDL**) and **XML**, which is file format exchange protocol

QuickTime Movie

Let's start with **QuickTime Movie**, the first in the **Export** list. Though you are exporting a QuickTime movie, FCP is still listed

Export	▶	QuickTime Movie...
Send To	▶	
Batch Export		Using Compressor...
		Using QuickTime Conversion...
Batch Capture...	^C	
Log and Capture...	⌘8	For Soundtrack
Media Manager...		For LiveType
Reconnect Media...		
Set Logging Bin		Audio to AIFF(s)...
		Audio to OMF...
Print to Video...	^M	Batch List...
Edit to Tape...		Cinema Tools Audio EDL...
		Cinema Tools Change List...
		Cinema Tools Film Lists...
		EDL...
		XML...

Save

Save As: Sequence 1

Where: 📁 Documents

Setting: Current Settings

Include: Audio and Video

Markers: None

☐ Recompress All Frames
☑ Make Movie Self-Contained

(Cancel)   (Save)

8.5   File > Export

8.6   QuickTime Movie Export Dialog

as its creator type. So if you launch the resulting movie, it will launch Final Cut Pro.

You can export a sequence as a digital file into a **QuickTime Movie** in several ways:

- From the active **Timeline** window directly from the sequence you're working in
- From an active **Viewer**
- From the **Browser**

You can also **Control**-click on an item in the **Browser** and go to **Export>QuickTime Movie**. Any way of navigation will bring up the dialog box in Figure 8.6. Here you can rename your sequence, if you wish, and you can set standard FCP settings from the **Settings** popup.

Settings can either be current or selected for anything in your **Sequence Presets Audio/Video Settings** panel. Or you can select **Custom**, which will actually call up the **Sequence Presets** window and let you create a custom preset right there.

A custom setting is useful if you want to export to the Animation codec. This important codec is a high data rate, lossless compression codec used to transfer material between various applications such as Motion and LiveType. The advantage the Animation codec offers is that it can carry alpha channel information with the video. This allows you to create a composition in LiveType, for instance, and bring it into FCP without loss. LiveType always renders into the Animation codec, though you can export from it to another codec if you wish.

8.7   Animation Color Depth Setting

With an alpha channel, your LiveType composition can be over-laid on other images. When you export from FCP using **Quick-Time Movie,** you can use a custom setting with the Animation codec with an alpha channel. This brings up the **Sequence Preset Editor** window. Set the frame size, frame rate, and other settings to match your material, and then set the **Compressor** in the **QuickTime Video Settings** to **Animation**. Click on the **Advanced** button, which brings up the window in Figure 8.7. Here you can set the color depth to **Millions of Colors+** . The plus setting will allow you to export your material with an alpha channel.

The **Audio/Video** popup allows you to export just audio, just video, or both.

The two checkboxes at the bottom of the dialog box are the cru-cial: **Recompress All Frames** and **Make Movie Self-Contained**. Normally you do not want to recompress the frames. You want to use the compression that's already there.

You would want to use **Recompress All Frames** only if you have material from different codecs or with different data rates in a single sequence and you want them to use a uniform, fixed codec and data rate. In such cases, you have to use **Make Movie Self-Contained** to create a single video file for your sequence.

But you have another choice. If you uncheck **Make Movie Self-Contained**, FCP will generate a reference movie. This is a rela-tively small file that points back to the original media source files. It will play the contents of the sequence as you laid them out. The reference movie will play back from the QT player, and it can also be imported into other applications such as Motion, DVD Studio Pro and even iDVD.

The real advantages to making reference movies are the speed in generating the file and the comparatively small file size. If anything in the FCP sequence needs to be rendered, it will still have to be rendered for the reference movie, and the audio files will also be duplicated as a mixdown of your tracks. The reference movie is treated just like any other QT clip inside your other QuickTime-based applications. FCP and the importing application do not need to be open at the same time for this to work. You do, of course, need to have access to all the source media included in the sequence, because a reference movie only points to existing media source files on your hard drives. It's not a complete video clip in itself. Be warned: if you delete any of the media needed for the reference movie, it will not play. It will be a broken QuickTime file.

Export to QuickTime Movie is an important tool because it is the only way to export a sequence from FCP without recompressing the video. All other exports, including export to **QuickTime Conversion**, will recompress the frames.

Creating a reference movie is probably the best way to get your material from FCP to iDVD. If you've set chapter markers in your timeline, these can be exported to iDVD by setting the **Markers** popup to **Chapter Markers** or **DVD Studio Pro Markers**. Either will work.

For Soundtrack and LiveType

Both of these export functions use the **QuickTime Movie** module, but they provide different presets.

For Soundtrack defaults to exporting a reference movie. That is, **Make Self-Contained Movie** is switched off. Also, the **Markers** popup is set to export **Audio Scoring Markers**. Scoring markers are useful for setting hit points in your score in Soundtrack.

For LiveType is similar. It also exports a reference movie that's not self-contained, only here the **Markers** are set to export **All Markers**.

8.8   Compressor Batch Window

Using Compressor

Export **Using Compressor** is a unique function. It doesn't actually export anything. You cannot export clips, only sequences. What the export function does is launch the Compressor application directly.

Because of its great flexibility and power, this should be the preferred method of export when you are doing a video or audio file conversion. Activating the function immediately brings up the **Compressor Batch** window (Figure 8.8). Notice the **Cluster** popup in the lower left that lets you use distributed rendering, which you can set up in the **Apple Qmaster** panel of **System Preferences**.

In Compressor you can either click on the **Click** popup to select a setting, or choose the **Presets** window from the **Windows** menu. The **Presets** window is divided into two tabs, the **Settings** tab (Figure 8.9) and the **Destinations** tab (Figure 8.10).

The **Destinations** tab lets you use selected preset destinations, or click on the button in the upper right to add a new destination and choose one from the navigation window it opens.

The **Settings** tab has an enormous selection of presets, 232 in all, pretty much anything you could want, all divided into groups. Note the **Advanced Format Conversion** group, which allows you to do standards conversion with Compressor using excellent optical flow technology to create intermediate frames. If these aren't enough, you can create your own preset for whatever you want. Just click the **Plus** button in the upper right add corner of the tab.

8.9 Compressor Settings

8.10 Compressor Destinations

Notice also that each of the DVD options has a Dolby 2.0 setting to compress audio for DVD use, doing away with the A.Pack application that accompanied DVD Studio Pro.

Export **Using Compressor** allows you to export to MPEG-2 with great precision and control for use in DVD Studio Pro, especially if you create your own presets to add in filters, which allow noise reduction, gamma correction, and others.

QuickTime Conversion

QuickTime Conversion is the catch-all for every form of file conversion and still export from FCP. I would have liked for **Still** export to be separated, but it's hidden in here as well (Figure 8.11).

Video Export

Final Cut Pro has a number of video export choices. They include:

- 3G, a format used for portable devices like cell phones
- FLC, an 8-bit format used for computer animations
- AVI, a PC video format

8.11 QuickTime Export

8.12 QuickTime Video & Audio Options

Animation
Apple Intermediate Codec
Apple Pixlet Video
Apple VC H.263
BMP
Cinepak
Component Video
DV – PAL
DV/DVCPRO – NTSC
DVCPRO – PAL
DVCPRO HD 1080i50
DVCPRO HD 1080i60
DVCPRO HD 720p60
DVCPRO50 – NTSC
DVCPRO50 – PAL
Graphics
H.261
H.263
✓ H.264
HDV 1080i50
HDV 1080i60
HDV 720p30
JPEG 2000
Motion JPEG A
Motion JPEG B
MPEG IMX 525/60 (30 Mb/s)
MPEG IMX 525/60 (40 Mb/s)
MPEG IMX 525/60 (50 Mb/s)
MPEG IMX 625/50 (30 Mb/s)
MPEG IMX 625/50 (40 Mb/s)
MPEG IMX 625/50 (50 Mb/s)
MPEG–4 Video
None
Photo – JPEG
Planar RGB
PNG
Sorenson Video
Sorenson Video 3
TGA
TIFF
Uncompressed 10–bit 4:2:2
Uncompressed 8–bit 4:2:2
Video

8.13 QuickTime Conversion Export

- DV Stream, DV audio and video encoded on a single track
- QuickTime

These are video formats. Some, such as AVI and QuickTime, allow you to use a number of different codecs. DV Stream is used by iMovie, not by FCP. Do not export to DV Stream if you're going to a video-editing application other than iMovie.

In **Quicktime Conversion**, the **User** popup offers a stack of common Internet or CD settings.

To export to a movie file, use the **Options** button and select the correct video and audio settings (Figure 8.12).

The default compressor is H.264, which is an outstanding codec that's highly scalable while preserving image quality. It's excellent for web use in particular. The only problem with it is that it requires the user to have QuickTime 7 installed, which will limit its availability, especially for PC-based users. You don't have to use H.264, but if you click on the **Settings** button, you get exactly the same **Settings** dialog box as you get when you press the **Advanced** button in **A/V Settings** for **Sequence Presets** and **Capture Presets**. You can set the compressor, quality, and frame rate just as before.

If you're doing a QuickTime conversion to DV be sure to set **DV's** **Quality** slider to **Best** for final output. The **Quality** slider will affect the recompression quality. Only use **Low** or **Medium** for a test output or some other intermediary use.

The **Audio** dialog box is also the same as you've seen in **Sequence Presets** and **Capture Presets**.

One setting that's slightly different in the QT export is the **Size**, which offers you either the current frame size or a custom size you can dial in.

Exporting with QuickTime allows you to use a great number of different codecs for compression, which can be seen in Figure 8.13.

H.264 and Sorenson Video 3 are excellent codecs for web compression. Photo-JPEG is used to reduce file size. It works with FCP's **OfflineRT** capability. Exporting to **QuickTime Conversion** allows you to add filters to your clips or sequences. Most QuickTime filters are available directly within FCP, with a notable exception, **Film Noise** (Figure 8.14). This filter adds an old-time film look to your video, as though it were scratched and dirty.

8.14 Film Noise Filter

In the **Film Noise** dialog, a small QT movie runs in the lower left corner, showing you how much schmutz you've added to the picture. Here you can set amounts of **Hair and Scratches** that appear on your video, from very low to fairly well-destroyed. You can't control the grain, but you can add that in FCP before you export. In addition to **Hair and Scratches**, the popup at the top will take you to another panel where you can set the color. The sepia is quite subtle, and the 1930's color film is suitably garish.

Image Sequence Export

Two other types of **QuickTime Conversion** export are often used: **Image Sequence** and **Still Image**. Image sequences are useful for rotoscoping and animation work. They provide high-quality output without loss. Select **Image Sequence** from the **Format** popup and click on the **Options** button to set the file type (Figure 8.15). You can set any frame rate, and exporting will create one frame of uncompressed video for every frame you specify. This can easily generate a huge number of files, so be sure to first create a folder in which to put your image sequence.

8.15 Image Sequence Export

Still Image Export

Quicktime Conversion export allows you to change the **Format** popup to export still images. This is how you get frames of video out to your computer for web or print use. Your stills will only be 72dpi, probably not good enough for fine printing. Photoshop plugins such as Genuine Fractals can help improve the image's appearance.

The **Options** button for **Still Image** export uses the same dialog box as **Image Sequence**, including frame rate. Don't be confused; leave the frame rate blank.

The still you're exporting may very well be in CCIR601 rectangular pixels. This is not a problem if you're going back to a video application, but in print or on a computer display, the stills will look squashed. Photoshop will fix this problem for you. If the still image comes from DV, in Photoshop go to **Image Size**. Switch off the **Constrain Proportions** checkbox, and either upsample the image by changing the size to 720×540 or, for better quality, downsample to 640×480. Either way, you'll end up with a 4:3 image in the correct pixel aspect ratio. If you're working with a 720×486 image, then downsample to 648×486. Check **Resampling** and select **Bicubic** whenever you resize in Photoshop.

If you're going to export stills for web or print work from video, especially video with a lot of motion in it, you'll probably want to de-interlace it. You can do this either in FCP before you export the frame by using **Effects>Video Filters>Video>De-interlace**. Or you can de-interlace in Photoshop as well. It's in the **Filters** menu under **Video>De-Interlace**. I normally do it in Photoshop because I think its **De-interlace** feature works better than FCP's built-in one, which simply drops one of the fields.

Audio Export

FCP can export to different audio formats:

- AIFF
- AU
- Wave

Below the **Format** popup is a contextually sensitive **Use** popup. So if you select **AIFF**, for instance, in the **Use** popup you'll get common audio file settings (Figure 8.16).

Notice that the selection does not include any of the DV sampling rates, although AIFF is the most commonly used format for audio files with Final Cut. Use the **Default Settings** option to give you the same sampling rate as that of your sequence.

Export Audio to AIFF(s)

This export module allows you to export your sequences tracks as pairs of audio. So if you have eight tracks of audio in your DV

8.17 Audio Outputs Panel (below)

8.16 AIFF Export Use Popup
(above)

sequence, you can export four tracks, either as stereo pairs or as channels into the AIFF format. How many tracks are exported is based on the settings in the **Audio Output** panel of your **Sequence Settings** (Figure 8.17). Notice that you can set the **Grouping** to be either **Stereo** mixes or **Dual Mono**. Switch off the **Downmix**, which defaults to −3dB, if you don't want it. When you set multiple track outputs for a DV sequence, you'll get a warning dialog box. Just ignore it.

If you want to export your audio using **Audio to AIFF(s)**, it is important that your tracks be organized and arranged logically— all the narration on a pair of tracks, the music on one or two pairs as needed, the natural sound on as many pairs as needed. Try to avoid jumbling up your tracks, so that you end up with music and natural sound and narration all scattered over the same track pairs.

To export **Audio to AIFF(s)**, select it from the **File** menu, which brings up the simple little dialog box in Figure 8.18. Here you can set the sampling rate, sampling size, and whether you want to export as **Channel Grouped** pairs or as a **Stereo Mix**. Using **Channel Group** will export your tracks as mixed pairs or as distinct mono tracks into separate AIFF files.

8.18 Audio to AIFF(s) Dialog

8.19 Exported AIFF tracks

> **Note**
> *Audio to AIFF(s)* uses a file-naming convention based on the sequence name. Stereo pairs are mixed into a single file with both track numbers, while mono tracks export each as a separate file as in Figure 8.19.

8.20 Export to OMF Dialog

Export Audio to OMF

OMF stands for *Open Media Format*, a file format that's widely recognized as an intermediary format for moving audio files between various applications. Exporting to OMF allows you to move your audio tracks as you've laid them out in FCP into a digital audio workstation such as Pro Tools. It works very well, as long as you bear a number of constraints in mind.

To export audio to OMF, select the sequence you want to export, and go to **File>Export>Audio to OMF**.

This brings up a dialog box that offers you a few choices (Figure 8.20). To be able to use your exported cross fades, you need to be working with Digidesign's DigiTranslator software.

It's important to note that the OMF file does not pass on pans, levels settings, or filters from FCP; all you get are the tracks and media handles. Levels settings and effects are supposed to be added in your audio-mixing software.

After you've exported to OMF, you then have to run OMFTools or DigiTranslator to convert your files into a Pro Tools project.

When you've finished working with your material in ProTools, or whatever audio finishing application you're using, you'll need to export the sound track as an AIFF file and bring it into FCP to marry it with your video.

Batch List

A *batch list* is basically a printout of the contents of a bin. You can only make a batch list when the **Browser** or bin is in List view. Select **File>Export>Batch List**, choose either **Tabbed** or **Formatted** output, and you're done (Figure 8.21).

8.21 Batch List Dialog Box (above)

8.22 Batch List in Excel (right)

The exported batch list will contain everything displayed in the List view columns, and not what's in the selected columns. If you don't want some information in the batch list, use the contextual menu in the bin header to hide the column. Choosing either **Tabbed** or **Formatted**, the list can be opened either in a word processing application or in a spreadsheet application such as Excel, where it is ready to print out (Figure 8.22).

Batch lists are useful for long-form projects. After you have all your material captured and subclipped with notes and comments added, printing out a Batch List gives you a hard copy of your bins. You can look it over in those spare moments while you're rendering or waiting for the coffee to brew.

What's great about batch lists is that they work both ways. Because they are just tab-delineated files, you can create them in Word, Excel, or other applications. This way you can log material outside of FCP, such as when you're on the road. Then you can use your list in FCP as a Batch Capture List. Because tab-delineated files are common to many applications, you can move logging lists from one application to another.

EDL

Final Cut Pro can export an Edit Decision List in a variety of common formats (Figure 8.23). CMX3600 is probably the most common carrier, but other systems use other formats. Because an EDL is a text file, you can readily, if laboriously, edit it in any word-processing application. EDLs are the last vestiges of linear systems, an arcane format that is limited to the types and numbers of tracks it can move, and to the types of transitions it will understand, often only dissolves and simple wipes. Sometimes it is the only tool available for moving between different types of edit systems, from offline to online, from nonlinear to linear.

Tip

Audio Sync: When exporting to OMF, it's a good idea to add an audio sync pop at the beginning and end of your tracks. Set a one-frame tone two seconds before the first audio and two seconds after the last audio. Just use the **Generators** to go to **Bars and Tone**, make the single frame, and throw away the video bars. This makes an easy sync point when you bring your audio back into FCP for final output.

8.23 EDL Export Dialog (left)

8.24 EDL Import Options (below)

EDLs normally export only one video track. Any additional tracks should be output as separate EDLs. Usually no more than four audio tracks are allowed. Neither effects nor motion information translates into EDLs. Titles do not export. Nested sequences do not export properly either. All in all, EDL export is a very limited format and should be avoided if at all possible.

Remember also that FCP can not only export EDLs, it can also import them from the **File>Import>EDL** menu. This will bring an EDL into the application and lay it out as a sequence ready for batch capture or reconnect (Figure 8.24).

XML

8.25 Export XML

XML is a much more sophisticated form of edit decision list export, a file interchange format that allows you to quickly and exactly export complex sequences and have them be recreated in another application. Multilayer sequences with titling and animation can all be exported quickly using XML and reopened as new projects within other applications that support this format. **Exporting to XML** opens up a deceptively simple-looking dialog (Figure 8.25). Click **OK** to name the file and pick the destination.

8.26 Import XML

8.27 Batch Export Queue

To use an XML file, open it in FCP. You'll get the dialog in Figure 8.26. This will allow you to create a new project that completely reconstitutes the exported material. If the media is not available, it will have to be recaptured. Other applications using the XML format will work similarly reconstituting your material or sequence within the application.

Batch Export

Batch Export is a good, comprehensive interface that allows you to set up a number of different export formats before beginning the export process. You can select a bin, a group of shots, or even a sequence to batch export. Once you've selected **Batch Export** from the **File** menu, the **Export Queue** window will open (Figure 8.27) at the bottom. Pressing the **Settings** button brings up an **Export** dialog box (Figure 8.28). Here you have all the usual settings options, like those in the **QuickTime Conversion export** windows. To trim video during batch export, check the box for **Use Item In/Out**.

The only two buttons that are slightly different from QT export are the **Set Destination** button at the top and the **Set Naming Options** button in the middle. **Set Destination** is pretty self-explanatory; it opens up navigation services and lets you pick a location on your hard drives for your material. Set **Naming Options** opens the dialog box in Figure 8.29.

Here you can remove any suffixes or add your own, as well as define the file type. When that's done, just press the **Export** button. Everything queued will be exported as specified in your set-

```
                     Batch 1
Destination:   Render Files
              ╭──────────────────────────────╮
              │        Set Destination...     │
              ╰──────────────────────────────╯
     Format:  ┌──────────────────────────┬──┐
              │  QuickTime Movie          │ ▲▼│
              └──────────────────────────┴──┘
   Settings:  ┌──────────────────────────┬──┐
              │  Item Settings            │ ▲▼│
              └──────────────────────────┴──┘
              ╭──────────────────────────────╮
              │        Options...             │
              ╰──────────────────────────────╯

    Naming:  ╭───────────────────────────────╮
             │      Set Naming Options...     │
             ╰───────────────────────────────╯
   Include:  ┌──────────────────────────┬──┐
             │  Audio and Video          │ ▲▼│
             └──────────────────────────┴──┘
             ☐ Recompress All Frames
             ☐ Make Self-Contained
             ☐ Use Item In/Out
        ╭──────────╮      ╭──────────╮
        │  Cancel  │      │    OK    │
        ╰──────────╯      ╰──────────╯
```

8.28 Batch Export Dialog (left)

8.29 Set Naming Options (below)

```
                  Set Naming Options
   Example File Name:   BaseName.ext

   ☐ Strip Existing Extension
   ☐ Add Custom Extension        [          ]
   ☐ Add File Type Extension
```

tings. If your naming convention duplicates with an existing file name, you'll get the error dialog box, which allows you to rename the file you're exporting.

Each set of batches can have different settings of course, so you can use it to set the same material to be exported in different formats, one for MPEG-2 perhaps for DVD creation, and another for H.264 or MPEG-4 for web creation. After exporting, clicking the **View Exported** button will open the clips in separate viewers within FCP. **Batch Export** is in many ways redundant now and has been superseded by the batch capabilities of Compressor.

⭐ *Tip*

FCP5 to FCP4: Older versions of FCP could not open projects created in newer versions, but now you can by using XML export. From FCP5, export using XML set to version 1. The generated file can be opened in FCP4 or 4.5, if you need to work on it in the older version.

Summary

We've now gone through the whole cycle of work in Final Cut Pro 5, using its essential editing tools, starting from raw tape material (either analog or digital), capturing, editing, working with audio, transitions, titling, and finally returning our finished project to tape. It's been a long journey, but I hope an exciting, interesting, and rewarding one.

The Yak is a delightful creature... rather like a visit with a bovine Confucious

Index

Updates

Want to receive e-mail updates for *Final Cut Pro 5 Editing Essentials*? Visit our web site www.cmpbooks.com/maillist and select from the desired categories. You'll automatically be added to our preferred customer list for new product announcements, special offers, and related news.

Your e-mail address will not be shared without your permission, so sign up today!